Economics in Action

Economics in Action

An Easy Guide for Development Practitioners

V. Santhakumar

SAGE   www.sagepublications.com
Los Angeles • London • New Delhi • Singapore • Washington DC

First published in 2013 by

 SAGE Publications India Pvt Ltd
B1/I-1 Mohan Cooperative Industrial Area
Mathura Road, New Delhi 110 044, India
www.sagepub.in

SAGE Publications Inc
2455 Teller Road
Thousand Oaks, California 91320, USA

SAGE Publications Ltd
1 Oliver's Yard, 55 City Road
London EC1Y 1SP, United Kingdom

SAGE Publications Asia-Pacific Pte Ltd
33 Pekin Street
#02-01 Far East Square
Singapore 048763

Published by Vivek Mehra for SAGE Publications India Pvt. Ltd, Phototypeset in 10/14pt Times-Roman by Diligent Typesetter, Delhi and printed at Saurabh Printers Pvt Ltd.

Library of Congress Cataloging-in-Publication Data

Santhakumar, V.
    Economics in action : an easy guide for development practitioners / V. Santhakumar.
        pages cm
    Includes bibliographical references and index.
    1. Economic development. 2. Development economics. 3. Economics. I. Title.
HD82.S346   338.9—dc23   2013   2013026823

ISBN: 978-81-321-1124-5 (PB)

The SAGE Team: Shambhu Sahu, Rohini Rangachari Karnik, Rajib Chatterjee and
                Rajinder Kaur

To Azim Premji Foundation

Thank you for choosing a SAGE product! If you have any comment, observation or feedback, I would like to personally hear from you. Please write to me at <u>contactceo@sagepub.in</u>

—Vivek Mehra, Managing Director and CEO,
SAGE Publications India Pvt Ltd, New Delhi

Bulk Sales

SAGE India offers special discounts for purchase of books in bulk. We also make available special imprints and excerpts from our books on demand.

For orders and enquiries, write to us at

Marketing Department
SAGE Publications India Pvt Ltd
B1/I-1, Mohan Cooperative Industrial Area
Mathura Road, Post Bag 7
New Delhi 110044, India
E-mail us at <u>marketing@sagepub.in</u>

Get to know more about SAGE, be invited to SAGE events, get on our mailing list. Write today to <u>marketing@sagepub.in</u>

This book is also available as an e-book.

CONTENTS

———◆●◆———

LIST OF BOXES, TABLES AND FIGURES

BOXES

TABLES

FIGURES

LIST OF ABBREVIATIONS

CFC   Chloro-Fluro Carbons
EGS   Employment Guarantee Schemes
GDP   Gross Domestic Product
GOI   Government of India
IMR   Infant Mortality Rates
IRR   Internal Rate of Return
NGO   Non-Governmental Organization
OPEC   Organization of Petroleum Exporting Countries
PCB   Pollution Control Board
PDS   Public Distribution System
SEWA   Self-Employed Women's Association
UN   United Nations
WCED   World Commission for Environment and Development

FOREWORD

———————◆•◆•◆———————

Even my 12-year-old daughter speaks the language of Development Economics. She is the average school-going child of her age, not one of those super rare, super-precocious students who have completed their PhD by the age of 18. It is just that she, like every one of us, is so much in the thick of development that, unknowingly, the language creeps in, picked up from the media, from her books and people around her. This is true of all of us; all of us are development practitioners and participants, to some degree.

The quest for development has become the dominant aligning pursuit for most of the world. People may have starkly differing views on what kind of development is desirable. They usually disagree on how it may happen, and they could have divergent views on its implications, but what they will have in common is the pursuit of development. And willy-nilly this pursuit makes all of us use the concepts, frameworks and assumptions of Economics. This usage of Economics is often unconscious, picked up from here and there, like my daughter.

Some of us have had a formal exposure to the field of Economics and may therefore be more conscious of our unstated assumptions and more cautious in drawing summary conclusions. While sometimes a brief exposure to any field may give a false sense of confidence and lead to its foolhardy usage, on the whole, people are better off with some exposure, rather than none.

Santhakumar's book is an attempt to provide such an exposure to Economics to the average development practitioner. It succeeds substantially in this attempt because of three reasons. First, it gives a comprehensive, end-to-end view of the field (as much as is possible in a slim volume). Second, its language is English, not Mathematics, which often seems to become the default language of Economics. Third, it uses the context of our here-and-now, not some distant past or unknown future.

I have been reading this book chapter by chapter, as Santha has been writing it. It is a pleasure to see it in its final form. It will certainly be helpful to all of us who are complicit in development.

In my own view, development is no development, unless accompanied in equal measure by justice, equity, humaneness and ecological sustainability. For those of us who hold such (or similar) views, understanding economics is a must, and this book is as good a start as any.

Anurag Behar
Vice Chancellor
Azim Premji University, Bengaluru

PREFACE

————◆•◆•◆————

Most government officials and politicians learn economics from articles in popular journals and newspapers. But often these articles are shallow and may not reflect the state of the understanding of the subject within the discipline. Popular notions and ideologies influence such articles and in turn these may influence the readers' understanding on development. For example, many officials think that private participation works well in any public service like roads, bridges and ports. Many others are sceptical of private participation even in what can be called private goods/services (like tertiary health care, higher education, electricity supply and so on). These divergent positions are not informed by any theory which can claim consistency.

Thus, there is a need for a general book on economics which can be read by all development practitioners (including doctors, engineers, politicians, other government officials and NGO volunteers) who have neither studied economics as a subject nor can now go through a full-fledged course covering different disciplines like micro, macro, development and institutional economics.

Such a book should provide a reasonable understanding of microeconomics, some knowledge of the role of the macroeconomic environment and the basic insights from the specialized area called Development Economics. Moreover, development itself is a contested concept and this and the debates on underdevelopment and its manifestations like poverty and inequality should be part of a 'knowledge package' for development practitioners.

National and international organizations have been helping the 'underdeveloped' regions by infusing capital and technology from elsewhere and also by facilitating internal changes like educational improvements. This was expected to help their development but the success of all these efforts is mixed. Recently, there is also a realization that development of a region or country depends on the internal

institutions (including formal legal systems and their enforcement) and the emergence of these institutions in turn depends on internal political factors and the
process of democratization. All these have to be discussed in such a book. But such
a book is not available in India and those available lack Indian issues in focus.

This is also the period of information explosion through the Internet and
other related sources. If somebody wants to see the definition of a term in economics or to get the data on an economic variable (like GDP or inflation) of a
country, these types of information are available almost instantly from the
Internet. Wikipedia provides extensive summaries of well-known concepts. Thus
there is so no social benefit in wasting the space of a book for repeated treatment
of such information or data. Hence such details are avoided generally in this
book. In fact it is expected that the readers would have access to such information
or data, and they are encouraged to collect such information as part of 'working
with' the ideas in this book. There is also a conception among many well-meaning
people that economics means quantitative assessment of development variables.
This is far from the truth. Economics is a way of looking at the relationships in
economy and society, and this way is based on a certain methodology. Thus this
book provides some ideas and relationships, which have a bearing on economic
and social development discussed in multiple sub-disciplines of economics. This
may help readers in using economics for analysing and implementing interventions that may influence social and human development.

Are these not explained in existing textbooks? Yes, but it may take a number
of years for someone to read different books to capture the essential ideas and
relationships given here. Moreover, such books do not communicate tips for practitioners in an easily comprehensible manner. A substantial part of these ideas are
discussed in standard textbooks on Development Economics (which are written
for students of economics) like Debraj Ray (1998) or Kaushik Basu (1997), Meier
and Stiglitz (2001), Hayami and Godo (2010) or Mookherjee (2006) or the multiple volumes of *Handbook on Development Economics* edited by T.N. Srinivasan
and J. Behrman (or H. Chenery). Those insights are rewritten here for non-econ-
omists and in a way that anybody interested in development can understand
without much difficulty. Moreover, the text here is connected with examples to
many well-known aspects of Indian development. This book, in general, tries to
relate the ideas and relationships described in economics with the real-world
problems that we may encounter as part of our life.

Understanding relationships alone is not sufficient for development practitioners. They should be able to infer, by reading such material, what they can do

to better development outcomes in the context in which they are working, informed by theory and empirical research. Thus, the focus of this book is on action. However, there are different levels of action. Changing or redesigning the economic policies of the country is also an action and it is expected that these will be carried out by those who have a more complete career/education in economics. This book does not address them. Instead, it addresses the requirements of two other realms of action.

- One, many people including development practitioners (politicians, NGO volunteers, civil society activists and government officials) participate in public debates on policies. In my view, some understanding of the economic imperatives and implications is extremely useful to make such public debates insightful and meaningful. This book is a modest attempt to contribute such knowledge to the participants of public debates.
- The second domain where this book is useful can be called 'micro-action'. This is where specific development interventions are designed and implemented. For those involved in the design of a village water supply project, a waste cleaning mechanism in a semi-urban area, in making the local government effective, in ensuring attendance of children in schools and so on, some insights of economics may be useful to them.

Conventional economics education does not produce many microactors of this kind. This is because of the nature of education in economics in general. Leading economists in world class universities work, on what I call, (economic) theoretical analysis of human behaviour. Shaping such economists is the objective of education in the discipline in most such schools. On the other hand, a large number of not so fortunate, foot-soldier researchers in economics analyse empirical data to test one or the other theoretical insights. Both these types are likely to be specialized in specific domains, methods or even theoretical issues in economics. Some of these economists may become macroactors in the design and advocacy of specific policies at the national level. Even here, excessive specialization makes some of them not so familiar with many other dimensions of the issue, which may in turn make their prescriptions narrower.

As noted by the well-known economist Raghuram Rajan recently,[1] there is a need for a greater number of general practitioners (like the GP in health care) in economics, more so in the case of microactions. In fact, a greater part of the development practice is taking place at the level of these microactions. The purpose of this book is to provide economic insights to the general practitioners of these microactions. Thus, the last two chapters of the book are specifically meant for providing tips for action to such development practitioners. The first of these chapters tells them how to use economics to analyse/design development activities/projects or interventions. The second one is more specific—on the analysis/ design of rules and organizations, since they are very much needed for effective implementation of development projects/programmes. The inefficiency or ineffectiveness of rules/organizations and governance is identified today as a major reason for the slow pace of social and human development.

THE BACKGROUND OF THE BOOK

This book partly depends on my own experience starting as a development professional (an irrigation engineer working in a watershed management programme) and then as a student of social science. I have studied economics as I saw it as an important way of analysing human behaviour and also as a crucial method for understanding some development puzzles that I faced as a development professional. This helped my practice as an academic and a consultant who applies economic theory for analysing real-world problems and designs possible solutions. My experience in training elected representatives and officials of the local governments of Kerala too reflects in this book.

The need for such a book became concrete as the Azim Premji University (APU) has launched a new teaching programme (MA) for development practitioners. The focus of this programme is not economics per se (but is multidisciplinary) and it is to empower students with a knowledge base that helps their development actions. The students of such a programme are not expected to have a basic training in economics (or even social sciences). This book is prepared to meet their needs. The book can also be used by development practitioners by self-reading or through some distant learning programmes. Parts of it can also be used for short-term training programmes aimed at development professionals.

A number of people have contributed to the writing of this book by reading different chapters. These include Anurag Behar, Namita Gupta, Lina Sonne, Sandali Takur and a number of others who showed interest in receiving the draft chapters. The students of the first batch of the MA Development Programme of the APU have contributed significantly to this book through their doubts and discussions, since the manuscript was used to teach them a full-semester course

on economics. Giridhar, the registrar of the APU arranged a copy editor and he—
Ananda—did an excellent job of reshaping the manuscript into a somewhat
decent form before sending it to the publishers. Praveena Kodoth has edited and
contributed to the chapter on gender. This book would not have become a reality
without the unstinted support of the Azim Premji Foundation.

NOTE

1. In an interview given to the Institute of New Economic Thinking recently.

PART I

INTRODUCTION

ONE

WHY SHOULD DEVELOPMENT PRACTITIONERS STUDY ECONOMICS?

————————⊸•⊙•⊸————————

S hould development practitioners study economics?
There are four arguments in its favour:

- Economic growth contributes to, but is not adequate for, social and human development.
- There are economic factors behind the underdevelopment of some societies and development practitioners need to learn about them.
- It is one of the important tools to analyse development interventions.
- Understanding economics helps in making effective rules and organizations and the lack of them is considered an important problem for underdeveloped societies.

Each of these arguments is detailed in the following sections.

ECONOMIC GROWTH CONTRIBUTING TO (BUT NOT ADEQUATE FOR) DEVELOPMENT

Let us think of a situation with the following features:

- Young children or infants do not die due to avoidable reasons.
- Everybody can read and write.

3

- Many people do not die as adults and most people live until 70 years or more.
- People have access to basic education and health care.
- Everybody can purchase basic items of consumption like food and minimal clothing.
- All people have access to basic amenities like a house, safe drinking water and toilets.
- People who can work have some employment opportunities.
- People who cannot work (like the disabled, the aged, the unhealthy and so on) are not deprived of basic consumption and amenities just because they cannot work.

One may consider such a society as 'developed' compared to the ones which do not have many of the above-mentioned characteristics. Are these features sufficient to consider a society as developed? That may not be so. We will consider the limitations in the following chapters.

However, even this limited concept of development is useful. Let us consider the number of children dying at a young age. This measure is called the infant mortality rate (IMR—the number of children below one year of age dying) and is an indicator of such limited concepts of development. If the number is too high, for example, 60 per 1,000 children, it is considered to be a manifestation of lower levels of development. However, not only developed economies but some developing societies also (including some Indian states like Tamil Nadu, Kerala and relatively low-income countries like Sri Lanka, Costa Rica and Cuba) have achieved an infant mortality rate, which is closer to 15–20 per 1,000. If a society can reduce the number of infants dying, it is a desirable achievement. The reduction of IMR per se is not a great indicator of development, but given its importance and reasonable achievability, it should be a priority for societies that currently have an IMR of 60 to 100. This may require only some reasonable and simple but effective steps on the part of the government and civil society. Hence there is merit in giving high priority to such achievable targets. Though this is not going to solve other complex problems of development, such as increasing inequality or the lack of happiness, a focus on all such complex issues should not cause a diversion of our current attention from those simple and easily solvable issues like infant mortality. This is the approach followed in this book.

The first and foremost lesson that we need to learn is that development cannot be achieved in a society without certain basic levels of economic growth. Here, economic growth is taken as the increase in the money value of all the economic activities (that may reflect the production of goods and services) in a context. This is what gives people income. Otherwise, people in this society should get income from outside the country. Such external income is possible if some foreign country is generously providing aid. It is also possible that some people of this society go out and work in other regions/countries and send remittances to those left behind. Economic growth is needed to create employment opportunities, so that those who can work generate income to meet their basic consumption, and have access to basic amenities and facilities. But more importantly, such economic growth is needed for a socially oriented government to generate (tax) revenue, so that these three key functions can be performed:

1. Provide support to people who cannot generate their own income.
2. Provide certain facilities like primary education or primary health care to all.
3. Provide some services which cannot be adequately provided by individuals themselves. These include roads, waste disposal and policing (we will discuss the reasons for this inadequacy later on).

Such functioning of the government is needed to achieve and sustain human development and also to sustain economic growth, which in turn generates revenue for the state and jobs for the people. Thus, economic growth (if not in one's own territory but then somewhere outside) is necessary for achieving human development.

The second most important lesson is that such an economic growth is, however, not adequate to achieve development. This is so since there can be an increase in the money value of economic activities (production of goods and services), even when a sizable section of people do not have basic consumption (of say food and clothing) and access to basic amenities (like housing, safe drinking water and toilets). Some people may not be able to work due to their disabilities and they cannot generate adequate income to meet their basic consumption. Even for those sections who can work physically, their income may be too low, if they do not have the basic skills or education, or if there are a lesser number of

job opportunities with the skills they have given the large number of people seeking such jobs. What they earn may not be sufficient to have access to basic consumption and amenities. There may be some clearly identifiable social groups
(based on caste/race or gender), which are subject to exclusion from the benefits
of economic growth. They may not have the political power to articulate their
demands effectively. Hence governments which respond to the needs of the poor
and the society at large are needed to achieve development. This can come about
only when people can demand effectively certain services from the state and
when it is forced to respond to the needs of the people. Thus, a certain level of
democratization by which even marginalized sections of people can articulate
their demands for public services effectively is needed.

There can also be social and cultural factors (beyond those related to the
state) that may also create a situation in which some sections of society do not
benefit much from economic growth. For example, if the society is highly patriarchal and sustains gender discrimination, it may not enable women to take up
jobs or acquire economic independence, even if economic growth takes place.
Similarly, the persistence of caste or racial prejudices may disable some sections
from gaining adequately from economic growth. Thus, not only a responsive state
and democratization, but a certain transformation of the social situation or social
change is also needed for achieving and sustaining development.

Thus, learning economics is needed to see the importance of (and to facilitate) economic growth as a necessary contributor to development. However, we
need to understand that economic growth by itself is not adequate to achieving
development and changes in the social and political sphere are also important.

ECONOMIC FACTORS AS CAUSES OF UNDERDEVELOPMENT

The discussion in the previous section gives us some clues about a few proximate factors that cause underdevelopment. Since economic growth is needed
(but not sufficient) for achieving development, lack of economic growth could
be an important proximate cause of underdevelopment. Hence, the factors that
slow down economic growth are also factors that may cause underdevelopment.
Economic growth would mean that income per person is increasing. If the
whole income of a country (a more accurate term can be used later on) is
increasing from ₹5,000 crores to ₹10,000 crores within a period of five years

but the population is also increasing from 5 to 10 crores during the same period, the income per person has not increased even though the whole income has doubled. In this case, there is no growth of income per person. Thus, income growth in the real sense is an increase in the income per person.

How can the income per person increase? A person may generate more income. This is often not possible when he/she is doing a particular kind of work in the same manner with the same set of skills over a long period of time, especially when the demand for his/her skills remains more or less the same. An increase in income per person is possible when that person uses his/her skill and labour with the help of better machines (more capital) and/or when he/she has better skills (better education or human capital) and/or when the work is carried out in better or more productive ways (or with better technology). A farmer using a tractor, a weaver using a machine and a carpenter using an electricity-driven driller are examples in this regard. Or there should be a situation where the money value of his/her output is increasing even when his/her physical quantity (or the amount) of output remains the same. This may happen in certain cases—like that of a teacher or a nurse. There may not be an increase in the output of a teacher/ nurse—the number of children/patients taught/cared for—but the value of this output may increase over time when the economy is growing.

Most of the early discussions on underdevelopment centred around the question of why some societies are unable to generate more output per person over a period of time; or, what prevents societies from having more capital, human capital or better technology? The following responses and solutions were given. Underdeveloped societies do not have better technology—so let the developed world give them better technology. There were some efforts in this direction. The Green Revolution and the consequent growth in Indian agriculture is an outcome of infusion of technology from elsewhere.

The other diagnosis of the problem of underdevelopment was that the people of the developing world lacked adequate money to make a capital investment and hence the prescription was to let the developed world give them capital. It may be noted that when people produce with their unskilled labour, they may generate just adequate income for their sustenance. Hence, they cannot save much money. Whatever is generated is needed for subsistence. If some money cannot be saved, there cannot be capital investments like setting up of factories or the creation/buying of better machines. Hence they need money from elsewhere to create capital investments including factories. Yet another diagnosis was that the people in poor countries do not have adequate education (or human capital) and hence the prescription was the spread of education. There have been some successes based on these prescriptions too.

However, the experience (which we will discuss in detail later) was that despite the infusion of capital and technology from elsewhere, many societies have not developed to the desired extent. This has led to a realization that external aid in terms of technology or capital has certain limitations in ushering in development in a context and it may depend on internal factors. Some of these limitations are: people in such societies may not have adequate incentives to limit population growth. The internal factors may not encourage the building up of human capital or education. There may not be adequate structures that encourage the development of appropriate innovations (better technology). (Even if technology is available from outside, innovation is needed to make them adaptable to a new situation.) These issues became the focus of thinking on underdevelopment later on.

Of late, there has also been a realization that societies do not take adequate steps towards development, not because of the lack of adequate capital or technology (since these can be acquired from elsewhere) but due to internal rules, norms and other social and political structures (or broadly, institutions). It may be noted that in this era of globalization, if people in a poor country are willing to work at lower wages—and this is the usual case when they are poor—capital may flow from the developed world to tap this cheap labour. The traditional constraint of lack of capital and technology need not exist in this period of globalization. If capital is not moving into a context where wage rates are lower, it may have something to do with other barriers. Hence, the argument is that internal institutions are not conducive for mobilizing/attracting capital or the appropriate technology to facilitate economic growth.

We have noted that economic growth is not adequate and changes in political and social spheres are also needed to accelerate development. But it may be possible that certain economic factors may prevent social and political change of the desired kind. Economists generally view material/economic/technological factors as the basis for social and institutional change. In this view, social and political change comes about in a context because of a demand for them from below (or people) and such demand is intensified whenever there are changes in technology and economic factors.

Hence, learning economics may be an important way of understanding underdevelopment.

ECONOMICS AS A TOOL TO ANALYSE DEVELOPMENT INTERVENTIONS

Economics also provides a tool kit to analyse specific development interventions. In one sense, any individual or firm taking an action goes through an implicit or explicit cost–benefit analysis. Any action requires certain costs or effort and the issue is whether spending this cost/effort is worth considering the benefits of that specific action. Such benefits and costs need not be material benefits to oneself—a common (mis)understanding about economics. Think of the following example: X wishes to help a young girl from the neighbourhood. There can be different ways of helping and all these can give only joy or happiness to X. However, this person would also be considering the best way of helping the girl taking into account the costs/efforts to do so. In the case of a private firm, this is to be an explicit affair. Before making any investments, the managers of the firm have to make a revenue–expenditure (or a financial) analysis of their alternative investment options. This may be important for someone who wants to start a social enterprise or becomes the manager responsible for such analysis in a company or organization.

However, such a financial analysis is not strictly a part of economics. Moreover, economists rarely bother whether private firms or individuals do a cost–benefit analysis of their own actions. The reason behind this attitude of economists is that if private individuals and firms are not doing it, they are going to bear the cost. Private firms who invest without carrying out such an analysis may lose or even close down if they continue to do so. Individuals may feel bad if they have taken wrong decisions and based on past lessons they may correct their behaviour.

On the other hand, there are some cases in which economists are particularly concerned about such analysis. Economic analysis is somewhat different from the financial analysis that firms and individuals carry out. Consider the case of a road. The decision to construct a road is taken usually by public organizations. There is a need for cost–benefit analysis here and unlike in the case of individuals or private firms, we cannot presume that public organizations have the incentive to do such an analysis. This is so because the costs of their actions are not borne by the officials or politicians who manage public organizations. Moreover, what public organizations have to consider as costs or benefits in the case of a road is not what they spend (as expenditure) or what they get as revenue. The organization constructing the road—for example, the highway department—may not get anything back as the revenue from the road. The benefits are to the people using it. They may get the benefits of spending a lesser time on the road (which may mean more time at work or for leisure). There are many such differences between economic and financial analysis and we will discuss them in detail later on. It is sufficient to note here that the cost–benefit analysis in the case of a road is much more difficult than what a private firm has to do while planning a new factory.

Whether we carry out a cost–benefit analysis in reality or not, the basic insights of such an analysis have to be internalized in all public decisions. One powerful tool that economics provide for development is those insights.

There are also other related tools. Since the resources are limited, both for a government and a non-governmental agency, we may want to see that the development interventions actually create the benefits intended. How do we ensure this? This is not an easy task as we presume.

Let us take a simple case. Farmers in a locality are facing a lot of hardship. Their income level is low. The government decided to provide them with an irrigation system on the presumption that the lack of irrigation is their main problem. A few years after the implementation of the irrigation system, their income increased. Is it then that the irrigation system was successful in enhancing their income? This may be true, but establishing this result needs a systematic analysis. This is because other socio-economic factors may have also changed during this period in the locality. The crops/cropping systems might have changed, children might have got educated/migrated and they may have got jobs, there could be other government interventions, or there may be an increase in the price of crops. All these may have contributed to the increase in their income. So it may be wrong to credit the increase in income to the irrigation system. How do we then separate out the impact of the irrigation system? There are techniques and methods in empirical research used as part of the economics discipline, which may help us in this regard. (Such methods establishing relationships are used in a number of disciplines doing empirical research and economics is one among them.)

Thus, an important use of studying economics is to internalize these tools or the insights behind them.

ECONOMICS AS A TOOL TO DESIGN BETTER RULES, ORGANIZATIONS AND GOVERNANCE FOR ACHIEVING HIGHER LEVELS OF DEVELOPMENT

There is a misconception among many people that economics deals with only markets. Market is one forum where people exchange goods and services voluntarily. Though markets perform reasonably well in certain situations (and it is harmful to avoid markets), there are many situations where such voluntary exchange would not produce most desirable results for the society. In such situations, an entity, beyond private individuals or private firms representing the wider interest of the society, needs to intervene. This may require a rule or a norm and/or a particular organizational intervention which needs to be abided by all the stakeholders. This is called an institution. Economics help us to identify where markets could be used and where institutions are needed. There are also multiple or alternative institutions to address one specific problem. For example, it is understood, based on theory and also from the experience in different parts of the world, that there should be some government intervention in school education. However, there can be multiple ways of intervention. There can be government-owned schools or there can be government financial support to private schools or there can also be government support to parents to send their children to whichever schools they like. There can also be different ways of supporting private schools like the payment of teachers' salary (a method widely practised in many Indian states) or there can be cash support to schools based on the number of children. Each of these can be reckoned as a particular type of intervention or a rule of the game.

There is also a need to evaluate these different 'institutions' with regard to public education if they exist or have been in use in a context. Or there may be a situation where we may have to pick up or design the most appropriate institution in a context before its implementation. For both these cases, we may need a criterion to evaluate different institutions. This evaluation need not be on the basis of one dimension. Economics can provide some insights in this regard. We will discuss this in detail in later chapters.

To some extent, this tool of economics is less understood in India. However, this is very important because there is a greater realization today that development outcomes in India and other developing countries are lethargic mainly due to poor institutions and mechanisms of governance and not just due to the lack of resources (money) or technology. The economic growth of India has generated substantial resources to be spent on the social sector both by the government and NGOs. Both central and state governments have been making larger allocations in this regard. Non-governmental initiatives are also increasing. Access to technology, in the broadest sense of the term, has also improved due to (*a*) globalization which facilitates faster movements of goods, services, people and ideas and (*b*) the revolutionary changes in information and communication technology. Information on the best practices in development (including those for poverty alleviation) from one part of the world reaches the other part without many hurdles these days.

However, all these developments have not led to a drastic improvement in development outcomes in many parts of India or of the developing world. There is a growing realization that internal institutions (including informal norms), or the lack of development-enabling institutions, are a major constraint. This can also be a reflection of the lack of social or political change including democratization. There can be political failures even in democratized states. All such institutional and political hurdles cannot be understood well using the framework of economics. However, there is an attempt to extend the method of economics to generate some insights on these issues as well.

QUESTIONS

1. Do you think that economic growth is adequate for achieving development? Give reasons.
2. Based on the limited understanding of this chapter, list three factors that may cause underdevelopment.
3. What is the need for a cost–benefit analysis for a public service like the construction of a road?
4. Children were found to be not attending school regularly in a village. An innovative teacher arranged the screening of Bollywood movies once in a week for those children who attended the school regularly. After a couple of years, school attendance went up substantially there. The teacher claims that this was due to her innovation. How do you respond to such a claim?

5. There are a significant number of infant deaths at the time of child delivery in a village. There is a perception that this was due to the absence of a trained midwife or doctor. The district government is planning to make one of the following interventions: (*a*) start a government hospital; (*b*) make payment to a trained doctor to visit the village at the time of child delivery; (*c*) provide financial support to villagers to go to the hospitals in district headquarters. Do you think that economics can be of any use in this decision? Give us your current understanding of the use of economics here.

⊰ TWO ⊱

WHAT IS ECONOMICS?

————◦◉◦————

This chapter provides a short introduction to the main focus of the discipline called economics. It tells us what economics is not about since there are many misconceptions even among well-meaning/educated people about the focus and methods of this discipline. The chapter starts with a very short summary of the origin and the historical emergence of different approaches of economics. It then moves to different sub-disciplines and issues covered (and not covered) within the discipline. It also gives a short summary of what is called the rational choice framework used in economics.

For economics as a discipline, though it may have roots in many cultural traditions (including in India where Kautilya is seen as a pioneer in this regard for his work namely, the *Arthasastra*), a more codified knowledge and disciplinary thinking emerged in the eighteenth and nineteenth centuries in Western Europe. One can identify a few early schools of thought in this regard. The first one can be attributed to the book titled, *An Inquiry into the Nature and Causes of the Wealth of Nations* by Adam Smith (first published in 1776). A major contribution of Smith is the codification of a major process in the economy—how the 'market' or invisible hand enables the process of coordination of the actions of disparate and self-interested individuals. However, he was also cautious to note that all such self-interest-based actions need not lead to desirable results. For example, what is currently considered as monopoly, when one particular company tries in different ways to avoid competition, was analysed critically by Adam Smith. He had also identified the 'division of labour' as a phenomenon of directing economic change over a long period of time. If most of the items required for making food in a traditional village household were made there, most of these items are 'bought' in an urban household. This is a manifestation of the division of labour. For example, if wheat was ground to make powder in most households earlier, currently we have firms specializing in making wheat powder. It may be cheaper to produce it in a factory rather than in all households spending effort to make wheat powder.

The second tradition was that of Karl Marx, whose publications came out in the middle of the nineteenth century. His interest was more in developing an economic theory of long-run social change. He focused on the dynamics between forces of production (or what can be crudely understood as technology) and relations of production (say between workers and owners of capital). For him, the changes in forces of production are somewhat autonomous and this may influence or induce changes in the relations of production. The inventions of the steam engine and factory mode of production are examples of such 'autonomous' change in forces of production, which in turn caused changes in relations of production. These inventions might have forced artisans who were producing artifacts in their own houses (as self-managed units) to move towards factories with owners and managers. Thus the organization of 'relations of production' may move from feudalism (where big landlords may be organizing agricultural production through tenants) to capitalism (where the main mode of production is factories with capitalist owners hiring workers). Based on this understanding of economic change, he predicted a sharpening of the conflicts between workers and capitalists and this, according to him, would lead to a transition towards socialism wherein workers gain control over the means of production like land or factories. This prescription was partly driven by the human suffering that he witnessed during the early phase of capitalism.

There were a number of economists then who followed the tradition of Adam Smith, with or without relating to the works of Marx, but all focused on the larger picture. Broadly, these set of studies can be called classical political economy. We will refer to them in a later chapter while discussing the changing ideas about economic growth. However, it is Alfred Marshal (1842–1924) who started developing economics into a way of analysing the decisions of individuals. It is easy to understand that the decisions of individuals are influenced by many factors. If one were to ask why a person bought 1 kilo of bananas (or why a set of people bought 50 kilos of bananas), it is difficult to explain this phenomenon. This is because such an action may be driven by their personal liking for banana; social conditioning that banana is good for health; the price at which banana is available; and because of their income.

One can take another social issue namely the farmers' suicides that we have seen in some Indian states recently. There are several factors that may influence such a phenomenon. These may include the increase in debt, reduction of the price of crops, loss of crop due to natural calamities, lack of support within the family or within the community, the lack of will power and other psychological factors and so on. Explaining why 50 farmers committed suicide in a village is almost impossible, since there are several factors influencing this outcome.

However, the marginal approach introduced by Alfred Marshal helped us in a different way. Though we cannot explain why 50 farmers committed suicide (or why somebody bought 10 bananas), it may be possible to explain why there is a reduction in farmers' suicide (or why some people who were buying 10 bananas have now decreased their purchase of bananas). This change in behaviour (reduced frequency of farmers' suicides or the reduction in banana consumption) can be analysed to see whether it is related to any change in one of the possible variables (which are visible/tangible/measurable) that may influence farmers' suicide (or banana consumption). For example, is the reduction in farmers' suicides related to an increase in the price of the crop that they cultivate? Is the reduction in banana consumption related to any change in price? Or is it due to any change in the income of the people? Such an analysis is possible only when other factors (say, psychological factors in the case of farmers' suicides or the liking for banana and social conditioning in the case of banana consumption) are not changing. With reasonable assumptions, a change in human behaviour/action/ choice can be related to a change in one observable variable (either by assuming reasonably that other factors are not changing at that point of time) or by using some methods to isolate the impact of change due to other variables. This is the important contribution of 'marginalism' in economics and this is generally seen as a tradition built by Alfred Marshal.

It is not that all economists focused on such individual behaviour (or what can be called microeconomics). There were also attempts to see the economy as a whole (all economic activities happening in a country at a point of time) as the unit of analysis or as a system driven by multiple forces such as consumption, savings, government investment and so on. How do the changes in some of these variables affect the performance of the economy? That was the approach used in what can be called macroeconomics. There are many traditions in macroeconomics. John Maynard Keynes was the one who analysed the economies at periods when these were shrinking (the total money value of the economic activities of a nation was decreasing and not increasing) and he came out with prescriptions of what governments can do during such periods. This had an impact on what governments did during what can be called recession (when the size of the economy is shrinking). Some economists have used these insights to tell us what the government can do in general to facilitate economic growth.

There was another tradition of macroeconomics, which saw the role of the state mainly in the form of regulating money supply. Money in every country is supplied by what is called the central bank (like the Reserve Bank of India). They found certain relationships between money supply and the performance of macroeconomic variables such as inflation (when prices of most commodities increase because more money is chasing fewer goods). They advised governments to 'regulate' money supply for macroeconomic management (say for controlling inflation). We do not touch upon these macroeconomic lessons in this textbook since we do not see any major role for development practitioners in such macroeconomic management. So we will mainly focus on microeconomics, even though there is one chapter in this book on macroeconomic variables that may have a bearing on development outcomes.

Issues of economic development (or underdevelopment) have also started attracting the attention of economists starting from the mid-twentieth century, when the world was confronted with problems arising out of world wars. It was also around that time that many countries gained independence from colonial rule. A number of such early development studies, following the classical political economy, focused on structural features (like the distribution/nature of asset ownership) and political economy factors (and the classes that wielded political power) and influenced the development process of these countries. However, such development theory was superseded later on by the microeconomic understanding of the issues of development. This was possible since microeconomics offered a better and consistent theoretical framework and predictive power.

Microeconomics has developed considerably during the last 70–80 years and a few of these major disciplinary developments need to be cited here. The analysis of the participation of individuals and firms in economic activities and the markets was the basic foundation of this microeconomics. Such an analysis was helpful not only to analyse situations where markets are useful, but also to know the conditions under which these may not perform well. Monopoly or other restrictive forms of markets have received substantial attention of the discipline. Microeconomics has also helped in identifying situations where the use of markets need not lead to socially desirable results. This led to the growth of public economics. Provision of 'public goods'—goods that benefit a wider society as a whole (and we discuss a rigorous definition of the term in a later chapter)— became an important concern.

Another area where the market 'fails' is in dealing with environmental pollution—leading to the development of environmental economics. There exist a number of contexts where incomplete information on the part of some parties hinders the smooth functioning of markets and a substantial part of economics today is devoted to such information-related issues. Microeconomics also gave a strong foundation to the growth theory—analysis of factors that may facilitate or decelerate economic growth of countries. Growth theory initially focused more on the inadequacy of capital and technology (which can be supplied from external sources) as barriers against development; but the recent focus is on internal factors such as population growth, education and innovation. Of late, microeconomics has started focusing on rules (which are called institutions) and organizations and the lack of appropriate institutions is viewed as an important constraint for achieving development. This textbook has some insights from all these branches of microeconomics.

WHAT IS NOT DEALT WITH IN ECONOMICS?

Economics does not deal with certain themes. Certain social, cultural or even psychological attitudes may enable individuals or groups of people to enhance their income or to achieve social mobility. For example, it is argued that the protestant ethics of North-Western Europe have facilitated the process of economic development there. By and large such factors are not analysed by economists. The natural environment, within which one lives, may have an impact on life and development. There was an argument that poverty is less miserable in a tropical environment, since one may not need the kind of clothes or energy as in a cold region. The humid tropical regions, where there is sunshine and lots of rain, generate substantial amounts of biological resources (flora and fauna) and such a biological environment can give life-sustaining food to a relatively higher level of population. Moreover, there may not be much scarcity of drinking water there. The natural environment, therefore, plays an important role in development or human life. The impact of nature on human life is not a major concern for economics, but it analyses the demand and availability of natural resources. It also analyses the situations where human impact leads to the destruction of natural resources or environment.

Similarly, science and technology play an important role in development. Though economics studies the policy environment that sustains such technological change or the economic impact of technology, development of science and technology per se is not a part of the economics discipline. It is clear that there are some issues of development (or some factors that influence development), which are not the main subject of the study of economics.

CORE ISSUES DEALT WITH IN ECONOMICS

A major aspect of study in economics is about how the production and consumption of goods and services are organized. We know that all people consume some goods and services, but normally only a few are involved in the production of each of these goods and services. How does the demand for consumption match with the supply of goods and services? Production takes place by mobilizing different inputs—money, workers, managers, electricity, other natural resources and so on. How does the demand for such inputs match with their availability? The production process is not static. Availability of new technologies (generated elsewhere or within the economy), over which economists do not have much to say, may change the production process. How does the demand for inputs to production match with their availability and how does this matching change with technological change? These are some of the core issues analysed within the discipline of economics.

An important entity that mediates this process is called the market. Thus, a major part of the attention of the economist is focused on the functioning of markets. However, there is a realization within economics that all exchanges cannot be organized as markets as well. For example, when a thief attacks our house, it may not be possible or desirable for us to run to the street to call a thug, though it is desirable to call a taxi/auto when we need to go somewhere. Similarly, it need not be desirable for a company to hire a worker as and when it is needed. It may require employees working on contract for a period of time. In both these cases 'markets' in the conventional sense of the term is not the best option. Thus, we need to think about non-market ways of organizing the supply of a good or service. When our house is robbed, we go to the police station. What is the best way of organizing services such as police or law and order? These are also the subject matter of economics. We know that it is the governments that usually provide the services of policing and law and order. Thus, what should be done by the government and how it can provide these services (by taxing people) too are important themes of economics. From these discussions, it is clear that what the government does or does not do may influence development. If a greater part of the resources of the government is used for buying arms for the military, or is used by the rulers themselves (say for building palaces) and only a smaller part of the resources are available for vaccination, provision of drinking water, education and many other such services, it may have a negative impact on development.

Over a period of time the subject matter of economics has also expanded. Conventionally, if a person believes that consumption of alcohol is good (or bad), having a large number of children is good (or bad), women are inferior to men, salvation comes from annihilating or destroying the other and so on, such beliefs are not considered the subject matter of economics. This is true to some extent even today. However, economists in the last two to three decades have 'struggled hard' to understand two aspects related to such beliefs: (*a*) what are the implications of such beliefs on the economy or on development? (*b*) Are there some 'economic' reasons behind the shaping and persistence of such beliefs?

Such expansion of the scope of economics was possible, since it is seen these days more as a way of analysing human behaviour and this is described in the following section.

ECONOMICS—A WAY OF ANALYSING HUMAN BEHAVIOUR AND SOCIAL INSTITUTIONS

Economics can also be viewed as a method of analysing or explaining human behaviour. The behaviour of a particular person or a group of people is influenced by a set of factors. For example, the decision to send a child to a particular school may depend on the cost (fees and travel), whether it is a public or a private school, the perceived quality of the school, personal preferences regarding the school, the religious/secular orientation of the management, social ideas about education internalized by the parent and so on. This wider set of factors can be divided into two. The first set includes those which can be measured or which are much more tangible. All those like personal preferences which cannot be measured or are intangible can be put under the second set. It is relatively easy to see, measure and perceive the changes in the first set; these are much more difficult, if not impossible, in the case of the second set of factors. But human behaviour depends on these two sets—tangible and intangible set—of factors. Economics tries to study the change in behaviour when there is a change in one of the tangible factors, by assuming that the intangible set of factors remains the same (unchanged) during the period which is studied. More specifically, it studies the direction of change, if there is a change—whether change takes place in the same direction as that of the factor changed or in the reverse direction. Take the example of admitting a child in the school, what change occurs when the fee goes up? Do more persons opt for schools with higher fees? Or is it the other way round? While doing so, our assumption is that factors other than fees and intangible ones like personal preferences or the internalized ideas of a good school remain the same. Such analysis is possible not only for explicitly 'economic' factors like fees. Take another variable. Will the change in the ownership of a school (having a new private school, a public becomes private, or vice versa) lead to a change in the approach of the parents? Are more parents opting for when private schools turned public or vice versa? Or the other way around? Such an analysis is possible with any of the tangible factors.

What we assess here is the change and its direction. There is a reason for this. If we set our job as to explain how many more children drop out when the fee increases or when the management changes, it may be an unviable project according to economics, since this depends on the human behaviour influenced by all—both tangible and intangible—factors. It is very difficult to study the impact of all factors influencing human behaviour, especially the intangible ones like personal preferences, which may vary from person to person. On the other hand, changes in tangible variables like the fees or ownership or a government law, or the content of curriculum or the gender of the majority of teachers, or the religion of the trust managing the school, or the role of the parent teachers' association (PTA) or local government in the management of school and so on, are visible. Once such a visible change takes place, we can then see whether there will be a corresponding change in the way the school is used or not.

In doing such an analysis, there are also underlying assumptions about human behaviour. It is presumed that people have some consistency in their behaviour. For example, if a person likes A over B and B is liked over C, then such a consistent position would mean that A would be liked over C (and not the other way around). People are expected to have some objectives, like say, to have more happiness or money. What is needed here is for people to prioritize different alternative choices (like actions or bundles of goods and services) in an ascending or descending order based on their objective (like say happiness). It is also assumed that there are no relevant options, which they cannot prioritize. If somebody thinks that getting 25 kilos of rice and 2 litres of vegetable oil is better than getting 20 kilos of rice and 2.5 litres of oil, then we presume that he/she can somehow evaluate 22 kilos of rice and 2.25 litres of oil (or any such combinations in between). It is also assumed that once individuals have an objective (say to get more leisure), they will try to maximize it within the constraints. Or more specifically, if they want happiness and if they get such happiness by making a specific choice and if they can indeed make that choice within their constraints, then it is expected that they would do so and not forgo that opportunity. For example, if they want to get happiness by travelling and they can order different travel plans on the basis of happiness that they get and if a particular plan is the one that would give them maximum happiness and they can, in fact, choose that travel plan given their resource constraints (like money and time), then it is expected that they would indeed make that choice. This is the essence of rational choice.

With these assumptions on human behaviour, we assess the direction of change in behaviour as one tangible factor changes (by reckoning that other factors remain the same). In most cases, only the direction of change is assessed (like whether people demand less or more of a good as its price increases) and the amount of change is not assessed (like how many more number of units of a particular good are consumed). There is one area where the amount of change is also assessed and that is the cost–benefit analysis. Here we assess the benefits of a particular amount of change in outcome. For example, if people start consuming more of an item because of a fall in its price, then the benefit of this change is measured. (In contrast, if people have to reduce the consumption of a good/service due to the increase in its price, this reduction in consumption may entail a loss and it may be assessed.)

Thus, if any project has resulted in such changes then all the benefits and losses due to such changes may be assessed and compared to see whether benefits outweigh the losses.

There is also a normative position in economics to evaluate different outcomes. If people know what they want (and let us call it happiness), then it is considered desirable to have actions that increase the happiness of one without reducing the happiness of others. It may be noted that when one's happiness is increasing without reducing others' happiness, the society's total happiness increases. This is called Pareto efficiency. Of course there is a problem of measuring happiness here. (See the discussion in Box 2.1.) One version of this efficiency

Box 2.1: On the Problem of Measuring Happiness or Utility

If we are thinking about the rational choice of only one person, then our inability to measure happiness should not matter. Then this person should be able to arrange all options before him/her, on the basis of the happiness that each option may give to him/her. Similarly, if there are choices that would enhance this person's (say X's) happiness without affecting the happiness of others in any manner, then operationalization of the efficiency argument that such pursuit of happiness by X should be allowed by the society, does not require a measurement of happiness. On the other hand, measurement is needed if we need to compare the happiness of two individuals. What would be the unit of measurement of happiness, which can work across individuals? How do we add the increased happiness of X and Y to see whether the aggregate is greater than the loss of happiness of Z? Such interpersonal comparison and aggregation may be required in certain cases, especially if we use the second version of Pareto efficiency. Thus, in reality, we need to convert the increase or decrease in happiness into something measurable and here income is the most widely used measure. Rather than measuring the increase in the happiness of a person (say by having a park in front of her house), we may ask what she would be willing to pay to have that park while keeping all other relevant factors constant? If somebody's ancestral property is destroyed, then we may measure his willingness to accept compensation in terms of money to avoid his unhappiness just arising out of this destruction. Once you have such money values (that is, willing to pay to get additional happiness or willing to accept as compensation for the reduced happiness), interpersonal comparisons and aggregations are possible.

Source: Author.

would argue that it is desirable to increase the happiness of A, even if that would reduce the happiness of B (or others), provided A can compensate B (and others) fully for the reduction in their happiness. This is Pareto efficiency with a compensation criterion. Similarly, if something (say X units of happiness) can be produced by spending 50 units of input, then doing so by spending anything more than 50 is not considered desirable. This is efficiency related to cost minimization. This is related to Pareto efficiency, since, if something which can be produced by 50 is in reality produced by spending 60, the process can be changed to produce it by 50 and the remaining 10 effectively used for something useful to enhance the happiness of the same person or of someone else.

Thus, a system or a rule is evaluated on the basis of whether it helps achieving Pareto efficiency and the cost minimization wherever it is relevant. Thus a rule which forbids increasing the happiness of A without reducing the happiness of others is considered less desirable. A system that does not encourage people to produce something with a minimum required amount of input is not reckoned as an efficient system. A rule which gives 'A' an additional income of 1,000 (or its equivalent of happiness or some other satisfaction) by reducing an income of 1,100 (or its equivalent of happiness or some other satisfaction) to others is also considered inefficient. This is not Pareto efficient since a society's total income (or satisfaction) declines here.

BIBLIOGRAPHIC NOTE

The first chapters of many standard textbooks on microeconomics would give a flavor of the method of economics. Two books that I have liked in this regard are Frank (2005) and Silberberg (1990).

QUESTIONS

You may refer to other writings too to answer these questions.

1. Why do we consider the contribution of economist Adam Smith as pioneering?
2. What is the economics behind the prediction of Karl Marx that socialism would come to exist?

3. What is the condition of economy that was analysed by John Maynard Keynes?

4. What is the importance of 'marginalism' in creating economic explanations?

5. What, in your view, is the crucial difference between microeconomics and macroeconomics?

6. List two sub-disciplines of economics which analyse the inadequacies of markets.

7. Assume that the score of a set of students in mathematics in a school depends on the innate interest of students, how good the teacher was, the number of mathematics teachers in the school, whether there was an active PTA or not, whether the headmistress is a woman or a man and many other factors. Think about an economic explanation, considering its focus on marginal change. What could be considered as a non-economic explanation?

8. What are the assumptions usually made behind an economic analysis of the choice of an individual? Think about a case where the choice is between electricity tariffs and power cuts. (Please note that under normal circumstances, if customers pay a higher tariff, the power cut can be reduced by the utility.) Some options before them are (₹5 per unit; 20 minutes of power cut per day); (₹4 per unit; 1 hour per day); and (₹3 per unit; 2 hours per day).

9. The average price of coffee beans in India in 2005 was ₹30 per kilo. An Indo-Sri Lanka Free Trade Agreement came into effect in 2006. The average price of coffee in 2007 was ₹25 a kilo. A farmers' organization argues that the decline in the price of the coffee bean is a negative impact of the trade agreement. Based on the method of economic analysis you have studied, what would be your response?

PART II

ANALYTICAL BOX OF ECONOMICS

THREE

RATIONAL CHOICE ANALYSIS OF INDIVIDUALS AND FIRMS

—————◆•◆•◆—————

Consumption and production are two important processes in the economy of a country or a region. Everybody consumes (certain types of goods and services) but usually a limited number of firms produce goods and services. This chapter analyses the behaviour of individuals and decisions of firms regarding their consumption and the supply of a product/service, respectively. This chapter is to be taken as a very concise summary, since the same subject is usually addressed in several chapters in a basic textbook of economics. Thus, the purpose of this section here is to make development practitioners aware of the need for and possible insights from, a demand and supply analysis. But the description in this section is not adequate to make one capable to carry out a methodologically rigorous analysis. This can be done only by a trained economist. Anybody interested to know more should refer to standard textbooks.

We have seen that economics helps us to analyse human behaviour. An important part of this analysis is to see whether there is some pattern in the way people use certain goods and services. This is called 'demand analysis' in the conventional economics syllabus. Such an analysis has to be a concern for not only those companies which sell goods/services but also for the government and NGOs, which provide services such as health care and education. Agencies concerned about people using certain substances like alcohol or not using a few others like clean fuels or hygienic toilets also need to know the demand patterns. If people reduce their consumption of alcohol when its price goes up, it may indicate that a higher tax on this commodity may reduce its use. On the other hand, if some people do not reduce their consumption of alcohol even when its price goes up (and reduce the consumption of other items like food for the household) then we may need a different kind of policy and not a tax.

Given the approach of economics described in Chapter 2, let us briefly discuss the insights of economics in analysing demand.

ANALYSING DEMAND FOR GOODS AND SERVICES

Given an opportunity, an individual may consume several commodities like food, cloth and so on and services like entertainment (watching TV), vacation travel and so on. There is a cost to each of these items of consumption. They may also want to have some leisure and this leisure is also 'costly' since (if they want leisure) they cannot work during that time. What they have as their money income may limit the total amount of commodities and services that they can purchase/consume. Similarly, if one opts for more leisure, it may reduce their income and hence what they can purchase.

Each individual is expected to consume to meet his or her satisfaction (or of those of the children or the members of the household. It can even be for the satisfaction of somebody else and that need not complicate the analysis much here). A crucial insight of economics in this regard is what can be called the 'trade-off'. One person (let us call her X) may like to have more clothes, even if that would mean some reduction of the quality of food. On the other hand, there may be another individual (say Y) who may give more importance to food. What each person may do when they have more income may depend on these 'preferences'. For both of them, more spending on food would mean less on clothing and vice versa. Thus the additional satisfaction that each person may get by spending say ₹100 more on food would depend upon the nature of the preferences of the person.

If basic food is already bought (without which no one can live), then spending more on food will give lesser satisfaction to X (compared with what she would have got, if that money is spent on clothes). Similarly, once the basic clothes are bought, spending more on flashy clothes would give less satisfaction to Y (compared with what he would have got if that money is spent on tastier food). Thus, there is a trade-off for both these (and for all) individuals regarding consumption. When some more money is available, whether to use it for one set of goods/services (or one basket) or on another set? We have seen that this may vary between individuals.

If one person has only consumed very minimal levels of food, then he/she may want to spend more of the additional money on food (since their need for food is less satisfied). On the other hand, if adequate food is already consumed, the urge to have more food may be low. This may be true for clothes but may not be at the same level as in the case of food. (We may see individuals spending more money on clothes even when they already have a significant amount of clothes. On the other hand, at least for some food stuff like rice or wheat, people may not be willing to spend more on it after they have these things adequately.) The trade-off (say between food and cloth) may change for the same individual, depending on the amount of these items that the person has already acquired.

We have seen some assumptions on human behaviour used in economics earlier. If a person (at a particular time) prefers an apple to an orange and prefers an orange more to a banana, then it is assumed that she/he will not prefer a banana more to an apple. This is an assumption on the consistency of the behaviour as part of a particular choice. Similarly, if one wants to have more food at a particular time and if they have the money in hand (and if the food is available), then it is expected that the person will pursue that want. Thus, it is assumed that individuals will not be lazy enough not to pursue what they want even when they have the means to do so. It is also assumed that they can make some ordering of what they want from the (available) choices based on their preference. If encountered by a set of options like watching a movie, buying a bottle of beer and going to a temple, to be done at a time and with some amount of money in hand, it is assumed that people are able to order these three from the most preferred to the least preferred one.

There are some taxing assumptions, which, in my view, may not limit the analysis of the rational choice of individuals on a number of occasions (but do so in certain other contexts). This has been already mentioned in the previous chapter. The first concerns the choice options which the individual can evaluate. The individual may encounter the following options, which we have considered as an exercise in the previous chapter: (₹5 per unit; 20 minutes of power cut per day), (₹ 4 per unit; 1 hour per day) and (₹ 3 per unit; 2 hours per day). Here, the consumer is expected to evaluate (or put as part of ordering) not only these three options but any in-between options (for example, ₹4.50, 40 minutes of power cut). Similarly, we have discussed the problem of measurement in Box 2.1 (Chapter 2). A money equivalent loss of moving from their more preferred option to the less preferred one (or the gains from moving from a less-preferred option to a more-preferred option) by keeping all other variables at the same level may also be necessary especially when interpersonal comparisons are needed.

Some insights emerge when these assumptions are used to analyse the behaviour of individuals with respect to their consumption. When a person spends some money on an item for consumption, he/she gets satisfaction. But the cost of this satisfaction is in terms of other items which she has to forgo due to spending the money on the chosen item. In the example given earlier, if a movie is selected, buying of a beer or visit to a temple may have to be given up. This is the cost of his/her satisfaction received from the chosen item. Thus, one can expect that people will choose an item to the extent that the satisfaction from it is at least as good as its 'cost'. This cost is defined as the satisfaction that could have been derived from the item given up due to the choice of a specified item. This is called the opportunity cost. Thus, cost is not merely the money to be spent on an item. It also includes a loss since this money could have been spent on some other item and this is not possible since it is (to be) spent on the chosen item.

We can consider the efficiency in consumption here. Given her resources, a set of decisions would be efficient if no other set of decisions that is feasible but gives greater utility exists. Take a simple example of consuming a banana (as one item of the consumption bundle). The consumption of bananas can be increased until the point where the additional pleasure or happiness becomes equal to the additional cost for procuring it. This depends crucially on two assumptions. The easy one says the additional (or, marginal as economists put it) cost of a banana is non-decreasing—the cost of a fifth banana is not less than the cost of the second banana. This is most often true if the bananas are bought from the market (and not gifted by somebody). The more non-trivial assumption is that the additional utility from the second banana is higher than the additional utility of the fifth banana.

This is called the declining marginal utility. Thus, if the individual is consuming five bananas, we can make the following observations:

1. When the individual consumes the third banana, the addition to utility from having the third banana is greater than the additional cost, that is, the price of the third banana.
2. If the individual consumes the sixth banana, the addition to utility from having the sixth banana is less than the additional cost, that is, the price of the sixth banana.
3. So, the individual buys the third, fourth and fifth banana, but does not buy the sixth banana.

So the consumption of bananas is at an efficient level when the additional utility of the last banana is equal to the cost of the additional banana or when marginal utility equals marginal cost (given the two assumptions stated above that marginal utility is decreasing and marginal cost is non-decreasing).

The consumers are likely to allocate money for different goods and services in such a way that for each item they would try to match the satisfaction derived from it with its cost. Hence they may reduce allocation on an item, if it is not very essential for some reason (and all such reasons are not studied by economics). For example, if cultural traits in a context discourage a person from consuming alcohol, he is less likely to spend money on it since he does not derive satisfaction from it (or gets dissatisfaction from its consumption due to the social aversion towards alcohol). A person is likely to spend less on more food, if she has already had enough food, since the additional satisfaction from more food is small. A person is likely to buy less of an item which costs more as she has to forgo more of other items to consume a given quantity of this item. For efficiency in consumption, matching of the additional satisfaction and the cost of each item in the consumption bundle is, though necessary, not adequate. There should be efficiency in the allocation of money between different items too. Take a very crude example as the following.

Assume that a person plans to spend Rs. 100 more per month on each of the following three items: (*a*) Tuition for the child; (*b*) vegetables and (*c*) alcohol. Let us assume that we use some way of measuring his additional happiness (by happiness units). The additional units of happiness for each of these items are:

(*a*) 45; (*b*) 20 and (*c*) 20. A situation like this is inefficient. This is so since by allocating more resources from (*b*) or (*c*), he may be able to achieve greater happiness. For example, by spending Rs. 50 less on vegetables or alcohol, he may lose say 8–10 units of happiness, whereas by spending this Rs. 50 more on tuition, his additional happiness may increase by say 18–20 units. Thus, some reallocation of money to one item from other item leads to a more efficient situation. Thus, efficiency is achieved only when all such gains by reallocation of money are derived, and no further gains can be made (by reallocation of resources).

The demand for a commodity by a person or a group of persons depends on a number of factors like gender, education, social background, geographical location and so on. Some of these factors are tangible (like gender or the number of years of education), but some others are intangible (like personal tastes sometimes determined by psychological or social/cultural conditioning). Using the economist's approach (as mentioned in Chapter 2), it may be possible to study (empirically) the changes in the demand of a commodity by a set of persons on the basis of a change in each of the tangible factors. For example, one can study whether persons with a higher level of education demand more of health care services (by keeping all other factors constant). The impact of the intangible factors is not studied, but it is assumed that such factors remain the same (do not change) during the period which is analysed.

It has already been mentioned that the demand for a good or service depends on how much of that good/service is already consumed. If we have already taken one or two bananas, then we may not like to have one more banana immediately. The urge to have the third banana is much less intense, compared with that for having the first banana. How do we say that the urge is less intense? This is expressed in economics as what is called the willingness to pay for the goods or services. (What if the person consuming is not the person who has to pay for the goods/ service? Usually children do not pay for the items they consume. People do not pay directly for many goods/services provided by the government....These are important issues but we will consider them in detail later.) If the urge to consume an item declines as the number of units of the same item already consumed increases, then their willingness to pay for each additional unit would come down (by keeping all other variables constant). People may be willing to pay more for the first banana, slightly less for the second banana and a much lesser amount for the third banana and so on. This is a manifestation of the declining marginal utility. This does not mean that for every good and service, the willingness to pay would come down as people consume more of the same item. It may remain constant or it may even increase during some range of consumption. This willingness to pay can also be interpreted as the price at which people are willing to buy one more unit of a commodity/service. If there is a declining marginal utility (declining additional satisfaction) operating for a particular range of consumption, the price at which they would be willing to pay would come down as more and more units of that item are bought.

A useful concept in this regard is what is called 'elasticity'. This is a measure of how much more or less a good/service would be consumed if there is an increase or decrease in the price or income. But this is a proportional measure. What is the percentage increase in the amount of consumption, if there is X (say 10) per cent increase in the price of a specific commodity? What percentage of decrease in the consumption of a good may happen due to a given (say X) per cent increase in the income of people? Thus, if a 5 per cent reduction in the quantity of consumption of an item has taken place due to a 10 per cent increase in its price, then the price elasticity is 5/10 (0.5). Similarly, one can calculate income elasticity by dividing the percentage (or ratio) of change in consumption by the percentage (or ratio) of the change in income. Higher price (or income) elasticity would mean that there is a higher change in consumption based on a change in its price (or the income of the people). On the other hand, goods for which people are less likely to reduce their consumption drastically when there is an increase in its price would have low elasticity. Basic goods whose consumption cannot be reduced (like food or drinking water) may be less elastic. People may continue to consume more or less a similar quantity of basic food or drinking water, even when the prices go up. Similarly, basic food or drinking water may have low income elasticity. This is because there may not be an increase in the quantum of the consumption of such goods even if the income of a person increases. On the other hand, for protein-rich foods or fruits and horticultural products, the income elasticity may be higher. As the income of people grows, people may be willing to buy more water for say gardening (but not for drinking) and here too, income elasticity could be higher.

The above discussion shows the kind of influences and the nature of people's behaviour in terms of demanding goods and services. This manifests in the form of a demand schedule—which can be simply represented in a graph as price versus quantity of each commodity (for an individual or a set of individuals)—which essentially would mean the additional quantity of a commodity that people are (or an individual is) willing to buy at a given price.

The demand schedules could be that of one individual or that of all individuals in a society. How do we get the demand schedule of the society from that of individuals? Let us take the case of two individuals A and B, whose demand schedules are given in Table 3.1. What A and B together are willing to buy are given in Column 4 and this is what the society's demand schedule (with the assumption in this case that there are only two individuals in the society).

The shape of this demand schedule (which indicates the elasticity too) represents the influence of the preferences and endowments of people with regard to the consumption of this specific good/service. In one sense, economists limit their analysis of individual behaviour to ascertaining the nature of the demand schedule and rarely go deep into what shapes their preferences.

It is assumed that all such variables (other than the price) remain constant as far as a particular demand schedule is concerned. If the income of a person (or a set of persons) increases, then there may be a new demand schedule depending on whether people with higher income demand more or less of this good. This is a shifting of demand schedule, whenever there is a change in factors other than the price of the good/service. This demand schedule is one important input for further economic analysis but that is not sufficient. We need a schedule that gives

Table 3.1
A Simple Demand Schedule

Price in ₹	Units A is willing to buy	Units B is willing to buy	Units A and B are willing to buy
40	1	0	1
30	2	1	3
20	3	2	5
10	4	3	7

SOURCE: Author.

us some insights about the supply of goods and services, which is discussed in the next section.

ANALYSIS OF PRODUCTION DECISIONS OF FIRMS

The goods and services are supplied by firms or organizations (and some of these are owned or controlled by the government). But we can take a very broad definition of the term called firms. It can include the farms selling agricultural products or an individual entrepreneur making/selling a product or a government or NGO providing health care. Their decisions are the subject matter of this section. The decisions of the firms on whether to supply an item or how much amount is to be supplied is much less complex compared with the decisions of individuals on whether to consume or how much to consume. This is so since supply decisions by firms are largely influenced by cost and profit considerations (or political considerations in the case of a government organization), while a number of social, cultural and psychological factors influence the decisions on consumption.

Let us consider the private firms or farms or the individuals producing and supplying goods and services. It is reasonable to assume that they are interested in profit (which is the revenue from the sale of goods minus the cost of production). There are multiple decisions and many factors influencing these decisions in this regard. Production of goods and services requires inputs like machine, workers, electricity, money for advertising, managers, factory space and so on. Some of these require major expenditure at the beginning—like that for the construction of a factory, whereas some others are recurring like the wages to be paid to the workers at the end of the month or the electricity bill to be paid to the utility. In order to understand the basic issues, we can categorize all these inputs into two categories—labour and money (capital).

A particular product, say a ready-made garment, can be produced in many ways. One way of making it is for a woman to stitch a shirt by using her hand; another possibility is to use manual sewing machine; and yet another possibility is to use an automatic sewing machine. In these three processes, the labour component is the highest in the first case, it is decreasing in the other two and it is the lowest in using an automatic sewing machine. On the other hand, the capital component is increasing from manual stitching to the use of automatic machine.

But we may note that in all these there is a combination of capital and labour being used. The only difference is that the amount of one of them (capital or labour) is more or less in each method of production. Ultimately, the entrepreneur is interested in producing the garment of a particular quality as cheaply as possible. (Why should that be the case? If some product of a specific quality can be produced at ₹50, why should a private entrepreneur be interested in producing it at ₹60?) We can presume that the costs of capital and labour influence the choice of the method of production. In a context where cost of labour is relatively higher than the cost of capital, capital-intensive technology may be used (automatic sewing machine is the capital-intensive technology in the above-mentioned example).

> What is this cost of capital? In one way, it is the cost of money. Money should be available from the banks or other lenders, and here the cost is interest rate. Money is also available in stock markets, and so on, and here the reward is dividends or appreciation on the value of shares. If the reward from the stock market is lower than the interest rates, then people may put their money in banks. Hence, interest rate may be taken as a benchmark cost of capital.

This is the reason why in developed countries, one can see automatic delivery machines replacing salesmen even in retail shops. On the other hand, in contexts where labour is cheaper than capital, one should be expecting the use of labour-intensive technologies like manually driven sewing machines or many saleswomen in retail shops.

There may be some situations where labour-intensive technologies may not be used even when there are many unemployed people (which would actually mean labour should be cheaper). Some of these situations are mentioned in Box 3.1.

There is some substitution between different inputs (capital and labour) possible often in a production process. Because of the urge to minimize cost, entrepreneurs may use an additional unit of a particular input only if the gain from doing so is greater than the cost of this additional input. This gain is to be seen in the increase in production. For example, if one more woman is employed in a garment factory, the additional gain is to be seen in the additional revenue from the production and/or sale of garments. The cost of the additional input in this case is the wage to be given to this worker. The entrepreneur is

Box 3.1: Why Do We See Labour-saving Technologies Being Used in Contexts Where Unemployment Is Very High?

There are multiple reasons: first, there may be some government rules which may discourage casual employment of unemployed people. If the cost of 'firing or dismissing' people is higher, entrepreneurs may be unwilling to hire many people. Moreover, management of many workers may be difficult and this may encourage the use of some machines. One can hear many middle class women complaining about the difficulty in managing the housemaids and this may encourage them to use machines (like washing machines) for household work. Preferences for certain quality or specific 'lifestyles' too may lead to the use of machines. There is an argument that economic liberalization in India has produced a middle class and the members of this class wish to have the lifestyle of Western countries and this may encourage them to use 'machines' and other facilities. This may have an impact on employment. However, the other cases wherein affluent middle class in India want to live in India rather than in the US or Europe are also visible. The fact that housemaids and car chauffeurs are available at affordable rates (compared with Western countries) and health care and nursing are also relatively cheaper here helps this process.

Source: Author.

likely to employ this woman only if the additional revenue (marginal revenue) from employing this person is at least a little greater than her wage. This is true with the input of capital too. The inputs are used in a production process only to the level wherein the additional gain from using one more unit of an input is equal to the cost of that (additional) input. Hence, the combination of capital and labour used in a production process will be determined by the relative prices of these two inputs.

Just like the demand schedule, there is a supply schedule. This is the additional quantity of a commodity that a firm is willing to supply at different prices. It is easy to see that this supply schedule is related to the cost of production. A firm would be willing to supply an additional X amount of an item when price changes from P1 to P2, only when each of these X units can be produced by spending an expenditure of P2 or less than that amount. Thus, the supply schedule can also be reinterpreted as the additional units of good that can be produced at different costs, implying that the firm would be willing to sell these additional units if they can at least recover the respective cost.

For a given commodity, it is reasonable to think that firms will be normally willing to produce more of it (willing to supply more of it) as the price at which it can be sold increases. Hence, a normal supply schedule is upward sloping when we draw it in a graph with the y axis depicting the price and the x axis depicting the additional quantity which the firms are willing to supply. This need not be true in all cases. If the supply of a good depends on some fixed (say some natural) resources, in such cases the supply need not increase even if the price goes up.

There is the concept of elasticity in production too. This is a measure of how much more (or less) of the good would be supplied when there is an increase (or decrease) in its price. Here too it is a proportional measure. What more percentage of the amount of the good would be produced, when there is a given (say 20) percentage increase in price? If there is a five per cent increase in the supply of the amount of the good when the price increases by 10 per cent, then the elasticity of supply is 5/10 (0.5). The elasticity will be very low or the supply inelastic if the supply of goods cannot be increased when there is an increase in price, as in the case of one depending on fixed (for example, natural) resources.

The shape of the supply schedule can be different during what can be called short term and long term. The production of a commodity may require capital investments like the building of a factory or the installation of machines. It also needs workers. Assume that there is a sudden increase in the demand for the commodity. The firm cannot increase the size of the factory or install machines quickly to meet the increased demand. It can only increase the number of work-ers. However, the additional production that can be made by the increased use of workers without having an expansion of factory can be limited or the per-unit cost may be higher due to such 'tight' or 'congested' expansion of production. Hence, the short term is the period during which all factors of production (including capital investments) cannot be changed and here the additional cost for each unit increase in production may be higher. Thus, a short-term supply curve can be steeper. On the other hand, in the long term, all factors can be changed to meet the change in demand, and then there can be greater efficiency and hence cost increase to meet additional production may then become moderate. The long-run supply schedule may be only moderately steep (less steep compared with the short-run supply schedule).

An important aspect that changes the supply schedule is technology. Technology in economics can be viewed in many ways. Each combination of capital and labour to produce a particular level of output can be viewed as one technology. In that sense, technology is selected on the basis of the relative cost of these inputs. But another manifestation of technology is when we can produce more with the same level of inputs for which entrepreneurs have to pay. In the case of printing, when we move from the manual printer to the computer-based printer, it may be possible to see that the number of pages printed by a given level of total input (by taking all inputs like money, workers and energy) going up. Or the total input needed per printout page comes down. This is a more efficient technology. When an efficient technology is used, entrepreneurs would be able to produce the same output at a lower cost (or more output at the same cost). Hence, they would be willing to supply more output at the same price (or the same output at lower price), compared with a situation where old technology is used. Thus, there is a new supply schedule. Sometimes, we call a new product (for example, 3G mobile phone) a new technology. This is more of a new product or a new quality or version of an existing product. This is usually treated in economics as a new good or service. Thus, when we talk about a shirt as a product, it is about a specific shirt, say 100 per cent cotton ready-made. On the other hand, another type of shirt made of 50 per cent cotton and the rest with polyester is a different product. The demand and supply schedules of different types of shirts have to be different, even though there may be some substitution of one shirt by the other at the consumers' side.

What will happen to the cost of production when more units of a good/service are produced? If one unit of a product costs ₹2 and two units cost ₹4 and so on, then there is a linear increase in cost. Or the additional cost per unit of production (or marginal cost) remains the same (₹2 in this case). There are three possibilities in this regard. The linear or proportional increase in total cost (or non-increasing marginal cost) that we have discussed here is one such case. There can also be situations where additional cost (cost per unit) comes down when more units of the output are produced. The per-unit cost of electricity may be lower with a 500 MW plant compared with a 50 MW plant. This is called scale economy—when something becomes more economical as a large-scale production is carried out. In certain cases, the cost of production per unit can go up as more units are produced. This is so since there can be congestion or additional management costs for the coordination of production as more inputs (including workers) need to be used for enhancing production. This can create some diseconomies in scale.

Whether there is a scale economy or not is a major issue in the decision on how to price a product. For the time being we can assume that the additional cost per unit either remains the same or is increasing. Such a situation is the least problematic for economic decision-making and a scale economy can create some complexity, hence, we will take that up in Chapter 5.

We have seen some factors influencing the decisions of consumers who demand goods/services and of firms which supply them. But these decisions have to be coordinated. The usual mechanism which coordinates them is the market. We will analyse it in the next chapter.

QUESTIONS

1. Consider the following two statements: 'Santhakumar consumes three bottles of beer a day'; 'Santhakumar consumes one more bottle of beer when its price comes down from ₹70 to ₹50 per bottle'. Which statement is more amenable to economic analysis? Why?
2. What is the elasticity of demand? Consider price and income elasticity. Give an example where you may be interested in knowing elasticity of demand as a development practitioner.
3. What are the factors that may influence the choice of labour-intensive (or capital-intensive) technology in production?
4. How does the cost of production change as more units of goods are produced? What are the different types in this regard?
5. List examples of goods which may have the following characteristics: (a) low income elasticity of demand; (b) low price elasticity of supply and (c) low price elasticity of demand.
6. We are talking about a land deal between Prestige Properties (PP—a real estate company) and a farmer living in suburban Bangalore who owns 10 acres of land. The farmer values his property at ₹100 million. Think about the following two situations:

   (a) PP buys land at ₹120 million and makes a profit from the real estate venture.

(*b*) PP uses political clout to buy the property forcefully from the farmer at ₹90 million and makes a profit greater than ₹10 million.

Discuss these two situations in terms of the economists' understanding of efficiency.

7. In a patriarchal society, women are not encouraged to take up paid labour outside the home. This is likely to have an impact on the choice of technology in that economy. Explain.

◄ FOUR ►

ANALYSIS OF MARKETS

———————•═◆═•———————

WHAT IS MARKET AND WHY IS IT IMPORTANT FOR ECONOMISTS?

Consumers get satisfaction only when there is somebody to sell what they want and producers get profit/income only when there are some buyers for their goods and services. Markets can be a place where the suppliers and the consumers meet. But we know that physical meeting is not needed for many markets to function. In this Internet age, online trading is possible even between anonymous buyers and traders. However, when economists talk about the markets, it is not much about this physical space of exchange.

We have seen that the basic components of an economy include producers, endowed with technology and consumers who have their own preferences and resources, which can be called endowments.[1] Consumers maximize their own welfare (which we call utility, derived from their preferences) and producers maximize profit. Let us start with a formal definition of market and then try to understand what it really means.

Economics define a competitive market (economy) as an equilibrium with a set of prices where, at those prices, consumers maximize their utility, producers their profit and, in the process, markets clear (that is, there is no unfulfilled demand for any good or service). Competition is a situation where no one agent's actions can affect the price of any commodity or service.

The above definition leads to two fundamental theorems in economics, which can be stated as follows: (*a*) any competitive economy is Pareto efficient and (*b*) any Pareto efficient outcome can be achieved in a competitive economy provided one is allowed to do a redistribution of the initial endowments.

First, what is Pareto efficiency, or efficiency, as it is more often known?

As mentioned earlier, measurement of happiness or utility is difficult and hence, we do not want to compare a person's utility with another's. If I give a banana to someone who likes bananas, his/her utility goes up. Alternatively, if I take away a banana that you consider consuming, I reduce your utility. If I take it away from you and give it to someone else, I do not know whether the other person's utility goes up by more than, equal to or less than by the amount you lose. This would require interpersonal utility comparisons and in economics we shy away from making such comparisons as much as we can. The concept of efficiency reflects this inability. Suppose we divide the resources in any society in either one of two ways, A and B. Suppose B is such that some people are better off than what they were under A, while others are no worse off than what they were under A. In other words, allocation B makes some people better off without making anyone worse off. We then describe A as an inefficient allocation of resources (because there is another allocation B that 'dominates' it). An allocation is efficient if it is not inefficient.

Let us consider a simple and somewhat trivial example. Suppose I had ₹100 and I divide it between two people X and Y (who together constitute our society). I denote an allocation by the ordered pair (x, y), where the first entry x goes to X and the second entry y goes to Y (hence, an 'ordered' pair since the order of the two entries is important to know who gets what). One such allocation could be (45, 50), meaning I give 45 to X and 50 to Y. Let me call this allocation A. Consider another allocation B, which is represented by the pair of (50, 50). We immediately know that A is inefficient since allocation B makes X better off without making Y worse off. But is allocation B efficient? If we were to make X better off than what she is getting now, we have to give her more than 50. However, our total amount of resource is ₹100. If we give X more than 50, we have to give Y less than 50. In other words, there exists no feasible allocation that makes B inefficient; hence, B is efficient. A feasible allocation A is inefficient if there exists another feasible allocation that makes some agents better off without making anyone else worse off. Any feasible allocation that is not inefficient is efficient.

This simple definition of efficiency has a very serious problem—it generates many efficient allocations. Even in our simple example with ₹100, there are too many efficient allocations. In fact, any (x, y) that satisfies $x + y = 100$ is an efficient allocation. In particular, both (100, 0) and (0, 100) are efficient allocations. Economists cannot survive as social scientists if they are satisfied with their result that giving everything in a society to one person is efficient. This is where the second theorem helps. It says that if you prefer an allocation (60, 40) and hate (100, 0), then a competitive economy will get you to the latter outcome (or very close to it) if you do an appropriate redistribution of the initial ownership of resources.

What does it mean in the context of development practice? Consider a village with agricultural land of 1,000 hectares. There are 50 families living there, but only 10 of them own these 1,000 hectares and the remaining 40 are farm workers. There could be a labour market within the village. Farmers will offer a wage rate at which they want to hire workers (if they offer less, they may not get them and if they offer more, that would reduce their profits). Workers would accept a wage which may be as good as what they can get elsewhere. If the wages in such out-side work is ₹60 per day, their wages as agricultural workers would also be at least ₹60. Thus, the labour market can efficiently determine wages here. However, it is possible that some are unhappy with such low wages and they want to increase them. The above-said second theorem says that it is possible to do it without manipulating or stopping the functioning of the labour markets there. What needs to be done is the redistribution of assets and here land is the main asset. If the land is redistributed, the landless will get a part of the land. After such distribution, the previously landless would work as agricultural workers only if the wage is higher than what they would have got from cultivation in their own plots (with the assumption that one cannot do both farming and working in others' farms). Or, there can be the distribution of another asset. If the children from landless families receive human capital (education) so that they can get skilled jobs elsewhere, this generation would take up farm work only at a much higher wage than that was prevailing in the absence of such education. Thus, by redistri-bution of endowments, one can achieve higher wages. In order to do so, there is no need to tweak labour markets. One such tweaking (instead of redistributing) occurs when the wages will be fixed by the government and not the market. This can lead to a certain level of inefficiency. One problem could be that the farmers may reduce cultivation and hire a lesser number of farm workers (since it may become less profitable or less viable to cultivate certain crops with such higher wages). Hence, the total gain for workers under the government-fixed wage system could be lesser than the market-determined system.

These two theorems allow economists to concentrate on two aspects—find out what makes markets non-competitive and then investigate the remedies for non-competitive markets. In other words, we study how to ensure that market outcomes are as close to what they will be if they are competitive markets. Contrary to popular belief in certain quarters, economists were the first to systematically study the conditions under which market outcomes are inefficient.

Why are economists then so much caught up with markets? This is because we believe that 'rational' people will voluntarily transact or trade, with each other only when it is in their interest to do so. And, if they voluntarily trade, it cannot be that any one of them will be worse off for they can always decide not to trade. Such voluntary trade takes place in what we call the markets and, hence, our obsession with them.

However, there are situations where market outcomes need not be perfect. We will discuss them in detail later on. But let us consider one example. If I listen to loud music and you are my neighbour, the satisfaction I derive in listening to music will decrease your satisfaction from silent meditation. This is called an externality—an action taken by a person or group affects another individual or group that was not a party to the original action. The fact that my neighbour and I are two different people is what causes the problem. If I like to listen to loud music and did silent meditation, I would solve this problem by listening to music when I liked it better than meditating and vice versa. Instead, if we are two people—one who likes loud music and the other meditation—we would have to coordinate our actions in such a way that I listen to music when he is not meditating. This understanding may be difficult to achieve voluntarily and this becomes evident when we consider that such coordination may have to be made not between two, but hundreds of individuals (for example, which side of the road to drive on).

WHAT ARE THE SOCIAL GAINS OF A MARKET EXCHANGE? AN EXAMPLE

It is easy for us to understand the gains from producing and supplying a useful product, and when some consumer uses it. But are there gains from mere exchange (a person selling something—say a house—to another person) in a situation where nothing new is produced? If so, how do we assess these gains?

Let us consider the following example.

Suppose A owns a house and money. The value of the assets (house and money), V_0^A, is given by $V_0^A = h^A + m^A$ where h^A is the value that A puts on her own house and m^A is the amount of money she possesses. It is important to understand that h^A is the personal value to A of the house; she must be given at least this amount of money if she was to voluntarily give up the house in exchange for money. This is known in economics as A's reservation price of the house. There are two other economic agents of interest to us, B who has an asset value $V_0^B = m^B$ and C who has an asset value $V_0^C = m^C$. The aggregate wealth among these three economic agents is given by $V_0 = V_0^A + V_0^B + V_0^C = h^A + m^A + m^B + m^C$.

One day, while going past A's house, B sees the house and immediately takes a fancy to it. He wants the house and convinces himself that he is willing to pay a maximum price of h^B for it; this is B's reservation price—any price below that and he will buy it. He knocks on her door and they sit down to bargain about the price. Let us suppose that $h^B > h^A$, that is, the maximum price B is willing to pay is greater than the minimum price A is willing to accept. Then one can safely say that unless something goes terribly wrong, the two will be able to reach some understanding and settle on a price p such that $h^A \leq p \leq h^B$.

If this transaction were to take place, then a number of economic principles would be satisfied. First, let us calculate the total valuation of assets resulting from this transaction. A now has $m^A + p$; B has $m^B - p + h^B$ and C continues to have m^C. Therefore, the total wealth of the economy is $V_1 = V_1^A + V_1^B + V_1^C = [m^A + p] + [m^B - p + h^B] + m^C = h^B + m^A + m^B + m^C > V_0$, as long as $h^B > h^A$, which was true to begin with. Here, a transaction that transfers an asset to one who values it more than the one from whom it is being transferred, increases the total wealth of the society. Hence, any society that allows, or enables, such transfers is desirable. Second, how does an asset market (or in this case, a market for houses) help? In a market, individuals transact voluntarily, that is, an individual will not go through with a transaction unless she benefits from it. In this case, as long as the price of the house, p, is greater than h^A or the reservation price of A, she would be willing to sell the house because she gets more than she gives up; similarly, as long as p is less than h^B, the buyer pays less than his reservation price or, again, loses less than what he gains. So, both are better off while C stays on at where he was before the transaction. Therefore, two are made better off while the third is no worse off than before.

CONDITIONS FOR MARKET TO FUNCTION

However, the fact that somebody demands a commodity does not necessarily create a market. Similarly, a market does not exist just because somebody is willing to supply. There are many real-world situations where a market or the actual provision of a good or service does not exist. For example, there are many villages where there are many people with some dental problems but no dental care is available. The reason for the absence of markets could be that what a person is willing to pay for a good or a service is lesser than the price at which any firm is willing to supply. This is especially so since there may be fixed costs in supplying a good/service in a locality and if there are not enough potential consumers willing to pay adequately, no firm may be willing to start serving there.

There also some conditions for the smooth functioning of the market. It is assumed that buyers have information on what they are buying and such information is cheap. It is also expected that sellers can communicate the nature of their product credibly to the consumers. However, there are many cases where such information gathering/communication is not cheap. Or there can be cases where such credible communication is not easy. This may have a bearing on the functioning of the markets. If someone is coming out with a new useful medicine, how do the consumers know whether it is really useful (before actually using it) or how can the producer tell the potential consumers in a convincing manner that medicine is indeed useful (this may require some government intervention and the point here is that a mere voluntary exchange is not possible or difficult)?

Another requirement for the market to function is that the additional costs required to buy something other than the price of a commodity are not high. What are these additional costs? If people want to buy land in a village, some money has to be paid to the local goon and this may restrain the market transactions. These additional costs are called transaction costs. In general, transaction costs include the following: search costs (for the buyer to look for a seller and vice versa), costs to assess the quality of the product, costs to see that the transaction is complete (to ensure that the good is transferred and money is paid) and also to take actions if one of the parties has violated any promised action. For example, the cost incurred by the buyer to get adequate remedy when found that the good supplied was not working properly is part of transaction costs. If these costs are very high, then either transaction may not take place or only a limited range of transactions would take place.

Let us consider the following example: in India, the current interest rate for bank loans is around 12 per cent. Thus, a farmer in a village should theoretically be able to get the loan at this rate. However, even when there are people who demand loans and when there is money (banks should be having money to lend at 12 per cent interest), a credit market need not function well in many Indian villages. People may not get a loan at this interest rate. This is due to the transaction costs, which may include the cost of what is to be done if the borrower did not pay back the loan. Such costs may lead to two outcomes: (a) some people may not get loans or (b) they may get loans only at much higher interest rates (say at 36 per cent from private money lenders) even when funds are available for 12 per cent. Thus, the scope of the credit market is reduced there.

HOW DOES THE MARKET WORK?

When a firm tries to produce something or expand an existing production unit, it needs to think about the possible demand from customers. Or it should have some information on the demand schedule of the potential customers (how much of the additional good will be bought at each change in the price of one unit of output). The suppliers are presumed to have information on their supply schedules (additional quantity they are willing to supply for each change in the price of one unit of output) based on an understanding of the costs (and with the interest in cost minimization).

Assume that there are a large number of firms trying to meet the demand for a specific commodity. The crucial issue here is that the amount of commodity supplied by a single firm is small enough so that it will not significantly change the total quantity of that particular good available in the market. Think about the market for rice and that supplied by a single farmer. Whatever be the size of the farm by this owner, his contribution can only be a miniscule part of the total quantity of the rice supplied in the market at a given point of time. Though the demand schedule for a set of consumers for rice may show a declining trend (the quantity of rice that people are willing to buy may increase as the price decreases), such a downward sloping demand curve is not relevant for a single supplier of rice. (Why do we call this a downward sloping curve? This is so when we plot a demand schedule in a two dimensional graph with the price on the y axis and the additional quantity willing to buy on the x axis, a typical demand schedule is a downward sloping one.)

It would mean that, for such a single supplier encountering a market populated by a large number of firms (and such a firm can be called a competing firm) it will encounter a price at which it can sell this product. This supplier may have some idea about this price. Once this price is known or expected (usually one can have only expectations of price), the firm will decide a quantity to be produced based on its supply schedule. After selecting this quantity, it will select inputs in such a way that the same quantity (of a particular quality) is produced with the minimum possible cost. An appropriate combination of inputs will be selected to achieve this cost minimization.

It may be true that, if only a few units of the good are available, people would be willing to pay a much higher price. As more and more quantities are available, the price that people would be willing to pay would come down (or as the price declines, people would be willing to buy more quantities). Consider the demand and supply schedules given in Table 4.1.

Table 4.1
A Demand and a Supply Schedule

Price per unit	Quantity that firms are willing to supply	Quantity that consumers are willing to buy
10	20	100
20	40	80
30	60	60
40	80	40
50	100	20

SOURCE: Author.

These schedules meet when the price is 30. Here the demand and supply schedules meet. If an exchange takes place at this point, there will not be any excess demand and excess supply (remember the definition of market). Here, the price per unit (p/u) that consumers are willing to pay is likely to be equal to the additional cost of producing one unit for the consumers. Here, customers buy 60 units at a price of 30. However, they were willing to buy 20 at ₹50 p/u, another 20 more at ₹40 and yet another 20 more at ₹30. Thus, when they buy all 60 at ₹30, they have gained ₹20 p/u for 20 units and ₹10 p/u for another 20 units. Thus, they gained ₹600. This is called consumer surplus.

Similarly, there is a producers' surplus when they could sell all 60 units at ₹30 p/u. They were willing to sell 20 at ₹10 p/u, another 20 more at ₹20 p/u and another 20 more at ₹30 p/u.

When they sold all 60 at ₹30 p/u, they gained ₹20 p/u for the first 20 units, another ₹10 p/u for the next 20 units. Thus, their surplus is also ₹600 (the same amount that consumers and producers gained here as surplus is only due to the specific example given here and that is not the general situation).

Producers and the consumers not only exchange some quantities of a good/service at a particular price but are also gaining a surplus from the process of exchange. Such surplus for the consumer and the producer arises when the price and the quantity are decided based on the meeting points of the supply and demand schedule.

When a consumer buys a unit of a commodity, she should be getting an additional satisfaction higher than her cost for that commodity (the price that she pays). If her satisfaction is 150 and the price is only 100, then it shows that probably her additional satisfaction from having one more unit could be say 125 (which is also higher than the cost). It indicates the possibility of a more efficient consumption (or that the current state—not consuming one more unit—as inefficient). Thus with efficiency it is expected that the consumers would go on consuming as long as their additional satisfaction from consumption is greater than price. For firms producing one more unit of the same commodity, they should get a price higher than the additional cost of producing this unit. If they get a price of 100 and the additional cost is only 80, it shows that they can probably produce one more unit (possibly at an additional cost of 90) and sell it at 100. This would enhance the profits. Thus, firms have an incentive to produce as long as the price they get is higher than the additional cost. Through this process the additional satisfaction that the consumer gets (by consuming one more unit) becomes equal to the additional cost of its production. This is efficient. Price and market are only intermediating this process, leading to efficiency. If there is some other interme- diating process, which can lead to efficiency, then it can be used (human attempts in this direction are not that successful, as evident from the central planning experiments in ex-socialist countries).

Let us now consider some specific markets.

Labour Markets

When firms want to hire workers, and people sell their labour, it becomes the labour market. Here, people at large become the suppliers and firms become the consumers. Some of the factors influencing the demand and supply are relevant here too. For example, social, cultural, educational and other factors, along with the wage rates (and other conditions of employment) influence the supply of labour. If the society is dominantly patriarchal, women may be socially/culturally compelled to work mainly within the household, which does not enable them to get any direct payment. Similarly, other social factors too may discourage the supply of workers for certain other work. In the case of a commodity, the usual pattern is that more of it will be supplied as the price goes up (though there can be exceptions). But in the case of labour supply, this upward sloping supply curve may not be visible all the times (needless to say that a supply schedule in labour market depicts how many more workers or how much more time a person would be willing to work as there is an increase in the wage rate). One well-known pat- tern is a backward bending supply curve—which essentially would mean that, as wages increase, people may not be willing to work as much as they would have done at low wage rates. This is due to the fact that they would like to have some leisure and with higher wage rates they can afford to have some more leisure. Such preference for leisure may be there not only among those with higher sala- ries but also among daily bread earners. This may lead to a peculiar impact. If the backward bending supply curve is prevalent, then one can see an increase in the supply of labour when wage rates become lower.

There is elasticity in this regard too. What percentage increase of labour will be forthcoming for a given percentage increase in wages would be one type of elasticity (price elasticity of labour supply). Similarly, there can be price elasticity of demand for labour. There can also be an income elasticity of labour supply. There can also be differences between long-run and short-run responses in terms of the demand for labour to changes in prices (wages). A short-run increase in wages may not lead to a drastic (short-run) reduction in the demand for labour. On the other hand, in the long-run firms may either use labour saving technologies or shift production to low-wage regions and thus the long-run reduction in labour demand in a region with an increase in wage could be sharper. If a government compels the firms to increase wages, or when such increase in wage is forced upon the firms by trade unions, the long-run effect could be a reduction in labour demand by the use of labour-saving technologies or through shifting of the factories to places with 'cheap labour'. In an open economy, high wages cannot be sustained in one particular region if lower wages prevail for the same job elsewhere.

Financial and Capital Markets

Like commodity and labour markets, there is also the capital market. Or, there are those who sell capital. Lenders and intermediaries like bankers are one such category. Lenders give people loans at a specified interest rate (which is the price of the loan). Banks mobilize deposits from those who save money and give this as loans to borrowers, again at a price called the interest rate. This price can become the additional cost of mobilizing and supplying capital, if there are a number of lenders/banks competing. Of course in a country like India, one can see many issues in the functioning of the financial market. One major problem is that, even if banks are available, everybody may not get loans. This is because banks want to ensure that the loans are repaid with interest. It is difficult to assess the quality of a person to know whether he/she would pay back the loan beforehand. Once the loan is given, then there is very little control that banks can exercise over the use of the money by the borrower. The banks have to use other strategies to ensure that they get their money back. Thus, they insist on collateral. The records of land, buildings or other such assets may have to be kept under the control of banks, so that in the case of default, they can sell these assets as a last resort to recover the money. Since these assets of the borrower are under the control of the banks, he/she has greater incentives to pay back the loan. However, this strategy creates another problem. Only those people who have such assets or those who can convince the banks through other means (like the guarantee of a salaried relative) can have loans from the bank. This would mean that in countries where many are landless and homeless, a significant part of the population may not have access to bank loans. Hence, there may be strategies needed on the part of the government to help with their needs for finance.

Land reforms, which provide land to landless or government supported and peer-monitored microfinance initiatives, may be useful in this regard. However, many informal money lenders give loans to poor people (who may not have collaterals) at very high interest rates (24–36 per cent per annum when bank rates are around 12 or 15). The fact is that some small borrowers may default loans since payback cannot be ensured through collaterals (since these poor people do not have assets to be shown as collaterals) or that the borrowers may have to use expensive strategies, including the use of thugs, to recover the money—all these may increase the effective interest rates from such informal lenders. There can also be other strategies used by these money lenders to ensure the return of loans. There could be some interlocking of loan and commodity markets. Farmers taking loans from a money lender/intermediary may commit to sell the farm products too to the same person. There is a loss of some freedom for the farmer and this is accepted to enhance the access to credit markets. All these specific problems arise primarily because of the limited access to capital markets and because capital markets may not have developed to meet the needs of the majority of the population.

Banks are controlled by the Government or the Central Banks (like the Reserve Bank of India) directly and indirectly and there may be some regulation in fixing interest rates. There is no such control over firms' functioning in other markets. Why should there be government or central-bank control over banks? What is so special about capital markets? See Box 4.2 for details.

Box 4.2: The Need for Regulating Banks

Unlike other market intermediaries, banks face a peculiar problem. They receive deposits from a large number of people and provide loans to another set of people. Out of the total loans, only a small part is based on banks' own finance and most of it is based on deposits. Those who borrow money from the bank are expected to return within specific durations. No bank will or can

(Box 4.2 contd.)

(Box 4.2 contd.)

keep all the deposits that it has collected in a treasury or a locker. It collects deposits with the thinking that depositors may demand money at different time points. For some reason, if all depositors reach the bank on the same day and ask for the return of their deposits, no bank can meet such a requirement. This is because a major part of the money is parked with borrowers and they need not return immediately. It is also not unusual for most depositors to demand money within a short period, especially if there are rumours on the viability of the bank. Because of this problem, many strategies are used by the governments and other regulatory organizations. This is so since banking is a useful service to the economy and society and their viability can be affected by such sudden demand for the withdrawal of money.

One such strategy is for the central bank to insist that all banks should park some money in its account. This cash reserve and with the money from many banks, the central bank may be able to give advances to any one bank or a few banks in trouble at a point of time to enable them to meet its depositors' sudden demand (cash reserve is also used for other purposes like to extract money from banks so that it may reduce the money supply in the economy and this is a strategy used to control inflation; we will discuss this in Chapter 7). There should also be ways to see that this support mechanism to save banks is not misused by them. If not controlled, banks may lend money to 'very risky' borrowers (who may not pay back the money with any level of certainty). Hence, there should be a mechanism to see that banks take only reasonable risks and costs of excessive risks are not passed on to the depositors or to the society at large. Thus, in addition to the mechanisms to save them from bank runs, regulations are also needed (to be enforced by central banks or other national regulatory bodies) to see that the banks internalize all the risks and do not pass them to society at large.

Source: Author.

The capital market also functions through stock exchanges. In order to understand the importance of stock exchanges or the share market as a financing mechanism, we need to understand one crucial aspect of bank finance. If a person took a loan from the bank to start a small enterprise and finally it failed (for external factors, that is, not mainly due to the fault of the person), he has to pay back the loan to the bank. Thus, the full risk of running the enterprise is taken by the borrower if he depends on bank loans. On the other hand, stock market helps to distribute the risk. Of course this avenue is not available to a new entrepreneur. An established entrepreneur can mobilize capital by selling a part of the ownership of the company as shares to the public. Those who buy shares expect the reward in the form of periodic dividends from the company and/or appreciated price of the shares that they hold. Since the entrepreneur does not have to return the money mobilized from the share market, he is not taking on the full risk in running the company. Thus, the company can take much more risk than what is possible only with bank finance. In order to have economic growth, there should be an environment which enables people to take appropriate risks and the functioning of stock markets and such financial markets are part of this enabling environment.

There can also be other specific markets, like say for land and other natural resources. One specific issue here is that the overall availability of the same type of resource (including land) is limited. Thus supply may not increase, even if there is an increase in demand. Hence there may be only price appreciation. Certain assets of this kind are also not mobile. Goods and services which are mobile can be imported from elsewhere, if there is scarcity in a particular context. But the immobile nature of assets like land may have an impact on the price increase and also the kind of development in certain contexts. We will discuss some of these issues in detail in Chapter 10.

QUESTIONS

1. There is an argument that economists are concerned only about efficiency and focus on the markets neglecting the inequality created by the markets. What is your response to this argument after reading this chapter?

2. Why do we need share markets which allow 'only speculation and not the creation of economic value'? Do you have an answer?

3. Though a company selling soap may not demand a government regulation, a private bank selling loans may require such regulation. Explain.

4. What can be a peculiar pattern in the supply schedule of labour? In general, firms would be willing to supply more when the price at which a commodity can be sold becomes higher. What is the fundamental reason that may make labour supply curve different in some situations?

5. Some entrepreneurs complain that people in the villages are lazy and that is why they do not get higher incomes. How do you analyse such a statement?

6. The market wage rate of agricultural workers is only $1 per day in the rural areas of the Chad Republic. The government thinks that such a low wage rate is not acceptable and that the low wage rate is due to the 'free market'. Instead of allowing the market to fix the wage rate, the government makes a law to the effect that the wage rate of the agricultural workers will be fixed by the local government. On the basis of your understanding of the fundamental theorems in economics, how would you respond to this policy of supporting agricultural workers?

NOTE

1. This part of the description is taken from Gangopadhyay and Santhakumar (2013).

⊰ FIVE ⊱

SITUATIONS WHERE MARKET IS INADEQUATE

———◆◉◆———

In certain contexts voluntary exchange between people by itself does not lead to a socially desirable outcome. What are these specific contexts?

LACK OF COMPETITION

If there is only one firm (or a few which collude with one another) supplying goods or service, then there is a problem. They can influence the price of that commodity in the market. If it supplies large quantities, people would be willing to buy them only at a lower price (based on the downward sloping demand schedule). On the other hand, if the supplier reduces the quantity, people may be willing to buy at a higher price. It is not that people will buy it at any price if the quantity supplied is reduced. Either they may decide not to use these goods if the price is too high, or they may use (cheaper) substitute goods and services to meet their requirement.

However, it is possible that if there is a single supplier, he/she can reduce the quantity (to some extent) to make people buy the goods at a higher price. Hence, such a single firm (which can be called a monopoly firm) interested in maximizing the profit has two options—minimize the cost and increase the price to an extent that it gives the maximum revenue (compare this with a competing firm: it has to take the price decided by the market and cannot change the price, hence, the quantity it can supply is fixed). The monopoly firm will try to produce a quantity at which its profits (total revenue minus total costs) are maximized. Usually, this amount of quantity is less than that which would have been produced if there were a number of competing firms in the same context.

Consider the same example given in Table 4.1 in the previous chapter. Let us assume that there is only one supplier. Through trial and error, the supplier understands that customers are willing to buy 20 units at ₹50 p/u, 20 more units at ₹40 p/u, another 20 more units at ₹30 p/u and 20 units more at ₹10 p/u. If he is selling these units at respective prices, then there will not be any consumer surplus. The whole surplus would be accrued to the producer. However, there is no reduction in the total surplus in this case and the only difference is that the part of the surplus to be accrued to the consumer is also captured by the producer. This is viewed as a distribution issue in economics and it is not considered as an efficiency loss. This is so since the total surplus that could be derived from exchange is anyway derived (but by the producer alone and not by the producer and customer together).

However, if there is only one supplier (or a monopoly), there could be some efficiency loss too. This supplier has an interest in reducing the output if such a reduction can increase the revenue. Here, the reduction of output by the supplier may enhance his profit since reduction in output also leads to an increase in the price at which people are willing to buy. However, he cannot reduce the output too much, since that may reduce the revenue too. There may be a particular output level at which the suppliers' total profit (total revenue minus cost) will be maximized and this output need not be the one corresponding to where the supply and demand schedules meet. This output level which maximizes the profit of the single supplier is usually lesser than that at which the supply and demand schedules meet.

The monopolist's impact is that production will not take place up to the point at which the additional cost of producing one more unit equals to what the consumers are willing to pay per unit. Hence, some output is not generated even when people are willing to pay a price per unit, which is greater than the additional cost of producing it. This is the social loss due to monopoly. Producing something for which the cost of production is less than what people are willing to pay for its consumption is a socially desirable step but this is not happening in the case of monopoly. The surplus associated with producing (and consuming) up to this socially desirable level is not derived in a context of monopoly. Thus, there is inefficiency here.

In this case, the exchange between the consumer and the seller need not lead to the full realization of the potential surplus from trade. Thus, there may be a need for some social intervention or rule here (to avoid/minimize monopoly). The crucial step here is to see whether it is possible to make (encourage) the monopoly firm to behave as if it is in a competitive environment. This is usually carried out through monopoly restriction policies (for example, MRTP—Monopoly and Restrictive Trade Practices Act, which existed in India and which has been replaced by a competition policy). These have clauses for punishment and penalties if firms are found indulging in practices which give them monopoly advantages. However, before attempting the regulation of monopoly, we may have to ask a number of other questions. Like, for example, how does this particular firm become a monopoly? Let us consider a hypothetical case.

In a specific context, a large number of firms were producing a particular item. However, one firm found an innovative way to reduce the cost of production—it could be a new technology or an organizational innovation. Hence, this particular firm could sell the product at a cheaper price. Consumers would then be willing to buy the product only from this seller, but there is monopoly here (a single firm dominating the market). However, if we artificially sustain competition, this particular firm may not have the incentive to reduce price through innovation. What is important here is to understand that there are social losses due to monopoly but society should interfere only when the social gains from controlling monopoly are greater than those when it is not controlled. There are situations when society may grant a certain level of monopoly. The case of patents is an example. Here there are social gains from innovations. The firms are allowed to use those innovations without allowing others to copy such innovations for a particular duration of time. It is expected that this innovating firm may continue to be a monopoly during that period. However, society may be better off suffering that social loss associated with the monopoly, since, in the absence of such patent protection, firms may not have the incentive to innovate, which in turn may create another type of social loss (forgone benefits of innovation).

On the other hand, if a firm operates as a monopoly because of some rules or policies (other than the likes of patent rules which internalizes explicitly this possibility of monopoly and its social costs), then there may be a case for removing such policies. Sometimes, monopoly is tolerated to some extent in developing economies. This is for allowing some firms to generate adequate surplus so that they can make higher levels of capital investments in the future. This may be done by considering the needs of long-run growth of their economies. Hence, competition policy in a developing country may have to take into account some of these needs (hence, some protection from competition from other countries is granted in many developing countries; developed countries enjoyed such a protection when they were less developed).

One issue of monopoly—important for development practitioners and even for those who are involved in the development of rural areas—is discussed below.

Let us consider a family that needs electricity but is living in a village that does not have power supply. They can buy a generator. In addition to the cost of the generator, they would have to buy fuel for, say ₹50 daily, to generate electricity for three to four hours. Instead, 10 such families could jointly buy a higher capacity generator. This might bring down the per-household expenditure on both the generator and power generation. This is the manifestation of economies of scale. If all households jointly petition the government through the elected representative, the State Electricity Board might supply power and the expenditure for each household would be much lower. This is so since an electricity board serving a large number of consumers can supply one unit of electricity at a much lower cost than that needed while using a small-size generator by 10 households (there are countries where rural electricity supply is mainly carried out by small private generating companies; for example, in Cambodia, people may have to pay up to ₹20 for one unit of electricity in the rural areas, whereas in India, even if we include government subsidies, the actual cost of supply may be ₹5 or 6 per unit).

Hence, there are cases where the per-household expenditure for the same service may come down when people come together (voluntarily or with the support of a public agency or government). This is one situation where each individual's or household's action in isolation may not lead to the 'maximum possible gain' for the society.

In such situations, a similar cost reduction can be obtained if one private firm provides electricity to all the households in the area. However, only one firm can function here since the operation of a number of firms will work against the cost reduction as each one may have to use a smaller capacity generator and a different distribution network. Similarly, a landline telephone or a centralized piped-water supply needs a very costly network to provide the service. Once this network is established, the additional cost of providing service to one more person is very low. Thus, it is cheaper for one company to use the existing network to provide additional service rather than a new company to establish a new network and provide connections. This is due to the large fixed costs in the provision of such services, which would make the per-unit cost of service smaller, as more and more clients are served. This is the problem of a natural monopoly.

However, such a firm with a natural monopoly will not have the incentive to charge only the minimum required price, or to provide as much service, as in the case of a situation where a number of firms compete with each other. There cannot be competition or there is a likelihood of monopoly, which in turn may create social losses. Thus, there is a need for society or government to interfere to see that such losses are minimized. There should be some role for the 'public' in compelling this single firm to operate as if it were in a competitive situation.

There are multiple ways of addressing this issue. For example, people can come together and form a collective organization and try to provide the service. Or the government (at the appropriate level) can start a company to provide the service. The government can allow a private company to provide the service but regulate the price or quantity of service. There can also be some regulated competition. Each of these has merits and demerits. We will discuss them in detail in Chapters 17 and 19 while discussing the role of the government and the institutions.

There is also some issue in deciding the appropriate charge for a service/good with a natural monopoly. Think about a village without an electricity connection. There is a substantial cost in bringing an electricity connection there. Hence, if only one person wants an electricity connection, he may have to bear the full cost. However, the additional cost of giving connection to one more person would be very small. When electricity is brought into the village, what should be the charge collected from different consumers? Is it the additional cost of serving one more consumer? Usually in a competitive economy, the efficient price of a commodity is the additional cost of supplying one more unit. If we follow the same rule here, how will the company recover the initial huge expenditure to bring in electricity lines there? Hence, 'marginal cost' pricing is not feasible here. There are different alternatives. Either all consumers will pay a part of the total cost (or average cost price). Or there can be a two-part tariff. Everybody pays a part of the initial cost (as installation charge) and then pays a price for units of service based on the additional cost of supplying one more unit.

Let us continue with other reasons whereby the market or voluntary exchange by itself need not lead to socially beneficial outcomes.

PUBLIC GOODS

Assume that people living in one part of a village badly need a road and are ready to put in some effort (or money) to construct it. Other households may then think that they would get the benefit of the new road, when those who need it badly, construct it. This is because once the road is built, it is difficult (or costly) to exclude anyone from using it and the additional cost due to allowing a few more persons to use it is very low, if not zero. Because of this, those who need the road badly are likely to wait till the time their benefits from the road (or losses due to its absence) are more than the effort (or relatively large amount of money) that they have to put in for the construction of road, without the support of others. On the other hand, the road could have been built much earlier, if everybody (or most households) in the village (are persuaded to) put in some effort (money) to con-struct it. Here too, socially, the best situation is achieved when most people come together or when some agency representing them acts on their behalf. This is called the 'public good' case in economics warranting social/state intervention.

These goods/services, once provided, can be used by a number of people. The consumption of one person does not reduce the availability of such good/ service for others until some limit is reached. This is called indivisibility. On the other hand, when one person uses a private item like a shirt or an ice cream, it is not available for use by others. Moreover, it could be expensive to exclude some-body from using public goods. This is called non-excludability. A street light is a typical example in a rural setting. Many people can use it without affecting others (provided there are not many people trying to use a street light at a time; if so, there can be congestion and hence one person may be blocking the light for the other). Moreover, it is costly to exclude somebody from using the street light (hir-ing a security guard to ensure that some people do not come near that light or only those who pay user charges get closer to it—but it costs a lot). There are many other examples such as culverts and drainage channels, improved law and order due to policing by the government, national defence, lighthouses and so on.

However, non-excludability and indivisibility may not exist in absolute terms. There can be degrees of indivisibility and non-excludability. Or certain goods can be somewhat divisible but costly to exclude. Or certain other goods are relatively cheaper to exclude but are indivisible. Hence, there can be varying degrees of 'public goods' character to different goods and services. For example, consider surface irrigation water. Strictly speaking, this is divisible—one person's use of irrigation water deprives others from using the same water. However, one may need a costly and elaborate mechanism to see that those who do not pay the fees/levy do not use canal irrigation. The same is the case of public water taps. On the other hand, a bridge can be used by many people (until congestion) without affecting the use of others. Thus there is indivisibility. But it is not costly to exclude some people from using the bridge. A simple toll gate is adequate.

The fact that some goods or services are non-excludable or indivisible does not mean that there will not be any provision of such goods and services if governmental or other societal interventions are absent. People who badly need such goods (and who can afford them) may create them. For example, a rural road can be created by a wealthy farmer and once it is created, others may also use it. However, such a private provision of public goods is not adequate. Similarly it is not that only the government can provide public goods adequately and efficiently. Community action or other forms of collective action are also used for the provision of public goods. We will take up some cases of non-governmental interventions, including cooperative interventions, in Chapter 18.

EXTERNALITY

For example, let us examine the market place in a rural area. There may be several shops selling vegetables, food, meat and fish. Each shop has some waste to dispose of at the end of the day. They may simply dump this waste outside the shop, most probably by the roadside. Usually the shops need no permission (or not pay) to dump this waste in a public area. This is because the 'roadside' is not owned by anyone and everybody can use it. The whole area now begins to stink. This pollution affects everybody. However, shop owners need not pay (or compensate) for the inconvenience suffered by others. If one shop owner feels that it is bad to dump waste like this and tries not to do so there may not be much improvement in the situation since all others are doing it. So this shop owner may lose interest in doing the right thing. This is another situation where one individual's action in isolation is not sufficient and hence some (public) agency (representing all or the majority) has to play a role. This is an issue of negative externality—dumping of waste affects others and not compensating for the inconveniences.

Voluntary exchange (or market) is inadequate in controlling externalities such as waste disposal. These types of externalities are widespread today. Factories or machines (like cars) emitting pollutants (including carbon dioxide, which is considered to be causing climate change), the discharge of harmful chemicals and biological waste at excessive levels to the water bodies are common these days. Cutting down forest or clearing wetlands is also creating externalities in the sense that it reduces the benefits enjoyed by someone else. When one person cuts down the forest, he will not take into account the shortage of water it may cause to the downstream inhabitants.

The crucial role of society is to ensure that the person creating externalities internalizes their cost. For example, if a factory pollutes a nearby river, there should be mechanisms to see that it pays for the damages caused by its pollution. Once such internalization takes place, then the factory bears the full cost of its pollution. Then it would pollute only at optimal levels, in the sense that it will pollute to the level at which the additional gain from pollution is greater than the cost (including the social damage) of pollution. This is socially desirable.

Here too the society can use different ways to control pollution. Giving this task to a government agency is an easier one. There can also be collective action (like those of the residents of an area) to control pollution. If in a particular case only one individual is affected, he/she may get into a negotiated solution with the polluter. However, such cases are very rare. Usually pollution affects a large number of people. Hence controlling pollution can become a public good. The benefit of reduced pollution is indivisible. When one person gets the benefit of controlling pollution, others also get the same benefit. Thus, there may be a tendency to free-ride over the benefits of pollution control. Some may think this way: why should I take the trouble of petitioning the government or filing a Public Interest Litigation (PIL) or conducting a sit-in strike in front of the factory if pollution would be controlled by the actions of others. Hence, rather than negative externality per se, the fact that controlling it becomes a public good makes a compelling reason for the society or government to intervene in this regard.

For the government, there are different options to compel the polluters to minimize pollution. Banning pollution could be an option. Enforcing standards— by which firms are allowed to emit waste up to a particular level (say like 'not more than 100 parts per million of sulphuric acid in discharged water') could be another option. If firms are found to be violating this standard, there can be penalties (fines and/or jail terms) according to law. Rather than fixing a rigid standard, there can also be quotas of pollution distributed among the firms considering what can be permitted to the atmosphere as a whole. Sometimes firms are allowed to trade the quotas so that some firm may buy quota from another one and pollute more but this will not increase the total pollution since those firms selling quotas cannot pollute to their full quota. There can also be taxes on pollution. If these taxes are designed to reflect the social damage due to pollution, then the firms may internalize the cost of pollution. Each of these mechanisms has some advantages and disadvantages and we will discuss them in the chapter which analyses different rules (or institutions).

A socially desirable control of pollution need not mean avoiding pollution completely. There may be small levels of pollution for which there is some social cost, but the cost of controlling such pollution could be much higher. We know that too much of suspended dust particles in the atmosphere cause health problem and we may take steps to reduce such dust. But the cost of reducing dust in the atmosphere to a very low level is high. Hence, there is an optimal point of controlling pollution. Then it is socially useful to pollute at lower doses. Let us try to understand this with another example. If we want to ensure that a stream is fully pollution free, it could be very costly. It may need several treatment plants. Also, a mechanism to see that no pollutants get transferred from the atmosphere to the stream is needed. Hence, the cost can be very high. On the other hand, even if a stream has some minor level of pollutants (say dust particles falling on it from the surrounding environment), the social benefit of avoiding such pollution may be lower. Thus, a certain level of pollution may be socially appropriate. I am reiterating this since many people presume that a 'zero' level of pollution is socially desirable in all contexts.

Another kind of social or governmental intervention is required in the case of certain negative externalities. In a small beach frequented by tourists, there may be an undesirable situation if the fishermen are allowed to dry their unsold fish. This will lead to the death of tourism. But fishermen too need space on the beach. However, it is not desirable to have both these activities on the same beach. Similarly, it may not be desirable to have residence and industry in the same part of a city. Under such conditions, it is better to set apart one place for one activity—one beach for tourism and another one for fishermen, one part of the city for residence and another part for industry. Such desirable allocation of space or 'zoning' for different activities needs to be carried out by an agency representing society at large.

MERIT GOODS

There are other situations too, especially in developing countries, where the intervention of a public agency may enhance the benefits of society as a whole. Poor people may continue to remain poor for a number of reasons in the absence of governmental intervention. This could be due to their inability to take the right decisions regarding education and health. If these people had to make their own decisions, they may not use primary education or vaccination facilities to the necessary extent. This could affect not only them but also the society as a whole. Thus in most societies, governments or public agencies provide certain services such as primary education or public health for the benefit and use of all. Or society is unwilling to leave it to the discretion of individuals whether to consume such services (such as primary education or vaccination) or not (these are called 'merit goods'). Governments may also intervene to see that people do not consume (or consume only specific varieties of) certain goods, which can be called 'merit bad'. For instance, such restrictions on narcotic drugs exist in most countries or restraints on alcohol consumption prevail in many Indian states (a public agency sells alcohol in the state of Kerala so as to avoid the sale and consumption of harmful illicit liquor).

These are goods and services for which societies are not ready to accept the idea of consumer sovereignty. To some extent, this is a paternalistic idea—even parents do not want their young children to do whatever they want. Most parents do not want their young children to smoke or drink alcohol. It is the extension of this parental responsibility to the level of society that we see in the merit goods. Societies want every child to have primary education or to have vaccinations (there are positive benefits—positive externalities—for the society when every child is educated or vaccinated; hence the provision of vaccination or primary education can also be seen as interventions necessitated by positive externalities). They may not like their citizens to use narcotic drugs and their children to consume alcohol (consumption of narcotic drugs or excessive alcohol by teenagers may have some negative externalities—like increased crime rates and controlling these can also be viewed as regulating negative externalities).

Here too, governments may have multiple options: in the case of merit goods like primary education, it can directly provide that service (through government schools) or it can ensure through other means (like direct financing to the parents) that every student gets education from any school (whether these are private or public). In the case of narcotic drugs or alcohol, different intervention strategies may range from a complete ban of these substances to a controlled provision of them to specific groups (like alcohol only to adults and narcotic drugs on small doses to registered addicts). Which option is better depends on specific circumstances and these are discussed in detail in Chapter 19.

INCOMPLETE INFORMATION PROBLEMS

The buying and selling of many goods and services are facilitated through quality control approved by the state or through its intervention to ensure the use of proper weights, measures and standards. In the absence of such intervention, the seller is unable to credibly communicate the real quality/quantity of the product sold or service delivered. The buyer is unable to secure proper information on (the quantity or quality of) the product sold and his/her excessive caution may affect (or reduce the volume of) voluntary transactions. These issues are due to private information that one party in a transaction has, which is not available to the other party. This is true even for the hiring of workers. Employers find it difficult to assess the quality or earnestness of people approaching them for employment. Thus, academic certificates issued by universities or other educational institutes not only provide information on their education, but also signal their ability to do hard/adequate work. In the absence of such certification systems, employers are forced to depend on people whom they know directly or through their friends or relatives. This is not a desirable situation since employers may not get the best workers on the one hand and people who are good and ready to do sincere work may not get appropriate jobs. To some extent, board examinations conducted by the government or its affiliated bodies or university examinations are also to address these information problems. Ensuring that all the firms listed in the stock market disclose some information (including audited statements) is another example of such an intervention. However, it is impossible for the government to solve all informational asymmetries. It can be seen in two ways: first, to view some information asymmetry as inevitable and the related inefficiency unavoidable. Hence, this can be accounted for in what is the maximum possible for a society to achieve given its resources and unavoidable extent of information problems. Second, there can also be some market-based mechanisms that may evolve since government intervention for addressing the problem of incomplete information is not adequate. For example, reputation is used by the firms to communicate information (regarding the quality of their products). Rating by private companies can be used to evaluate the performance of firms listed in stock exchanges. Some of these mechanisms are also discussed in detail in Chapter 19.

There is another manifestation of incomplete information. Poor people may remain poor if they cannot get loans to support their economic activities. Their children may not have access to quality education if educational loans are not available (and if the government or charitable agencies do not provide enough opportunities for higher education). However, those who give loans want to ensure that these will be repaid. So lenders insist on collateral. The poor may not have enough assets to pledge as collateral. This may prevent them from getting loans. This is also due to asymmetric information since lenders cannot judge the repayment ability of the borrowers. Thus the problems within loan markets (or imperfections in capital markets) may prevent asset-poor households from participating in economic and market activities to enhance their income and quality of life. Governments or public agencies intervene in most societies to solve such problems.

RULE OF LAW

As mentioned earlier, voluntary exchange between individuals is possible only if the state/community ensures property rights, enforcement of contracts and also the general rule of law. For example, if people can steal electricity in an area without being caught and punished, then no agency may be willing to supply the power there. If people in a village attack travelling salesmen and steal their goods, then salesmen may not go there. Even the voluntary transaction between villagers and salesmen takes place in the background of a government/community that ensures the rule of law.

QUESTIONS

1. Should there be government or social intervention in the case of following goods and services? If so, what is the type of intervention? Justify your answers: tea shop; ironing clothes; cable TV; washing soap; house maid; electricity supply; washing machine; sewerage disposal; vaccinating animals; milk supply; hotels.

2. What could be the economic logic of government intervention in the following cases? Registration of land titles; primary schools; hospitals; police; traffic control; cigarettes; TV broadcasting; watershed management; agricultural extension; issuing of birth certificates; universities.

3. Why do economists say that 'zero-level of pollution' need not be desirable in all contexts?

4. How does 'controlling pollution' become a public good?

5. Will government or other public agencies be able to solve all issues of incomplete information? If not, what are the alternatives?

6. Explain specifically the reasons cited in economics for government intervention in the following cases:

   (a) Primary education
   (b) Road
   (c) Water Supply
   (d) Vaccinating Animals
   (e) Issuing birth certificate

◄ SIX ►

ANALYSIS OF STRATEGIES
IN RELATIONSHIPS

━━━━━•◦•━━━━━

In daily life people interact strategically. For example, in a government office, bribing an official to get the work done is a strategic decision. Likewise, collecting bribes is also a strategic decision for an official. Such strategic interaction is possible when a person has more than one option and he chooses one depending on what the other person might do. But there is no such strategic interaction in a normal market setting: we go to a shop and look for an item for which the price is exhibited. We then either decide to buy or not to buy it; we may also try another shop. In shops/places, where bargaining is allowed, there is scope for strategic interaction. Similarly, when we exchange 'something' on the basis of a contract— like paying now to get a flat later or borrowing money now to be paid back later— strategic interactions are possible.

Another area where strategic interaction is predominant is when there are only a few suppliers for a commodity or service. Either they can form a cartel and act like a monopoly, or one may compete against other and create a situation similar to that of (but not perfect) competition. This is called monopolistic competition. The problem is that if they have to cooperate (collude), it should be in their own interest. Otherwise, one may cheat, after giving some false promise of cooperation.

72

TWO TYPES OF INTERACTION AND THE WAYS OF ANALYSING THEM

Here, interactions are analysed as 'games' and the tool used for such a strategic analysis is called game theory. It is a part of mathematics and is being used in several disciplines. Economics is one among them. There are mainly two types of such games. One type is when two people act simultaneously. Here, one person does not act after observing the action of the other. Two vehicles approaching a junction simultaneously could be one such case. Different people using a stretch of grass land or a patch of an unprotected forest, or fishing in a public pond and so on can also be viewed as such situations of simultaneous actions. The other category is sequential interactions. The relationship between a factory owner (or a polluter) and the inspector (of the pollution control board) is an example. Here, the action of the inspector comes after the action of the polluter (whether polluting or not) and this action depends on what the polluter perceives as the response of the inspector (whether she imposes fines or demands bribes or behaves indifferently to the pollution). The interactions between the robber and the robbed (before the escape of the robber), the police and the thief (or the law breaker and the law enforcer in general) and so on come under such sequential interactions. The ways of analysing these two types of interactions (simultaneous and sequential) are somewhat different. Let us take the sequential interaction first.

Consider a polluter (A) and the pollution inspector (B). For the time being, we consider two options for the polluter. Either he can control pollution and hence he gains nothing from pollution or he can pollute and let the gain from polluting (say on a given day) be ₹1,000 (from this amount he may have to bribe the inspector, if she demands). These gains from pollution could be that he does not have to operate the pollution control equipment on that day and hence can save electricity charges. We consider three options for the inspector, which are: (a) be indifferent to the pollution; (b) take action against the polluter and (c) demand and collect a bribe. All these options can be represented in the form of a tree diagram as in Figure 6.1.

Option (a) may give a negative gain or loss to the inspector. Let this be a loss of ₹100. This may be worked out as follows. There is a very low probability that her superiors would find her not acting against pollution. If her inaction is found out, there may be some disciplinary action and it can be costly. Let us assume she would lose, say ₹10,000 (by way of delayed increments as part of disciplinary

Figure 6.1
A Sequential Game

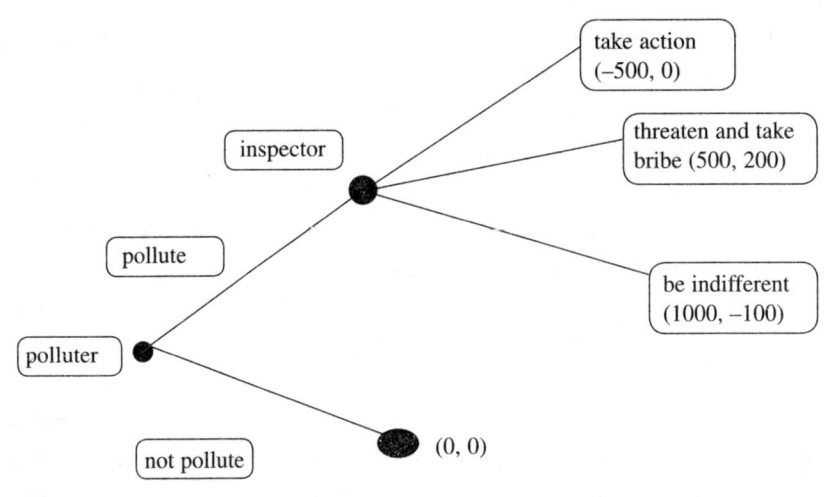

action) in this case. However, she thinks that the probability of getting caught is only 1 out of 100, on an average. Thus, her expected loss is calculated by multiplying the probability of the event (of finding out her inaction) with the actual loss if that event occurs. Thus ₹10,000 multiplied by 1/100 leads to an expected loss of ₹100. If the inspector does not take any action, the gains to the polluter would be ₹1,000.

[This is the way expected gains or losses of uncertain events are assessed in economics. If somebody expects to get a heart attack with a probability of 1/1000, and the actual cost of treatment of that disease is 200,000, then the expected cost is 200 [that is, 200,000 × (1/1000)]. More specifically it should be calculated as follows: the probability of getting the disease is 1/1,000 and hence the probability of not getting the disease is 999/1,000. The cost if there is disease is ₹2,00,000 and the cost if there is no disease is zero. Hence, the expected cost *E* is given by *E* = (probability of getting disease × actual cost of treatment) + (probability of not getting the disease × the cost if there is no disease)].

Option (*b*) for the inspector may not give her any loss or gain, since that is her expected job. In this case, the polluter may suffer a loss, say ₹500 as fine (and he has to stop the attempted pollution). On the other hand, let us take that option

(c) will give the inspector a net gain of ₹200. Here, we need to consider the bribe that she may get from the polluter and the potential loss that she may incur if she is caught by the law enforcement machinery. Let us assume that she gets a bribe of ₹500. She may have to suffer a loss of 3,000,000 if arrested for corruption, but the chance of getting arrested according to her is only 1 in 10,000. Thus, the expected loss of arrest is 300 and hence the net gain from corruption is ₹200 (that is, ₹500 – ₹300). If the inspector opts for option (c), the gains of polluter would be ₹500 (that is, ₹1,000 – ₹500, which is the bribe).

All these gains for the polluter and the inspector are given in ordered pairs given as a part of the tree diagram. The first term in the pair gives the gain to the polluter and the second term represents that of the inspector. In such sequential interactions, we need to start from the right-most end of the tree. This node (or the second one in this particular case) is where the inspector takes a decision. She may find that among her three options, (c) is the most beneficial as it gives her a gain of ₹200 [compared with '0' of (b), and a loss of ₹100 in (a)]. Thus, she may decide to opt for option (c). Now, we have to work backwards to analyse the rationality of the polluter. When he decides to pollute, the interaction reaches the second node and then the inspector chooses the option (c) and hence the gain of the polluter under the option of pollution is ₹500. Hence, the potential gains for the polluter are as follows: if he pollutes, he would get ₹500. If he does not pollute, he would get 0. Thus, he has an interest in polluting.

Why do we do such elaborate calculations? This is essentially to understand the rationality of the situation and what can be done to ensure that a socially desirable outcome is achieved. What would be a socially desirable outcome in this regard? It is to avoid pollution. This cannot be achieved by a pep talk on morality that she should act against pollution whenever she sees such a case, or by telling the polluter that it is socially harmful to pollute. We may have to take certain steps that may change the pay offs described here. How do we go about it then? We want to make 'not pollute' the best option for the polluter. This can happen if the gain from pollution to him (which is currently ₹500) is reduced to zero (or lower, so that it becomes a net loss). This may happen if the inspector takes action against him. If we want the inspector to take action against the polluter, then she should find option (b) as the best one. This is possible when the expected loss for her while choosing option (c) (the corrupt deal) becomes greater than under (a) and (b). This may occur if the expected cost of action against corruption is much greater (say more than ₹600) than the bribe (₹500). Then there will not be any gain from corruption and moreover the loss from doing so may become greater than that of inaction. Such an increase in the expected cost of corruption may arise due to the following reasons:

1. An increase in the probability of action against corruption. If that probability increases from 1 in 10,000 to say, 1 in 1,000 (an increase by 10 times) then the loss for the inspector in this regard would be ₹3,000. This would make her choose option (b).
2. An increase in loss in the case of action against corruption can also lead to a similar effect. For example, if it increases from 3,000,000 to 6,100,000, then even without any increase in the probability of her arrest, her loss in choosing the option increases to ₹610. This too would make her select option (b).
3. An appropriate combination of '1' and '2' can also be used to have the same effect.

Thus, the policy lesson would be the need to increase the probability of arrest or losses if arrested (maybe through an increased jail term and the loss of job and so on) or a combination of these policies to see that the inspector selects the option of taking action against the polluter and hence compelling the firm not to pollute (it may be noted that each of these strategies may require different costs from society and depending on that, the society/government can design an economically more appropriate strategy).

In this simple case of interaction, one may argue that such policy lessons can be arrived at without doing these elaborate calculations. However, such analysis may be useful in a little more complex interactions (for example, when there is one more stage in the interaction).

There can also be simultaneous interactions and an example of this type is taken up in the following section.

GAINS OF COOPERATION BUT TEMPTATION TO BE SELF-CENTRED

To understand the fruits of cooperation and the temptation to cheat in strategic interactions, let us consider a simultaneous interaction situation. One such game is called the prisoner's dilemma. This can be used to picture several situations in real life.

Two farmers living nearby may need to coordinate on many things: it can be for water control or not to extract too much of ground water. It may be to see that their cattle are not destroying the crop. It may be to ensure that fishing in a common pond is not leading to the catch (or killing) of the young fish. It can even be to avoid dumping waste in a public place. There can be many such situations where coordination can enhance social welfare for all but there may be a slight increase in the gain for the person who cheats (when the other person sticks to a cooperative strategy). Hence, it may be tempting for one person to cheat in the expectation that the other is sticking to a cooperative understanding. But the other too may be thinking in the same way. Thus, both will try to cheat the other. Hence, both may end up being worse off, compared with what they would have gained if they were cooperating. This game can be presented as a table with potential pay offs for two people as follows (see Table 6.1):

Table 6.1
A Simultaneous Game

		B	
		Cooperate	*Cheat*
	Cooperate	(8, 8)	(0, 10)
A			
	Cheat	(10, 0)	(0, 0)

SOURCE: Author.

Here we consider two people—*A* and *B*—interacting for one time point. Each person has two options: to either cooperate with the other or to cheat. If both people cooperate, each can make a gain of 8. On the other hand, if one cheats the other, the former gets 10, whereas the other does not get anything. These gains are mentioned within brackets, with the first one being that of *A* and the second term being the gain of *B*. Let us consider the incentive for each person. For *A*, the best option when the other person cooperates is to cheat. This is so since he can get 10 by cheating, whereas the gains from cooperation are only 8. Similarly, *A* can be indifferent between the options when *B* cheats (since *A* would get '0' under both the options). Since the numbers are symmetrical, *B* too has the same incentive. It may be noted that the socially desirable situation is for both to cooperate, since that will lead to a maximum gain for both together or society constituted by these two individuals and the social gains are 16 (whereas if one cheats, the total for both is only 10).

If we analyse the action of both *A* and *B* and the possible 'natural' outcome (or the equilibrium), *A* is likely to select the 'cheat' option since it is individually better for him and *B* too would choose the 'cheat' option and hence, both of them would end up with the pay off matrix (0, 0). Assume that *A* and *B* had some informal talk beforehand and both had agreed to cooperate. But *A* may think that it is better to cheat when *B* sticks to the cooperative option (since the former can get two more than when they both cooperate) and vice versa. Hence, even when they agree to cooperate, the temptation to cheat can be higher.

If these two people play this game (or are at such a situation of interaction) only one time and they are sure that they are not going to interact in the future, then the temptation for each is to cheat but by doing so, both may end up not getting anything (or losing heavily). There are many social situations like this, whereby the pursuit of individual interest (of maximizing individual returns) may encourage people not to stick to an agreed cooperative understanding and in that process people becoming much worse off than what they would have been if all of them had stuck to the cooperative option.

This example should not give the impression that all such one shot interactions between two persons are of this kind. There can be some games wherein coordination would have given a little more gain to both compared with the lack of coordination (compared with the heavy loss in the case discussed here). There can also be others where the pay off structure is such that coordination emerges as the equilibrium outcome. There can be cases where it is in the interest of one person to stick to cooperation whatever be the option of the other. There may be many real-world cases representing each of these interactions. There are multiple kinds of such interactive situations that can be analysed using game theory. We are not covering all these here. There are interesting books like the one by Dixit et al. (2009).[1]

WHAT IF PEOPLE INTERACT OVER A VERY LONG PERIOD OF TIME?

Let us slightly change the situation described above. Assume that these are two people living in the village as neighbours. They may be living there for their entire life and probably their children may live there afterwards. Are they likely to cheat like this? If no, can there be a rational reason for not cheating? There can be moral or emotional reasons: one person may not want to be known as a cheat in the community. There can be rational interpretations of such behaviour and we may take up some of these explanations later. Let us confine ourselves to a much more explicitly rational reason in this section.

Let us assume that they have agreed to cooperate. However, one has cheated. But here they are not interacting just once. Had they cooperated once, they could have cooperated for a long period of time (or forever if we consider their future generations who are expected to live there). Let us use the numbers given above to see the implications of cheating in a context of successive interactions.

Assume that A has cheated B at the first time (it is not necessary that cheating takes place at the first interaction, it may occur at any intermediate time, say the fifth interaction; but what we consider is the outcome of cheating). Thus, B has decided not to cooperate with A after being cheated. What is important here is that if A decides to cheat B in the first instance and B decides not to cooperate afterwards, then the total gain of A would be 10. This is what A would get when he cheats, while the other sticks to cooperation, as the numbers discussed above. On the other hand, if A was not cheating and they were cooperating, then the (present value of the) gains of A and B would be as follows:

$$Y = 8 + 8/\Delta + 8/\Delta^{**}2 + 8/\Delta^{**}3 + 8/\Delta^{**}4 + \dots$$

Each will get 8 as the gain from the first interaction, plus 8 as the gain of the second interaction, plus 8 as the gain of the third interaction and so on. But there can also be time difference between the first and the second and between the first and the third and so on. Thus, if we want to calculate the total present value of all these gains, then we need to do, what is called, discounting. This is so since ₹100 today is more valuable than ₹100 given after a year. The latter may be as good as, say ₹92 given to you today (since if you deposit this amount ₹92 in a bank or put in a productive enterprise, you may get ₹100 next year). Whatever be the duration between different interactions, a series of gains like 8 today, 8 during the second interaction, 8 during the third interaction and so on, also needs to be discounted appropriately to get the present value. Based on the mathematics of discounting, if Δ is the discounting factor, the present value of the gain received today will be the gain itself, the present value of X received during the next interaction is X/Δ, the present value of X received after two time periods is X divided by the square of Δ, the present value of X received after three time periods is X divided by the cube of Δ and so on.

It is likely that Y (gains to each when A and B continue to cooperate) is greater than 10 (under some conditions). This may encourage A to continue cooperation and discourage him from cheating at the first instance. Here we have discussed one threat strategy of B in response to the cheating of A, that is, not to interact with him afterwards. What is important here is that when people have multiple interactions over a long period of time, one may use a threat strategy (as one may decide never to interact with the other after being cheated upon). This may encourage the other to stick to the cooperative agreement. There can also be other threat strategies that may lead to a similar result. For example, B can decide that if A cheats him once, he will not interact with A the next five times. Or another strategy could be that if A cheats once, B will interact with him only if he returns a sum (which may be equal to the additional gain he made through cheating with or without a fine). Thus, there could be any number of such threat strategies that may encourage A to stick to the cooperative option.

However, such sustenance of cooperation depends on two conditions. We have mentioned that this happens when these people interact over a long period of time or forever (or for an infinite period). Instead, let us assume that the interaction is for a fixed (finite) number of times. Let us take it as 10. Both the parties know that the interaction is going to end the tenth time. Thus during the tenth interaction, if one cheats, the other cannot use the threat strategy of punishing the cheat in the future (by not cooperating with him in the future). Hence, nobody has the incentive to continue the relationship after the tenth interaction and here each (or one) may try to maximize what he can get from that interaction. This would mean that cheating, in the expectation that the other would stick to cooperation, is the best option (by considering the pay offs mentioned above) at the tenth interaction. Both may try to cheat at the tenth interaction. At the ninth interaction, both know that the other is likely to cheat during the tenth interaction. Hence, they do not have the incentive to pursue cooperation even during the ninth interaction. By following the same logic, cooperation may not occur even during the eighth interaction, the seventh interaction and so on. It may work backward even up to the first interaction. Thus, if the interaction is for a finite number of interactions, then cooperation need not be a natural outcome (or an equilibrium solution). This is so if we assume that the people who interact are 'rational' and self-interested. We may say that one of the conditions for sustaining cooperative interactions is that they should 'interact' forever. The village setting that we mentioned, where different generations of the same families are likely to interact over a long period of time, may be an approximation of this condition. However, when the people from the village move out or strangers come and stay there for shorter durations or when they start to depend on wider markets (that is, moving from the local to regional/national/international markets) for commodities, capital or jobs, the interaction or mutual dependence between the villagers may become less intense or would exist only for shorter periods of time. Then, there may be difficulties in sustaining cooperation in such contexts.

We have also talked about discounting. Assume that the rate at which future gains are discounted is very high for some reason. This would mean that the value of Y (present value of the series of gains from a number of interactions) may become smaller. In extreme cases, this may make Y equal to or even less than the gain from a one-time cheating. This is another case where cheating may become more likely in the place of cooperation. If cooperation is to be sustained, people should not discount future gains heavily. There is an argument that the poor (especially those who are exposed to the temptations of the wider world) may discount future gains heavily and in that case, it may become a disincentive against sustaining cooperation among such people.

When these two conditions are satisfied—that the interaction is for a very long period (approximating infinity) and also that the parties do not discount the future heavily—then it may be possible to sustain cooperation through a number of threat strategies. This basic result described here is based on what is called 'folk theorem' in game theory literature in economics.

So far, we have talked about the interactions between two people. Most real-world situations may have many people interacting with one another. Will there be a change in results if there are more than two people in such games? Yes and then there is a possibility of a coalition among some stakeholders. Instead of one equilibrium solution in such cases, there can be, what is called, a core (a set of equilibrium solutions). But by and large the insights from two person interactions are useful to understand the strategic interactions in many real-world situations.

DIVIDING THE SURPLUS OF COLLABORATION

Consider this: a one acre plot of land just by the side of a busy highway is owned by a small farmer. A businessman from the city wants to collaborate with the farmer to start a petrol pump on that land (let us assume that the businessman knows how to get the license for a petrol pump through genuine or not so genuine means). The businessman does not want (or he does not have the money) to buy the land nor is the farmer willing to sell the land. The proposal is to develop a joint enterprise—the farmer giving the land and the businessman investing the money to start the petrol pump. The farmer was getting an annual net income (after deducting the cost of cultivation) of ₹10,000 from this land through cultivation. The market value of this land is ₹100,000. The businessman may have to spend ₹500,000 to start the petrol pump. This amount, as savings deposit in a bank, would have fetched an annual interest of ₹40,000. One reasonable estimate is that the petrol bunk would fetch an annual income of ₹100,000. This will help us to identify the surplus generated by the joint venture— ₹50,000 (that is, ₹100,000 – ₹40, 000 – ₹10,000). How do they divide the surplus? There is no single for-mula for division here. But we can analyse the strategies of these two parties. Negotiation over the division of surplus is fundamental to economic growth (which essentially would require people coming together to create surpluses like those derived from the petrol pump).[2]

If the businessman offers ₹10,000 as the share of the farmer, he may not agree. He can get the same income from farming. If the farmer wants ₹60,000, the businessman will walk out of the proposal. Why? Because he will be left with just ₹40,000—the amount he would earn from the bank as interest. These points can be taken as the threat points of both the farmer and the businessman. Each would be interested in getting more than what they were already getting.

If the farmer is offered ₹11,000 (or ₹1,000 from the surplus) and the rest ₹49,000 is taken by the businessman, what would be the farmer's response? If the farmer is 'rational', he should accept the offer if it is an ultimatum (and there is no further possibility of bargaining). This is so since the farmer is better off compared with the 'no project' situation. However, since a major part of the surplus is with one party, this offer can be reckoned as an exploitative one.

Will people accept such offers? There are many experiments conducted in economics, which are called dividing the pie. Consider two persons A and B.

Somebody gives A ₹10 and asks him to share it with B. But A can offer a sum and B can accept or reject it and that is the end of the game. Strictly speaking, even if A offers ₹0.1 a rational B should accept it, since he would be better off accepting such an offer (rather than rejecting it). However, in experiments, it was seen that people reject such 'demeaning' offers, even though they can be better off by accepting it. The pattern is that people tend to reject offers of amounts which are less than around 30 per cent of the pie divided. This shows that there is some sense of fairness in the minds of people, or that they are willing to forgo something if it is not a fair deal.

There can be another offer in the case of the joint enterprise of petrol station. If the businessman is very conscious of equity, he may offer 50 per cent of the surplus to the farmer. Hence the latter will get ₹35,000 per annum, and the rest (₹65,000) will go to the businessman. Probably this is the best that the farmer can hope for. It can be considered an equitable share of the surplus.

The value of this whole joint venture is ₹600,000 – ₹500,000 invested by the businessman and ₹100,000, value of the land belonging to the farmer. The endowments of these two people are of different levels and therefore, to some extent, give differential bargaining power to both the parties. Through bargaining they can reach any one of the many points of sharing this surplus. John Nash identified one equilibrium division of surplus. The importance of such an equilibrium is that this would be reached by the bargaining of rational individuals. This equilibrium, which is a complex mathematical formulation, can be crudely translated as follows: consider the amount ₹100,000 which is the new annual income. Consider any point between 0 and 100,000, and let it be X. Then the threat points of the farmer and businessman respectively are 10,000 and 40,000. Consider the following product: $(X - 10{,}000)*(X - 40{,}000)$. There would be a value of X which would maximize the value of this product. (This can be calculated using calculus). That value of X (say X^*) would be taken for the division of surplus. Then $(X^* - 10{,}000)$ would go to the farmer and $(X^* - 40{,}000)$ would go to the businessman.

This bargaining over the division of surplus is fundamental to economic exchange. Such bargaining can take place between the farmer and an industrialist trying to locate a factory over a stretch of land, between workers and owners of a company or between a domestic firm and an international investor and so on. Each of them would be creating a surplus. If not, either or both the parties would not be interested in such a deal. However, for economists, how these parties share the surplus is not hugely important, except in one case. This is when the bargaining over the division of surplus leads to a breakdown situation and hence such surplus generating deals are not taking place. That would reduce the surplus and hence not be efficient.

THE RELATIONSHIP BETWEEN THE PRINCIPAL AND THE AGENT

Another strategic relationship that the economists are concerned about is the one between principal and agent. The relationship between a land owner and a tenant can be one such relation. The relationship between citizens and politicians can also be a principal–agent relationship. The same is true about the relationship between a politician and an official. In all these relationships, the principal wants the agent to do something. The principal has an objective. He/she uses the agent to achieve that objective. But the agent's own objective can be different. Thus, the principal–agent problem is how to motivate the agent to do the task in such a way that it meets the objective of the principal. Let us take a case to explain the problem.

Our university has a lot of photocopying work. It hires a person as a worker and the university owns the photocopying machine. The salary is fixed at ₹10,000 per month. She copies 500 pages per day but the university's objective is to see that the maximum number of pages are copied daily. Is she taking too much rest in between? One possibility is to hire a supervisor but that costs money as salary of the supervisor. So what is the solution? Can she be paid according to the number of pages copied instead of a fixed salary? She would then have an incentive to maximize the number of pages copied. But there can be a problem here. She may take copies too fast and without adequate care, which will bring down the quality of copied pages. One may need some quality cum quantity-based wage rate. The principal has a problem of observing the effort of the agent. Hence, the principal uses alternative payment options to encourage the agent to act in a manner compatible with the interests of the former.

Let us consider the relationship between the landlord and the tenant. A conventional contract is for the tenant to cultivate and return a percentage of the revenue. Let us assume that in a particular contract, the tenant has to return 50 per cent of the revenue. The tenant is expected to meet all the costs from his (50 per cent) share of the revenue. One more de-weeding, at a cost of ₹2,000, might increase the production giving an additional return of ₹3,800 bringing an extra profit of ₹1,800; if the owner was cultivating the land he would have gone in for additional de-weeding. Let us consider the incentive of the tenant. By doing this additional de-weeding she may have to spend ₹2,000 more but she will lose ₹100 because she will have to pay ₹1,900 to the land owner as the share of this additional revenue of ₹3,800. Thus, the tenant may not be interested in doing the de-weeding (if she cannot have a separate new contract clause for this additional work) even though this additional work is efficient. This happens since the land owner cannot easily judge whether the tenant has carried out this additional de-weeding (if he wants, he may have to employ a full time supervisor and that may become costlier than the potential gains). Hence, a percentage sharing tenant contract may not lead to efficiency in a tenancy relationship.

An alternative contract between the landlord and the tenant could be that the tenant pays a lump sum amount to the landlord from the revenue of cultivation. Such lump sum payment back to the land owner (say like ₹5,000 per acre per year) is relatively more efficient. This is so since the tenant has to pay this amount to the owner whatever be the profit from cultivation and the gains from and cost of each additional work are fully taken by the tenant. The lump sum payment does not alter the calculations on the level of inputs used for this cultivation. For example, in the case of additional de-weeding that we mentioned above, all benefits of it (₹3,800 – ₹2,000) goes to the tenant and she has to pay the lump sum amount to the landlord whether she has carried out this de-weeding or not. Hence, she has the incentive to carry out de-weeding and this leads to an efficient outcome.

However, the situation may change if the cultivation is a very risky operation. In such a case, the payment of lump sum amount would mean that the full risk is borne by the tenant. On the other hand, a percentage sharing contract would make the owner to bear a part of the risk. This is so since he will get only a lesser amount if there is a crop loss or a reduction in the revenue due to a fall in price. Similarly such a percentage sharing contract is feasible if the actions of the tenant regarding cultivation can be monitored cheaply or additional contract clauses can be made for each additional work.

QUESTIONS

1. Frame a game based on a real-world situation like that between the polluter and the inspector given in this chapter.

2. Think about the pay off structure of a one shot interaction of two persons, where one of them sticks to cooperation, whatever be the option taken by the other. Can you think about a real-world situation of this kind?

3. Some activists and environmentalists argue that it is possible to achieve cooperation in communities for managing natural resources. This may be for community irrigation schemes or community forest management and so on. What would be your response to such a claim based on the reading of this chapter?

4. There is an argument that capitalist investments do not take place adequately in Kerala due to the high bargaining power of the trade unions. How do you analyse the problem based on the strategic analysis mentioned here?

5. Think about the relationship between citizens and the elected representative as a principal–agent problem. Is it possible to change the incentives of the agent here?

6. You are in charge of extending primary education in a district. Can you identify a principal–agent problem that you may encounter in this regard? What 'payment mechanisms' would you consider to address this problem?

7. Extractable iron ore deposits are located in the village of Rowepada. Salisco Private Limited is interested in extracting these mineral deposits but about 1,000 households own land in this area. The villagers' current income from the land is from rain-fed agriculture. Some members of the village argue that they will not allow the company to establish mines in the area whatever the amount of compensation offered for the land. Discuss the situation using the insights of the bargaining game and surplus division.

8. An anthropologist who studied tank irrigation in Tamil Nadu has documented the informal mechanisms that existed in the past to ensure the cooperation of the villagers to maintain and protect the irrigation systems. These systems are currently witnessing degradation (due to a lack of

proper maintenance). One observer has attributed this degeneration to the changing morality of the villagers. Do you have an alternative explanation?

NOTES

1. Avinash K. Dixit, Susan Skeath and David Reiley (2009). *Games of Strategy*, 3rd Edition, illustrated, reprint. New York: W.W. Norton & Company Incorporated.
2. This is part of what is called cooperative games in game theory. Some of you may have heard that the major insights of game theory are generated by mathematician John Nash and most of his insightful works were based on his doctoral thesis written in his late twenties. He received the Nobel Prize in Economics. The movie *A Beautiful Mind* was based on his life.

SEVEN

A BRIEF UNDERSTANDING OF MACROECONOMIC ENVIRONMENT

———————•◦◉◦•———————

You may have heard some debates on what the government should or should not do when there is high inflation, which is a general increase in the prices of most commodities. Inflation hurts the poor the most since their ability to consume even basic items like food may come down if there is a steep increase in prices. Some people just above the poor in terms of income/consumption may become poor due to inflation. Thus, inflation and what governments do to address it may have implications for poverty.

Similarly, development depends on what the government spends on services like health care, primary education, the Public Distribution System (PDS) and so on. However, no government can spend an unlimited amount on such services. What happens if a socially committed government tries to print more money to spend on such social services? Economists call it a bad idea as it may become counterproductive. Even in developed countries, many become jobless when there is a 'recession'—a shrinking of economic activities. What can governments do under such circumstances? Inflation or recession or policies like printing more money may have an impact on development outcomes. Such issues are dealt with in the sub-discipline of economics, namely macroeconomics.

Some understanding of macroeconomics is essential for development professionals/practitioners to understand the impact of different policies on development outcomes. This is the purpose of this chapter. A different pedagogic approach is followed here. Instead of building on ideas from fundamental concepts, most of the insights on the relationships in macroeconomics and approaches are described by taking two events, that is, recession (in the context of a developed economy) and inflation (in the context of a developing economy). But before that we need to have a more precise understanding of what is meant by economic growth and why macroeconomists are concerned about it.

We have seen that the money value of the final goods and services produced within a country in a given year is measured in terms of Gross Domestic Product (GDP). Broadly, it is the sum of the market value of all final goods and services produced within a country in a given year. In addition to the goods and services consumed within the country, it includes goods and service exported, but it keeps out the goods and services imported. GDP is considered as an indicator of the standard of living. It is generally considered desirable to have an increase in the size of the GDP. Growth rate of GDP (for example, between 2010–11 and 2011–12) can be calculated by the following formula: [GDP (2011–12) – GDP (2010–11)]/GDP (2010–11)].

However, the prices of commodities in general may change over a period of time. This is called inflation. Hence there can be an increase in GDP due to an inflationary increase in prices even if there is no increase in the quantum of the economic activity. We may be interested in knowing whether there was a 'real' increase in GDP or whether the increase could be attributed to an increase in prices. Thus, GDP at real prices and current prices is computed. When the GDP of 2011–12 is computed at the averages prices of year 2011–12, it is called GDP at current prices. But we may be interested in computing GDP of 2011–12 at the prices of 2010–11, to see if there was any real increase in GDP between these two years.

COMPUTATION OF PRICE INCREASE

A general increase in price is computed by using the index numbers. For example, if the price of rice in 2000 is ₹20 and it has increased to ₹22 in 2001, ₹26 in 2002, the corresponding index numbers can be calculated as follows (see Table 7.1):

Table 7.1
Index Numbers

Year	Actual price	Index number
2000	20	100 (here we take the starting number as 100)
2001	22	$(100/20) \times 22 = 110$
2002	26	$(100/20) \times 26 = 130$

SOURCE: Author.

Here, we have considered only one commodity (rice). This is not sufficient to compute inflation, since inflation is general price rise. Thus, we may have to consider many commodities. But people may spend a major part of their income on food and only a small part on say electricity. If food price has increased by 50 per cent and electricity price has increased by only 5 per cent, giving equal weight to both these items may not give us a correct picture of the intensity of inflation based on its potential impact on people. Thus, an index number of inflation should be based on a number of commodities and based on a weight assigned to each commodity reckoning its importance on the lives of the people (for example, the share of income spent on it).

We have defined GDP, but thinking of development in terms of GDP is problematic for a number of reasons. We have already mentioned in the first chapter that what is important may be GDP per capita and not the overall GDP. This is because there can be a 10 per cent increase in GDP but if there is a 5 per cent increase in population during the period, we need to consider the population growth to see the size of the economy per person, if we take GDP as an indicator of the standard of living. Another problem of GDP is that it does not take into account the impact on the environment. The GDP may have gone up with the export of timber but it may have reduced the country's forest cover and this latter impact is not explicitly taken into account in the calculation of GDP. Attempts are now being made to calculate green GDP and we will consider some of these issues in a later chapter.

GDP does not take an account of who benefits from such growth. Agricultural GDP may constitute 20 per cent of an economy but it sustains 60 per cent of the population, whereas services and industry may account for 80 per cent of GDP sustaining 40 per cent of the population. However, with all these limitations it is not unreasonable to consider GDP as a measure of economic opportunities available in a society, since such opportunities may translate into employment. Employment is the source of income generation for a major section of the population in any country; only a small section of the population in any society can make a living by earning profits from their capital investments or by rents from their property. To the extent that the size and growth of the economy lead to an increase in employment, it may have desirable impacts on the vast (but not all) sections of the society. Hence, increasing the size of the economy as measured in terms of GDP (or not decreasing it) can be a major concern of macroeconomic policies.

The economic activity of a country can be divided mainly into three components: consumption, investment and government expenditure. Consumption can be for both the domestic economy and for exports. Since imports are not based on economic activity within the region, it has to be kept out from the calculation of GDP.

Private action alone is not adequate for maximizing social benefits for certain goods and services. We need a government and a part of the expenditure has to be spent through the government. Economic growth requires investments. If an economy consumes all that is produced, then there cannot be any growth (in fact there can be a negative growth since the depreciation of the existing capital assets would lead to a reduction of output later on) and hence for the growth of the economy, a part of the current production is to be saved and used as investments. Thus, the savings rate of the economy as a whole (and this can be done by households or private firms or even by the government) is another important macroeconomic variable.

UNDERSTANDING CYCLICAL CHANGES IN DEVELOPED ECONOMIES

We have mentioned that increasing or sustaining a reasonable growth rate is an important goal of macroeconomic policies. However, we can see this concern operating differently in two contexts—(a) in developed economies whose economies are already advanced with significant levels of capital investments and (b) in developing or poorer economies which are yet to see adequate capital investments.

We will consider these two sets of countries differently. For countries of type (*a*), a major problem is that their economies may go through a cyclical change. There may be periods of growth (or boom) and this may be followed by periods of negative growth or recession (shrinking of the size of the economy as measured in terms of GDP). To some extent, such a cycle is somewhat inevitable in market-based capitalist economies. This is so since production, consumption and investments in such an economy are driven by the decentralized decisions of individuals and firms, based on their expectations on the future of the economy and also what others are doing. The expectations of some of these people can turn out to be incorrect. Each person is taking some level of risk (for example, he may be buying a house in the hope that its price is going to increase). Or banks may be lending more loans to a particular section of people thinking that they can repay them. There can also be incorrect judgements about other people's risks. The organization of the economy may be such that some persons or firms may be able to transfer the cost of their risk to others. Thus, when a big company starts a new factory thinking that it can sell more cars but fails to do so and collapses because of the inability to pay back loans, it may impose some costs on the society. Ideally, the economy should have rules and organizations to see that the cost of risk is internalized by the actors who are taking such risky decisions. There may be lapses in this regard.

To understand this issue, let us consider the recession that has occurred in the recent past. Some of you may have heard about the subprime crisis in the housing market that led to a financial crisis in the US and Europe and created an economic recession in the developed world as a whole. The developing world, including India, too bore the brunt. Let us try to understand this crisis in a little more detail. I am using this example of recession as a pedagogic tool to understand some of the interconnections in macroeconomics.

The last decade has seen a foreign exchange crisis affecting South East Asian countries (for example, South Korea, Thailand, Indonesia, Malaysia and China to some extent). Foreigners who had invested money in the stock markets or even in the production systems of these countries withdrew their money suddenly and wanted it paid in an international currency like the US dollar. Thus, they all wanted to buy dollars by paying local currency. The value of the local currency declined drastically when there was a sudden increase in the demand for dollars. The central banks of these governments may not have enough dollars in their kitty to meet the demand. Buying dollars in the international market will become an expensive proposition then. Producers from these countries who import items from elsewhere may have to give a lot more in local currency to buy those items and this may affect their production system. Thus, factories may reduce their production leading to a layoff of labour. This was the 'foreign exchange crisis' encountered by South East Asian countries.

Learning from this, the governments in these countries became very cautious and started saving more in US dollars or investing in US banks and other financial organizations. The increase in oil price and the consequent wealth accumulated by the oil-producing countries has also accelerated this process. Though interest rates in the US were lower, the need to have dollar deposits led to a substantial flow of money to US banks or bank like organizations. When they get more deposits, they need to give more loans. Thus, there was a generous disbursement of housing loans in the US. For the banks which disbursed these loans, these are 'assets' over which they get return (interests) to be recovered over a period of time. Hence they can disburse more loans, if they 'sell' these assets now itself. This is the motivation behind what is called securitization. Thus, the primary lending banks which have disbursed loans directly to the consumers convert these loans (or assets) into securities and these are sold to other financial intermediaries. They buy securities (assets over which they get a return in the future) and there can be a market for the exchange of such securities (this can be called the primary security market). There can also be a secondary market for securities. Financial institutions which bought securities from primary lending banks may sell the securities they bought to yet another set of financial intermediaries.

The crucial issue here is that the primary lending banks may have some information on the actual borrower (whether he or she can repay the loan) and have some control over whether to disburse loans to a risky borrower. The financial institutions which bought the securities from primary lending agencies have much lesser information and control. This issue becomes much more complex if we think about those who bought securities in the secondary market. These institutions were making investments on the basis of incomplete information on the final borrower.

This generous disbursement of housing loans led to a housing boom. Many people were willing to buy homes and that increased the price of the houses. A guarantee for a housing loan is the house itself. The banks are supposed to recover the loans from the defaulters by selling the house which was provided as collateral. While showing these as collateral, the price of the house is taken into account. When there is a housing boom, that price may be much higher and this price cannot be received by the bank when it sells it at a time when many people have defaulted on the loan and when there is a slump in the housing market.

When many people did not pay back loans and consequently there was a glut in the housing market, the price of houses started to decline drastically. In other words, the value of the collaterals came down. Hence, the primary lending banks reached a position where they could not recover their loans. Thus the value of their securities, which they had sold to others, fell sharply. The value of securities bought by financial intermediaries also came down.

This sort of a situation leads to some banks becoming bankrupt, since they cannot recover loans, which is needed to repay the depositors. This would make depositors nervous and they would be careful in depositing money in banks or buying shares of financial firms including banks. The banks would be extra cautious and stringent in the disbursal of loans—not only housing loans but also for all purposes. Thus, firms and consumers may not get adequate loans. This will reduce production and consumption. It will reduce the volume of economic activities and this may persist for some time. This, in a nutshell, is the story behind the recent recession in the developed world.

Impact of the Recession on the Developing World

Recession in the developed world may affect developing countries too, if they are exporting a lot of goods to the developed world. The fall in consumption there would reduce the demand for exports. Export-dependent units in the developing world may have to reduce their production (or some of them may close down) and there can be a consequent impact on employment. There can also be some reduction in investment from the developed world in developing countries too (but this is not so obvious; if the developing countries continue to grow, then the developed world investors may see an opportunity in investing there). People from the developing world, working in richer countries may lose jobs or get reduced salary due to recession. Thus even if there is no recession (reduction in the volume of economic activities) in the developing world, it may still get affected by the recession in the developed world.

HOW DO GOVERNMENTS IN THE DEVELOPED WORLD ADDRESS RECESSION?

While looking back at the recent recession, one can say that its effects could have been minimized but not completely avoided. The inflow of money to the US depends on some imbalances in the world economy and correction of this may require tightening of economic policies in countries like China (in fact, the US economy is in such a situation that it cannot attract this much of money from elsewhere; we will discuss this later). The idea that the government needs to facilitate credit to the poor and lower income groups for housing (the strategy used in the US) may not be the best way to either help the poor or to maintain the health of the economy. (Probably other ways of helping the poor like improving access to education have to be pursued in countries like the US.) The use of information technology facilitated online transactions of securities at primary, secondary and higher levels. Such quick transactions taking place at different levels without adequate information of the repayment probability at the level of the primary borrower may create a boom situation which can also bust with higher probability. Hence, regulation of financial transactions and organizations may have to evolve considering these changes in technology. However, it may be unrealistic to think that all such reasons that would have caused a recession could have been prevented in a market-dependent economy. (One may ask if recession is prevented in non-market economies like socialist countries; to some extent it is prevented but the wealth creation is also limited in such economies and thus many societies may opt for a market economy that enables wealth creation even if that would mean an increase in instability).

As mentioned earlier, an important objective of macroeconomics is to tackle this recession. The political reason is that such recession may create large-scale unemployment and societies may want to avoid this situation. Once an economy is in recession, production systems which were functioning at a particular level are working now at a lower level, since the demand for goods and services has declined. Machines and factories were set up (and were working at a higher capacity) but a part of that becomes idle since there is reduced demand as part of recession. Thus, an intervention strategy to tackle recession is to increase the demand. This is first advocated by John Maynard Keynes. It was suggested that in such situations, the government should spend money so that the income of the people would increase and hence they can demand more goods and services, so that these idle machines and factories can work in full capacity, which in turn will increase employment. When the government spends ₹100,000 on a road, ₹70,000 may reach road workers. Out of this they may spend ₹50,000 on food and ₹10,000 on clothes. Farmers who produce food (who get ₹50,000) may spend ₹20,000 on farm workers. Similarly, cloth makers may spend money on their workers. They will also demand more food and so on. Thus, there can be a multiplier effect. This may gradually make idle capacities in different production systems to work in full and may lead to an increased employment.

Increased government spending (even if that is for paying people 'who count waves') is advocated as a strategy to come out of recession. But this is relevant mostly in the case of the developed world where capital investments are already made (and hence there are machines and factories, a part of which has become idle due to recession). Even in the developed world there are concerns about the validity of this solution. For example, in the context of an open economy, if the US government spends money to increase the purchasing power of its citizens, a substantial part will flow to countries like China. This is because US citizens may be interested in buying cheaper goods from China rather than buying domestic goods/services and hence such a strategy may not increase the demand of goods and services of the domestic economy of the US. Thus, the expected improvement in employment situation in the US may not take place. However, following Keynes' ideas for a developed economy in recession times, there have been suggestions for an increased government spending in the developing world too, even during non-recession periods. Let us consider government spending in these developing countries in the following section.

Government Spending in the Developing World

There are many areas for the government to spend money. These include public goods (like physical infrastructure), services like education and health care and also poverty alleviation. But will a government spending of the type carried out in a recession-affected developed economy make the same impact in a developing economy (which is not in recession)? One view is that such spending is useful. But one needs to be careful about some other impact too. We have mentioned that the situation in a recessionary economy is that machines and factories (and other production systems) are developed, but a part of that is currently idle due to a fall in demand for the goods and services. Such a situation is not a general picture in the economies of developing countries. There, the real challenge is how to build adequate factories and machines and other production systems (and these can be called capital investments, in general) so that more goods and services can be produced and workers' productivity enhanced. When the government spends more money in an economy where adequate capital investments are not in place, production will not increase (since more capital investments are not in place for increasing production). Hence, people now having more money will try to buy the same amount of goods and services produced in the country at a higher price. Thus, there will be inflation—a general increase in the price of most commodities. Inflation can also be harmful, affecting the very poor severely (an unemployed person from a middle class family may not be deprived of basic needs). Inflation affects people whose incomes are low. They may not get the same amount of basic goods for the price they were paying earlier. Thus, inflation is also a major concern in macroeconomic policies.

Inflation is also related to the supply of money. Assume that a government prints and supplies more currency in an economy where there is no growth in the total value of domestic economic activities. This would mean that people have more cash but the quantum of goods and services has not increased. Thus, there will be an increase in the (nominal) price of the goods and services as people would be willing to pay more (since they have more cash). This increase in money supply can cause inflation. Using the reverse logic, one can see that if the government can somehow 'suck in' the money available with people, it may have a negative impact on inflation. How does the government suck in money? It can increase interest rates so that people may put more money in banks as deposits. It may also reduce the money available with the banks to lend. This is usually done by the central bank (every country has a central bank and in India it is the RBI). The RBI may increase the cash reserve—each bank is to keep a part of its deposit with the central bank. An increase in the cash reserve would mean a reduction in the liquidity (cash) available with the bank to lend out. The central bank also may increase the interest rate that it pays to banks for deposits. When that interest rate goes up, banks may increase the interest rate it pays to the depositor or charges for the lender. All these may reduce the money available within the economy and it may help reducing inflation. Thus, one set of tools used to control inflation is these monetary policies.

Even if money is not printed, governments can borrow money and spend it. When the government spends more than its revenue, it creates a deficit. There are two types of deficits. Some kinds of expenditure are routine—for example, the salaries and the travel allowances of the officials. This is called revenue expenditure. When governments have to borrow even to meet this routine expenditure it is called revenue deficit. Governments also spend money on projects and programmes from which the benefits are derived over a period of time. These can be called capital expenditure. Even if a government does not have to borrow for revenue expenditure, it may have to borrow for capital expenditure. When such borrowing is done, it leads to fiscal deficit. In order to consider the consequences of these two deficits, consider household expenditure. If you have to borrow for food and regular expenditure, then it implies that your finance is in real bad shape. On the other hand, it is reasonable for some people to borrow for constructing a house or financing education. This is so since this house or education is going to give returns over a longer period of time, using which, one can pay back the loans. (The return from a house is that you can avoid paying rent and that from education is increased salary/wages.) Similarly, revenue deficit is a manifestation of real financial trouble for a government, whereas fiscal deficit is not so. The real concern about fiscal deficit should be that the returns to society from capital investments made should be greater than the cost of the capital (or interest rates and other costs if any) paid for the loans taken for these investments. If a country decides to meet its fiscal deficit through printing money, it leads to inflation. If countries borrow today and use it for current consumption, future generations have to repay the debt from their income and it may have a negative impact on their consumption. Thus, there can be an issue of intergenerational inequity created by higher government deficits.

However, higher deficits of the government can be problematic for some other reasons too. If the government is not printing money, it has to borrow. If it is borrowing from its own people—people give money to the government as loans (directly through government bonds) or indirectly through banks (where people deposit and governments borrow from banks). This is done from the savings of people. The overall savings in an economy at a time may be, by and large, fixed. It is from this savings that the government is borrowing. If a government borrows a bigger chunk of the savings of people, the money available for private firms to borrow from people or to mobilize through financial intermediaries may shrink. Private firms too need capital for investments and this cannot be done solely based on their own savings. Thus, the excessive use of savings of the society by the government may reduce the money available for private investments. This can also work in a different way. When the government tries to borrow along with the existing private firms, the interest rate will increase. When the interest rate goes up, the cost of borrowing by private firms or the cost of capital goes up. Moreover, when the interest rate in banks goes up, a greater part of the savings of people would flow towards banks as deposits and only a smaller part may move towards other financial intermediaries like the share market. Thus, the amount of money that can be mobilized by private firms through the share market also shrinks. In essence, when the government borrows more from its own citizens, the capital that can be mobilized by the private sector from the domestic economy may decline. This may affect their production or expansion plans. Thus they may not expand production, compared with a situation where government borrowings are smaller. This is called crowding out of private investment due to excessive government borrowings.

When the production by private firms does not expand much (as a consequence of excessive government borrowings), the supply of many goods and services available in the economy may not increase. On the other hand, due to increased government expenditure (since the government borrows more money) some people may have more money in their hands. (When the government spends money on projects, the money will be distributed to the workers, at different points of the production chain.) This may encourage them to demand more goods. This, when combined with a situation where the supply of goods/services is not increasing, may cause inflation. Thus, excessive government borrowings and expenditure can also lead to inflation.

Let us consider another scenario where the government borrows excessively from external sources. This may not create inflation or the crowding out of private investments, as mentioned above. But there could be another problem. When a government borrows heavily from outside and it cannot pay back enough in time, the credit worthiness of the country will fall. This may reduce the credit availability from outside. In addition, the external investors [these may include three types: (*a*) those who lend money to the government; (*b*) those who invest in a country's stock markets and (*c*) those who invest in factories and production units in the country] will be closely watching the financial situation of the country. Excessive borrowings and fiscal deficits (including the one financed by excessive printing of money, if this is attempted) will send a signal of poor financial health of this country to external investors. If they get worried too much, they may withdraw their investments from the country (like by selling the shares of the companies of the country). Any drastic outflow of capital from one country can create the foreign exchange crisis like the one that happened in East Asian countries (that we mentioned in the note on recession). For this reason too, excessive fiscal deficits and financing of those by internal or excessive borrowings is not a sound economic policy. Hence, countries would try to balance their fiscal deficits. This can be done in many ways. There can be a fiscal responsibility act, which may limit the percentage of fiscal deficit to say three per cent of the GDP.

On the other hand, governments have to spend a substantial amount of money for public goods, services such as education and health care (which are not public goods but there are other reasons why a government should spend money for these purposes) and also for helping the poor and vulnerable sections. This is needed for social security as well as economic growth. But the tax income available in a developing country is much lower than that of a developed country. For example, if around 50 per cent of the GDP is available as tax income to a government in Western Europe, the corresponding figure in India is around 15 per cent. This is due to many reasons: incomes of many people are low and hence only a small section of people is considered taxable by governments; the tax collection system is not full-proof, there is a high level of tax evasion; governments may provide tax concessions to firms so that they can expand operations and create employment and so on. With such low tax incomes and with the burden to alleviate poverty of a large section of people, governments, in countries like India, have to spend more on the social sector. This may create a situation where adequate amounts of public goods may not be provided and also the government may have to borrow a large part of domestic savings. This may create instability in the macroeconomic environment. Let us try to understand this in the Indian context.

In India, there is not only a general inflation but also a price increase across food and related commodities creating tension in society. The RBI has been increasing interest rates but these efforts have not been very successful so far. There are several factors behind this phase of inflation. There has been a substantial increase in spending by the government on the social sector in the last few years. The National Rural Employment Guarantee Scheme is one such spending programme. This has helped partially in bringing more money to the hands of the poor and other vulnerable sections. More money means an increased demand for more commodities, including food. However, our food production and distribution (especially the supply chain) face a number of problems. That is why we can see wastage of food grains on the one hand and an increase in their prices, on the other hand. It is also not uncommon to see a drastic reduction in supply (and hence increase in price) in one place or one season, even when farmers find it difficult to sell these commodities at other places and other seasons. Adequate investments in infrastructure and the supply chain management are not taking place for several reasons. When demand increases, when people have money but when supply is not increasing there will be inflation. There are also external factors. The country has no control over fuel prices. Though the government has tried not to pass on the burden to end consumers, it is forced to do so, albeit, partially. All these have contributed to inflation.

Spending programmes of the Government of India have also contributed to fiscal deficits. On an average ₹4 out of ₹10 it spends is based on borrowing. In addition, state governments also borrow money from the market. These borrowings increase the interest rate. It is difficult for governments to control deficits. The recession in the developed world two years ago forced the government in India (and other countries) to spend more on the one hand and also not to follow deficit control measures. The increase in interest rate works against investments by all, including private firms. This too has an impact on the supply of goods and services. When there is an inadequate increase in supply compared with that of demand, there can be inflation.

It is in this context that the RBI is increasing interest rates to control inflation. But it hurts investments and further reduces the expansion of supply of goods and services. Also, governments cannot take steps to control fiscal deficits or rationalize their spending programmes. Thus, inflation remains uncontrolled.

The other major challenge that governments in the developing world face is that they are not able to spend enough money on activities to be funded by the government and the absence of such adequate spending may have an impact on development outcomes. Let us consider the following two important impacts on development:

1. Inadequate investments on infrastructure and public goods will have an adverse impact on the sustained growth of the economy. This would also affect the development and create inflation, as we have seen in the case of supply chain problems. Poor and other vulnerable sections may be affected by such inflation.

2. Governments cannot spend adequately on health care and education. Health care expenditure has become a major spending which makes non-poor poor. Similarly, a lack of education in general and also a lack of appropriate education which imparts employable skills for a substantial section of the population have serious impact on their welfare. Though the private sector is showing some interest in education, this is still not adequate. The absence of education for some accelerates inequality in society. Moreover, it is only through education that people belonging to economically backward sections can hope to achieve social and economic mobility.

Hence, understanding some of these macroeconomic challenges is important for development practitioners.

QUESTIONS

1. What is inflation? When does it occur?
2. What could be the relationship between the deficits of the government and inflation?
3. What is the rationale behind the use of monetary policy to control inflation?
4. What is recession? How does government spending help in coming out of recession? What are the factors which may make such spending less effective?
5. What are the factors that one should consider before using the Keynesian solution of increased government spending as a strategy in a developing world?
6. How does recession in the developed world affect developing countries?

PART III

DEVELOPMENT AND GROWTH

⊰ EIGHT ⊱

HUMAN DEVELOPMENT

————•◆•————

In the introductory chapter, we have seen that economic growth can take place even when a substantial section of the population lives in absolute poverty—with high illiteracy, infant mortality or people dying before they are 50 years old. There can also be other manifestations like inadequate nutrition, unhealthy growth of children and so on. There may be a systematic pattern in these symptoms of ill-development. Some social groups (like certain caste groups in India), some regions or women in general may have more of these vulnerable people. Thus, there is a general consensus that economic growth is not adequate to achieve development.

What is development then? People have tried with different approaches. One way is to consider whether the entire population in a society gets certain basic items for consumption—the definition of such basic items may vary, but food, minimal clothing, house, water supply and basic energy have to be included in such assessments. If a significant section of the society is deprived of these basic items, it is a measure of underdevelopment. There were also attempts to develop aggregate measures considering the status of some of these items. One such measure developed in the seventies is called Physical Quality of Life Index (PQLI). However, ensuring basic goods or services (for example, drinking water or energy) may not be adequate if our objective is to see that people are capable

of functioning normally. Taking an active role in economic life is one such functioning and this may require certain abilities like literacy or schooling. Such a
functioning can also be viewed as part of the pursuit of human freedom. Amartya
Sen, the Nobel laureate, has analysed the importance of such capabilities and
functioning in understanding development.[1] As a way of translating this concept
into reality, Professor Sen and his colleagues have contributed to the measurement (and improvements in the methodology) of, what is called, the Human
Development Index (HDI). We will focus on this idea of human development in
this chapter.

HUMAN DEVELOPMENT INDEX

This concept is based on three factors: education, health and living standards.
Hence, certain variables such as mean and expected years of schooling, life
expectancy at birth—the number of years one can expect to live at the time of
birth in a society and the Gross National Income (GNI) per person are taken into
account. GNI includes GDP, which we have already defined. In addition, it
includes the income received by people from other sources. For example, if an
Indian has invested in a company in West Asia and he/she has received profits
from that company, it would also become part of the GNI of India. The HDI is
not an absolute but a relative measure. Each country's achievement in terms of
each of these factors is compared with the most successful country in terms of the
same factor and a rank is prepared. The ranks in terms of these different factors
are aggregated to get a combined index. The detailed method of calculating this
index is given in the following section.

Calculation of HDI

The methodology is fairly standard now and one can get this from many sources,
including Wikipedia. The following indicators were used for calculating HDI in
2010 (there being improvements/changes in the methodology over a period of
time):

- life expectancy at birth;
- mean years of schooling and expected years of schooling; and

- per-capita income at what is called, 'purchasing power parity' (PPP). This PPP is considered because what one person can purchase in India with a given amount of money (for example, ₹100) is different from what a person can purchase with $2 (an almost equivalent amount as per the exchange rate) in the US. One may not get a cup of coffee in the US with $2, but one can have a decent lunch with ₹100 in India. Thus, the purchasing power of a particular value of international currency in each country may vary and this can be calculated by comparing the prices of a set of commodities in different countries.

The value of each factor in a given country/region is converted into an Index by taking the maximum value of that factor (among the countries) and the minimum value. For example, the life expectancy (LE) index of a particular country in 2010 is calculated as:

[LE (of the country)—its minimum value among the countries (20 in 2010)]/ [maximum value of LE (83.2 in 2010)—its minimum value (20 in 2010)]

There are some differences in the way education indicators are used.

Education Index is based on Mean Years of Schooling (MYS) Index and the Expected Years of Schooling (EYS) Index. These are calculated as follows:

MYS index = (MYS of the country – 0)/(13.2 – 0): please note that 13.2 and 0 are maximum and minimum values of MYS among different countries. MYS is defined as the number of years a 25-year-old person or older has spent in schools on an average in that country.

Similarly, EYS Index = (EYS of the country – 0)/(20.6 – 0). Here, EYS is defined as the number of years a 5-year-old child can expect to spend on education in the whole life (on average). The maximum and minimum values are 20.6 and 0, respectively.

Combining MYS and EYS indices, an education index is prepared as follows:

[√(MYSI*EYSI) – 0]/(0.951 – 0): 0.951 is calculated by taking the square root of the product of the maximum values of MYSI and EYSI.

Please note that there are different ways of taking averages: for two values, A and B, $(A + B)/2$ is one average and it is called the arithmetic average. There can also be other averages. $\sqrt{(A*B)}$ is another average and it is called geometric average. There are some properties for each of these averages and based on the nature of the units of measurement of these numbers, a particular way of calculating the average is better than the other in a specific context.

Income Index is calculated as follows:

[Natural Log (GNP per Capita of the Country in PPP) – Natural Log (163)]/ [Natural Log (108,211) – Natural Log (163)]: 108,211 and 163 are maximum and minimum values among the countries in 2010.

Combining the indices of education, life expectancy and income, the HDI of a particular country is calculated as

$$\sqrt[3]{(\text{Life Expectancy Index} \times \text{Education Index} \times \text{Income Index})}$$

ECONOMIC GROWTH WITHOUT HD AND HD WITHOUT ECONOMIC GROWTH—DEBATES AND CASES

In the seventies, it was noted by a number of scholars that some countries or regions had achieved relatively higher levels of human development, though they were poor countries/regions in terms of per-capita income. Sri Lanka, Costa Rica (in Central America) and Kerala were such countries/regions. The literacy rate, infant mortality rate, enrolment rate and life expectancy of these areas were found to be comparable to those of some developed nations, even though their per-capita incomes were far lesser than those of the developed world. That created a debate on human development—more specifically whether countries can achieve higher levels of human development even without substantial economic growth.

There were other counter examples too. Some countries in the Middle East/ Latin America had a per-capita incomes comparable to middle income countries (thus, they were not really poor or developing countries in the conventional sense). However, a section of people like the urban poor in Latin American countries were living in very inhuman conditions. For example, until some years ago, children from urban slums in the cities of Latin America—like Rio or Sao

Paulo—were not attending schools and became part of violent gangs, and instances of police shooting them were quite common. Hence, the idea that economic growth need not lead to human development also got strengthened.

How did some relatively poorer countries/regions achieve a higher level of human development? An accessible public distribution system, which provided basic food grains to all, was an important instrument there. There were schools accessible to the whole population. Primary health care was also made accessible and affordable. There may be several specific reasons that made each country/region adopt these policies.

What Made the HDI Higher in Kerala?

There are many historical and other factors that helped Kerala. Geography and the climate of Kerala are unique compared with many other Indian states. Very high rainfall in this tropical region has created a higher degree of biodiversity. This itself has made some impact. Water is abundantly available—both for drinking and maintaining personal hygiene; also some cultivation is done without irrigation. People with even small plots of land could grow tubers, fruits, nuts, and this, along with the paddy grown in naturally marshy areas, ensured a minimum sustenance for a sizable population. This climate has also facilitated the growth of many plants whose produce is not so easily available in several parts of the world (or available only in similar climatic regions, which are not many). Thus, spices like pepper and cardamom were growing in the forests as part of the natural vegetation in Kerala. This had attracted traders from the Arab and Roman world for a very long time. These traders were also bringing in cultural and other ideas. Christianity reached Kerala very early (probably) through the traders. Islam also arrived nearly 1,200 years ago. The interests of European explorers like the Portuguese (starting from Vasco de Gamma) and then the Dutch, French and finally the British to establish bases in Kerala were also driven by the interests in monopolizing this trade. The presence of precolonial Christianity in the state encouraged a much higher level of missionary activity there. The precolonial states were also interested in revenues from trade (of spices) and thus they adopted a collaborative attitude towards the colonial traders who became rulers of the country later on. The trade also created a large number of intermediaries and there was an interest in acquiring basic numeracy.

The educated got supervisory positions in other outposts of colonial trade in Sri Lanka and Malaya. The collaboration between colonial rulers and missionary activity led to the starting of a number of schools. The rulers of the princely states also collaborated in this venture. The usefulness of education in trade, supervisory jobs within and outside states and so on encouraged many people to access schools. Along with this, the state bureaucracy encouraged some sections to acquire education.

In Kerala, each caste group started movements to address some issues within the community and also to fight for a greater share of resources from the state. The movement within Brahmins was aimed at facilitating widow remarriage within the community and also to avoid restrictions against intra-caste marriage for all the siblings. Nairs had their own struggle to move away from the matrilineal system and also to fight for more jobs within the government which was in the control of non-Keralites. Another group, namely Ezhavas, had undergone a major transformation under the leadership of Sri Narayana Guru, encouraging them to acquire education and engage in business other than their traditional occupation of tapping and selling toddy—liquor from the coconut tree. They also fought against untouchability and this boosted their esteem. Even the Dalits fought for their rights (under the leadership of people like Ayyankali) during the pre-Independence period and made efforts to establish their own schools. The wide network of Christianity and Islam in Kerala also encouraged many people from the Hindu religion (or the outcastes) to convert themselves into these religions to save them from the caste discrimination prevalent among the Hindus. This also helped them to access opportunities in education and health care provided by missionaries and religious establishments. Thus, even before Indian Independence, there was competition by different communities and groups of people to have schools or to corner a part of the resources provided by the state to start schools.

It is in this social context that the socialists who were initially part of the Indian National Congress and who later became a part of the communist parties, mobilized small (tenant) peasants and agricultural workers (belonging to backward communities) and other sections of the working class. This mobilization too helped enhancing the self-respect of the oppressed and vulnerable sections. When the Communist parties came to power in the fifties and the sixties, they implemented land reforms (albeit partially) and bestowed ownership rights on the landless people who were living in huts on the land owned by their landlords. This too enhanced their self-respect and this led to their demanding/participating in governmental provisions of education and health care. The political mobilization by the left parties has also helped different sections of people demanding the extension of public services to them. The Public Distribution System was an integral part of these expanded government services. Competitive politics which brought in Congress-led and Communist-led coalitions to power encouraged successive governments to respond to the people's demands favourably. The decision of the first Kerala government to pay the salary of the teachers of private schools directly and the consequent practice of private school managers to appoint teachers by taking money from them (since they got government salaries) created some perverse incentives but in turn led to the expansion of school education systems.

The level of education in Kerala was better when compared with many other Indian states even at the time of Indian Independence. This was true even in the case of female education. All the efforts mentioned above led to the spread of school education to most regions, caste groups and classes and covered both men and women. The spread of education to women had other positive impacts. Hygienic practices that help reduce infant mortality got popularized. This reduction in infant mortality combined with social campaigns to encourage small family influenced women and through them, the families. This has led to a faster demographic transition in Kerala. All this has contributed to a higher human development there. Thus, we have to note that a number of geographical and socio-political factors have helped in creating a conducive environment for this process.

Higher levels of human development have been achieved by a few other Indian states too. Goa is an example. Its geographical features are akin to Kerala. Christianity reached Goa nearly 500 years ago. This and colonial contacts have given them an outward orientation. Job opportunities elsewhere encouraged people to acquire education. Similarly, such factors may have enabled some North Eastern states like Meghalaya or Mizoram to achieve mass literacy.

Of late, states like Tamil Nadu have adopted effective public policies, which have helped in recording higher human development. It may be noted that Tamil Nadu has many disadvantages when compared with Kerala—the need for irrigation, the relatively large size of landholdings and a high level of landlessness and so on. Though reform movements were very successful among the middle caste groups, it had not touched the Dalits until recently. Even today untouchability is practised in few villages. The spread of education to backward social groups and women has taken place at a much slower pace. Mid-day meal schemes attracted more kids to school and also helped retain them in classes. Family planning schemes, though these were somewhat supply driven and top down, met with success in the eighties and nineties. A higher economic growth and tax revenues available to the state, combined with the competitive populism of the two main contending parties, led to a large number of schemes that transferred money or benefits to the poorer and vulnerable families. However, a discomforting feature of Tamil Nadu, in terms of human development, is in terms of the sex ratio, which continues to be unfavourable to women with reports of female infanticide coming from parts of the state. But the experience of Tamil Nadu shows what a state can do in terms of human development with effective public policies, even if it did not enjoy advantageous factors like Kerala.

CHALLENGES TO SUSTAINING HIGHER LEVELS OF HUMAN DEVELOPMENT

To some extent, the former socialist countries like the USSR or those in East Europe, or countries like China or Cuba (which continued to be ruled by the communist parties), too had higher levels of indicators in terms of literacy rate, enrolment and life expectancy. However, unrelated to the debate mentioned here, these countries became non-socialist over a period of time. The USSR and East European countries have changed the political system (removed the monopoly of communist parties) and the economic system (by moving from a centrally planned one to a market-driven capitalist system). China has not changed the political system but has transformed the economy into a market-based one (which they call market socialism). Of late, even Cuba is trying to change its economic system. Thus, the experience of these countries show that they have not been able to sustain state interventions in the economy to the extent they were doing in the past, even though they could achieve higher levels of human development due to such interventions.

Though not pronounced as socialist countries, countries like Costa Rica or states like Kerala have realized that despite their achievements in terms of human development, they have not been able to usher in economic growth to the level desired. Economic growth is needed for governments to get adequate tax income for meeting social needs (for example, for running a large number of schools or health care centres or to continue with an elaborate public distribution system). In the absence of such a growth of the domestic economy, the region with a higher human development may encounter several challenges, or they may have to overcome them with the help of some external factors. The case of Kerala in terms of the challenges it faced in sustaining human development may be a pointer in this regard. This is detailed in the following section.

The Challenges to the Kerala Model

The spread of basic education to all sections of the population encouraged them to seek better jobs. People were not willing to continue with conventional low-skilled jobs such as those of farm workers. However, there were not enough jobs in the industrial and service sectors and there was also a stagnation of industrial growth caused by several factors. The spread of minimal social security and labour mobilization discouraged people from working at low wages as in other Indian states and thus the relative cost of labour increased in Kerala. This forced some industries to move out and discouraged others from investing in Kerala. Militant labour mobilization gave an impression to investors that there would be many 'no work' days in factories. Successive governments did not take a pro-investor view and not using police against militant trade unionism in factories and the consequent threat to life and the property of investors too discouraged potential investors. Some other inputs, like land, were also costly in Kerala due to high population density and the uses for plantation, agriculture, residence and so on. Industrial growth has some cluster effect, that is, when there are many industries in an area, there will be a tendency to open more and more new units in the same area. This is because the demand for industrial goods/service in an area creates a nearby market for new units. Similarly, the supply of industrial goods/services in a nearby area may reduce the cost of production and this too adds new units to an already industrialized area. The corollary of this is that if a region is less industrialized, it may become more backward in terms of industrialization in the absence of this 'clustering effect'. All these factors slowed down the pace of industrialization of Kerala.

This forced people to search for jobs outside the state and white collar jobs like typists, teachers and nurses in other Indian states beckoned the Keralites who were more qualified than the locals there. The economic boom in the Gulf countries (financed by the oil revenue) became another source of jobs for the Keralites. The spread of education and the long-standing trade connections enabled Keralites to use these opportunities more than other Indians. Thus, remittances from these Keralites boosted consumption in Kerala and gave a big boost to the service sector growth within the state. The growth of banks (which deal with remittances), travel business (facilitating migration), construction (of houses and shops financed by the remittances) and so on are part of this service sector growth. Thus, there is an economic growth fuelled by remittances even though there is lack of industrial growth/investments in Kerala. In summary, even though higher human development caused a stagnation of industrial growth within the domestic economy, 'remittances' benefited many Keralites.

Of course, there are also costs associated with these processes. A large part of the population has to depend on jobs/remittance from foreign countries, where they cannot expect any meaningful future as full citizens, is one issue. There are sections within the state which could not benefit much from the jobs available elsewhere. These include scheduled castes and tribes who did not have the money to meet the cost of migration. It also included certain sections of women who, for social or cultural reasons, are not that mobile or are forced to be at home to take care of the children in the absence of their fathers (who work elsewhere). The social costs associated with the families and parents left within the state, whose bread earners live elsewhere, could be another issue. The most crucial issue is that the internal resource mobilization of the government is not going up to meet the growing needs of public services. Thus, the state has been grappling with a huge burden in terms of meeting the costs of public education, health care and public distribution but the taxable income is not increasing at the rate at which expenditure is going up. Rationalization of these expenditures even to accommodate changing needs is also not that easy. It is difficult to reduce the number of public schools though the number of children enrolling is decreasing (due to demographic changes and the exodus of some sections of children to privately funded schools). Charging even a minimal fee in public hospitals for those sections who can afford them is not easy, although more than 60 per cent of people use private health care facilities. The strategies for human development have also enhanced public employment and the expectations surrounding them. The government cannot easily change these expectations (and thus cannot change pension schemes or increase the retirement age and so on). Thus, the government of Kerala is in a debt-ridden situation and the revenue deficit of the state is high even though many other Indian states are presenting a surplus budget.

Sri Lanka and Costa Rica, which had reported higher human development without a significant increase in per-capita income, have also encountered similar challenges. These two countries have also adopted, over a period of time, growth-oriented policies, or have tried to rationalize their public expenditure in tune with their current needs. Their experience shows that economic growth by itself will not enhance human development. However, it also shows at the same time that focusing only on human development without facilitating economic growth or efficiency in public expenditure may not be desirable.

We can consider the challenges faced by other Indian states too. Goa did not develop an elaborate social security network (of government funded/aided schools, public health care and public distribution system) as widespread as Kerala. Similarly, Goa did not encounter similar challenges to industrial investments as those in Kerala (even though land prices are higher in certain areas of Goa). Thus, Goa could go ahead with some industrialization, migration, remittances, backpacker tourism (which allows the percolation of the benefits of tourism to lower income groups in a major way) and so on.

Both Kerala and West Bengal had a long history of social and political movements, which helped in mobilizing the less privileged sections of society. Though such mobilization has helped in achieving higher human development in Kerala, the favourable impact of such forces on human development is yet to become visible in West Bengal. However, both these states faced challenges in terms of industrialization, partly driven by the political and trade union mobilization led by the left parties. These states are also facing challenges in mobilizing enough tax resources to meet public expenditure.

There can also be a comparison between West Bengal and Tamil Nadu. Though West Bengal could implement land reforms reasonably well, such a transformation is yet to take place in Tamil Nadu. The state of Tamil Nadu did not face challenges in terms of industrialization and it is probably one of the states which attract higher levels of industrial investments. It could also mobilize substantial tax resources. The government of Tamil Nadu used these tax resources and implemented some schemes (in a top–down manner) like the mid-day meal scheme and all these have enabled them to achieve higher levels of human development in a relatively shorter period. Competitive politics have also encouraged each party to offer a wider set of resources to households (especially those who are below the poverty line) and this too may have helped the process of enhancing human development. Compared with Tamil Nadu, the slow pace of industrialization (or deindustrialization to some extent) and the absence of competitive politics (until recently) may have worked against the achievement of human development in West Bengal.

SOME LESSONS ON HUMAN DEVELOPMENT

What are the broad lessons that we get from these comparisons? First, we should consider human development itself as a very limited achievement, as it takes into account only a few minimal factors such as life expectancy and schooling along with per-capita income. So the achievement of human development (in terms of higher HDI) can be taken as a minimal but important social task. This does not mean that other transformations in society are less desirable. For example, land reforms may be an important strategy and it may have indirect linkages with the social indicators mentioned. However, some societies may be able to achieve higher levels of human development even without fundamental changes like land reforms. The lack of implementation of land reforms need not be seen as a barrier against achieving higher levels of human development. This may be an important lesson for the BIMARU states. Since policies which aim at fundamental social transformation like land reforms could not be implemented quickly, they may adopt policies which help achieve higher levels of human development.

The comparison also shows that states which have not had a long history of social and political mobilization can also achieve higher levels of human development through appropriate public policies. This is not to underplay the importance of such mobilization. It may be important for more fundamental socio-political transformation, including the deepening of democratization. But we need not wait for such transformation to achieve human development.

Another lesson could be that different kinds of social opportunities may facilitate the achievement of human development. The outward orientation (in terms of culture and material opportunities) provided by the spread of Christianity has also played an important role in the achievement of human development.

Yet another lesson could be that the people benefiting from human development need to participate in a growing economy, whether within the region or outside, to sustain their gains. If opportunities for migration or employment in other regions are available, the lack of adequate jobs within the region may not be a major constraint for some people. However, there may be some social sections, which may not be able to utilize the opportunities elsewhere and for them lack of employment opportunities within the region may be a serious constraint.

The experience of Kerala and also the experience of former socialist states show that, even if they achieve higher levels of human development, they may face challenges if the internal economy is not sustaining industrial development through private investments and the economy/society is not adopting policies that enhance efficiency. This can happen even if the human development of the society is at a lower level, as in the case of West Bengal.

Human development is only one way of conceptualizing development of society. There are criticisms of the human development approach. For example, questions on the impact of the development on the happiness of individuals or on the environment are more vocal now. Some of these issues will be discussed while taking up issues of inequality and environmental impact later.

QUESTIONS/EXERCISES

1. Get the human development indices of different countries and different Indian states for the latest available year from different sources. Discuss the states/countries with very high human development and those with very low values. Are there some surprises, given your current knowledge of the issues?
2. Calculate the HDI of your district from the data available from different sources.
3. Is HDI an adequate formulation of development? Give reasons.
4. Do you think that your state (if it happens to be one with a lower HDI) can learn from other regions which have recorded higher HDI? What are the key lessons that you will take home in this regard?
5. What are the global regions with a concentration of countries with low HDI? Try to develop an argument based on reading literature.

6. Based on your reading of literature, write a 300-word short essay on capabilities, functioning and their relationship to freedom.

7. A feminist economist argues that the HDI fails to take into account gender discrimination that exists in many societies. Is it true? Explain.

NOTE

1. The idea of capabilities and functioning are much more important even beyond the notion of human development. Those interested may read some original writings in this regard, such as Sen (1999).

NINE

ECONOMICS OF GROWTH: PART I

INTRODUCTION

Economic growth means that a country is producing more and more goods and services (in terms of their value) every year. How can this happen? If the adult population increases, then more goods and services can be produced by making use of these additional workers. But income per person may not increase then. This is not a good indication of growth. For a growth of income per person, the value of the goods and services produced per person should increase. The total value of the goods and services may increase even if there is a general increase in prices but that is also not an indication of improvement in income in a real sense, since, in such a case, the quantum of goods and services available per person is not increasing.

A country can produce more goods/services per person, only when each person (on an average) can produce more goods/services. This is possible when people use better machines, skills or technology, which help them produce more with the same level of inputs. Thus more capital (including human capital) and/or technology is to be infused into the production process if a country has to produce more goods and services per person. If we take capital, one option is to generate such capital (in simple terms, money to buy machines or mechanical power or to acquire human capital or education) from within the country. This is possible only when people 'save' a part of their current income. The machines that we use may rust and degrade over time (and this is called depreciation) and a part of the saved money is needed to repair or replace existing machines. We need to have more savings than those required to compensate for depreciation if we want to have a higher level of capital in the production process in the next time period (to produce a greater volume of goods and services per person).

So, how much savings are needed to attain a particular growth rate? How does one deploy these savings to ensure maximum growth?

THEORIES ON ECONOMIC GROWTH

We will consider briefly how different strands of economists have thought about economic growth at different points of time in the following sections. We may start with those pioneers who started thinking about it in the eighteenth and nineteenth centuries.

Classical Economists

The importance of savings for growth was recognized even by first generation economists including Adam Smith and Karl Marx.[1] Adam Smith considered industrialists as one group having the incentive to suppress their own consumption and generate savings for capital investments for enhancing production. The workers could not do so since their earnings were just adequate to meet their needs. Smith argued for withdrawing protection and the privileges enjoyed by landlords/royalty and traders who spent more money on luxuries. Other economists like Ricardo too saw the distinction between workers and capitalists in terms of their saving power. The population growth among workers was seen by these economists as a factor that would increase the number of workers.

How does population growth affect economic growth? See Box 9.1 for details. When a large number of workers compete for jobs, their income will be just enough to meet their minimum needs and workers cannot save much money, and investments may have to depend on the savings of the capitalist class. This class can save because even at low wages, they are able to attract a large number

Box 9.1: Population Growth versus Economic Growth

Malthus (eighteenth century) postulated that the population would grow at an exponential rate (like, 2, 4, 8, 16 and so on) while food production may take place at an arithmetical rate like 2, 4, 6, 8 and so on, leading to a catastrophic situation. But this view did not take into account the possibility of technological change. Ester Boserup noted, on empirical evidence, that the size of the population played an important role in technological change or the production system. For example, as population expanded, the area of land increased by bringing in territories which were not used for cultivation earlier. But such extensive cultivation has limits. Once such an extensive cultivation was found to be costly, the changed human strategy was to intensify cultivation in the same area. This could be achieved by different means. Irrigation systems were developed so that the cultivation can be carried even in the absence of rainfall. Thus, the same area can be used twice or thrice in a year for cultivating short-term crops like paddy. The use of high-yielding varieties, fertilizers and so on could also be a part of such intensive cultivation. What is important to note is that as the population grows, societies come out with different strategies to meet their increased requirements.

Source: Author.

of workers. However, Ricardo saw the slow pace of increase in food production (as against the growth of population) putting a pressure on capitalist savings. According to him, the scarcity of food production (compared with demand) may increase the minimum sustenance wage to be given to the workers, reducing the surplus available with the capitalists posing a threat to their savings and capital investments in the future.

Karl Marx, too, highlighted the need for capital investment for economic growth. Besides population growth, he saw two other factors, which created surplus labour (a reserve army) leading to more number of people competing for fewer jobs in industries bringing wages almost closer to the minimum needed for subsistence. First among them is the breaking down of subsistence agriculture dominated by a large number of peasants. According to him, inroads of capital into agriculture and enhanced productivity would make large farms economical and peasant agriculture and artisan-based production in rural areas less productive. This would lead to more workers being available in urban or industrial areas. Second, engines (including steam engines) were being deployed in the production system then. Marx postulated that capitalists would use labour-saving machines in such a way that there would always be a situation where the wages to workers could be suppressed. The industrial reserve army created by the population growth, breaking down of traditional rural production and the use of labour-saving technologies would help capitalists to keep the wages lower (or almost close to the minimum needed for sustenance). Thus, capitalists saved more money and went ahead with more and more capital investments. Marx did not see the growth of food production as a major problem like Ricardo, probably due to his conceptualization and experience that capital investments in agriculture would lead to an increase in the production of food grains, possibly overcoming the growth of population.

However, the political part of Marx's argument is that such a production system would lead to a widening inequality between workers and capitalists and create conflict overturning the capitalist system by bringing productive assets under public or workers' ownership. However, such a revolution did not occur in the industrial economies of that time but were seen in relatively backward economies of Russia, East Europe, China and so on. On the other hand, real wages went up in the industrialized West proving Marx wrong. This could be due to the changes in the institutional and governance system, which would like to avoid extreme inequality that was predicted by Marx. (Possibilities of revolutions like the ones that happened in socialist countries may have encouraged the political and economic elite of Western countries to part with a greater part of the surplus with the working class.) There were more legal measures ensuring social security and other related support measures in almost all these countries. But there are also economic reasons why capitalists wanted to give a wage rate higher than the subsistence rates. One idea was that higher wages and higher consumption of workers could increase the productivity of workers. There was also an argument that higher wages would reduce the need for costly supervision at the shop floor level. Workers getting higher wages do not want to lose them by shirking since an alternative job would only fetch them a lower wage. Thus, they would be more productive and loyal to the current employer even without explicit supervision. In general, Marx underestimated the possibilities within the capitalist economies to contain the tension and conflicts emerging from the growing inequality. Hence his political prediction did not turn out to be very valid.[2]

It is important to note here that both Adam Smith and Marx (and other classical economists) have seen capital investments as the important driver of economic growth. However, another important classical economist, Schumpeter, focused on another dimension called 'creative destruction'. He argued that, in Western economies, the crucial factor fuelling economic growth is innovations. Here, innovation needs to be seen in a wider context. For example, a new entrepreneur could come out with a new product (or it could be the improved version of an existing product). If he could sell it, he might make more profits as long as he enjoys the monopoly. But this may encourage others to emulate him (in making the same product). This may eventually lead to competition and the disappearance of his extra profits. But this will benefit consumers—they got a new product, initially and at competitive prices, later. Thus, economic growth requires a wider set of actors to come out with periodic innovations as the reward from each of these innovations may taper off.

Development Theorists of the Twentieth Century

Classical economists were considering a context where substantial industrialization had taken place (or was taking place at a significant rate). But countries like India, which got independence in the first half of the twentieth century, had a large population surviving on subsistence agriculture (with very low savings). These countries were not industrialized and the capitalist class who could mobilize resources was also small then. Some development theorists like Rosenstein-Rodan and Nurkse have identified an important problem of these poorer (newly independent) economies. Even if a capitalist mobilized savings and started producing a product (say footwear), it cannot be sold on a large scale because the majority cannot afford to buy. So the demand for commodities and services within the society itself could be a limiting factor for the expansion of production (This is, to some extent, based on the idea of Keynes—see the chapter on macroeconomic environment.) According to them, there is a need for coordinated investments in productive activities. This may help the workers who are employed in one sector to demand the goods produced by other sectors, for example, the worker in the cloth factory is likely to buy footwear and vice versa. But where is the money for such coordinated investments in several sectors? Due to low savings rate and the absence of an adequate size of the capitalist class, the state is expected to take the role of forcing people to save (and to reduce consumption). This can be done in many ways. Direct taxes can be one source, if such tax revenues are used for industrial investments. Limiting the sale of certain other products (for example, banning the exports of food grains) can also help. Limiting exports would mean that more is supplied in the domestic market and prices will be lower. Such low prices for food grains would reduce the cost of living for industrial workers. This would help keep the wage rates lower if the minimum wages paid are to meet sustenance. The other strategy for the government to extract money is to sell certain commodities mandatorily to government companies so that the profits they make can be ploughed back into industrial investments. Certain natural resources can be brought under the ownership of the state so that it can use them 'cheaply' in their investments. Hence, an overwhelming role for the state/government was envisaged in the framework, which saw the need for coordinated industrial investments.

Scholars have also postulated that, if the economic growth rate is too low, it may not lead to any growth in income per person, since the population rate is higher. This may even lead to a 'trap' wherein population increases along with or faster than income growth and keeping the society perpetually at a low level of consumption and hence savings (without adequate capital investments). Even for overcoming this trap, it was envisaged that substantial savings should be mobilized (by the state) to facilitate increased capital investments which may eventually lead to higher per-capita incomes.

To some extent, such theories, which saw the need for 'forced savings' imposed by the state and the need for coordinated growth, were also by and large in tune with the Soviet Union's central planning experiment that was then going on. One can view the Soviet experiment as an extreme version of such a state-led growth. But many countries, including India, opted for a state-led growth with forced savings with different degrees of freedom for the private sector. We will review the experience of these countries in Chapter 10.

Such an important role for savings rate (and capital investment) was seen by theorists like Harrod–Domar. They worked with a model where the growth in national income depended on the percentage of the income saved and also the additional capital required to produce one more unit of national income. This can be represented as follows:

$y = \Delta Y/Y$ (ratio of growth of national income = change in national income divided by national income).

$s = S/Y$ (ratio of savings = total savings divided by national income).

c = capital–output ratio (additional capital divided by the additional income produced by this additional capital).

Thus, the model can be described as $y = s/c$.

Thus, the growth rate increases proportionately to the savings rate, especially if we take the capital–output ratio to be constant for the period.

However, the heavy emphasis on savings rate and the role assigned to the state to mobilize such savings (and use them through government controlled industrial investments) were partly driven by a neglect of a few other aspects of the real world. There are different combinations at which capital and labour can be combined to produce an output. (Note our discussion on technology in Chapter 3.) In such a view, a given output can be produced with more capital and less labour or with more labour and less capital. Here, there is a presumption that labour can be used to substitute for the (less availability or higher cost) capital. This would mean that there could be capital investments using labour-intensive technology. For example, dams and canals can be built by using labour-intensive technology but such an investment may increase agricultural productivity (production of food grain per worker). Moreover, there are some technologies, which try to produce more output with a lesser use of capital and technology. For example, more grains can be produced from a given amount of land and labour if a high-yielding variety of seed is used. A greater number of bikes can be produced with the same labour if the different production processes are arranged in the most optimal manner. The cost of supplying soaps to retail shops can be reduced (and hence the cost of supply can be reduced) if an optimal way of distributing stocks from different godowns to retail stores is put in place.

There were studies in the fifties to know what factors have contributed to the growth of income in developed economies like those of the US or Europe. Let us consider a very simplistic way of doing growth accounting. If a country's income has grown by 70 per cent between 1900 and 1950 and if we know the percentages by which the use of labour and capital has to grow to achieve this increase in income, one can cross-check if that much real growth in labour and capital had really occurred during the period. The studies found that the income growth rate was much more than what could be accounted for the growth in labour and capital. Or, there is some residual of growth in the income of these countries, which cannot be explained by the growth of labour and capital. Different estimates at different points of time indicate that about 70–90 per cent of the income in the US needs to be attributed to factors other than the growth of capital and labour. This is reckoned as the contribution of technological progress, which enhanced productivity per worker (which is different from the increase in productivity per worker due to the use of more capital).

Though this 'residual'—the unaccounted factor that causes economic growth (after separating out the impact of growth of labour and capital)—is called technological progress, it is in reality a combination of several factors. This can include even primary schooling, which may enable people to increase their efficiency. It may include the level of higher education and the overall knowledge base in the economy. Technology need not be viewed always as an artefact or as equipment like steam engine (and of course, such equipments are an important part of technological progress when these are newly available). It can also be organizational innovations. How does one organize production better in a factory? How does one best manage people in a company? And how can one be creative in marketing one's own product? All such strategies are a part of what can be called technological progress.

NEOCLASSICAL GROWTH MODELS

This awareness of the importance of technological progress has changed the growth theories from the sixties onwards. Robert Solow's neoclassical growth theory is an important one. The essence of his theory is: it incorporates the possibility that more labour can be used to produce more income even with lesser amounts of capital investments. Thus capital can be substituted by labour to some extent. However, if workers are greater in number because of a higher population growth rate, it would mean a reduction in the income per worker. On the other hand, if there are not many workers (or a lower population growth rate), the possibility of substituting capital by labour is also limited. Moreover, there can also be 'decreasing returns to scale' for capital investments. This would mean that even though the use of more capital would increase income, the rate of such increase may keep declining. This can also imply that after a certain stage (for a given level of other factors like labour), further addition of capital investments need not increase income. On the other hand, there may be an increase in income with the use of more labour but then the income per worker may not increase. Thus if we assume that there is no technological progress and the substitution of capital by labour is taking place with the same technology, one can see a saturation point (or a steady state) in terms of income per worker because of the operation of these trends: more population reduces the income per worker but enhances substitution possibilities (that is, one can produce more output with even lesser capital); and less population would mean that the substitution possibilities are restricted and also the decreasing returns to capital. Hence if technology is stagnant, one should not expect a sustained increase in income per worker.

On the other hand, the steady state may shift to a higher level if the production technology changes. This opens up a different level of substitution possibilities. The gains from substituting capital by one unit of labour under a new (better) technology would be higher. Thus, the income per worker that can be generated even with the same level of workers or population would become higher under this new technological regime. What are these different technological possibilities? For understanding them, let us take the example of farm production. We consider the following two technological regimes:

A. Let us consider a cultivation practice where traditional seed, tractor and human power are used. It is possible to avoid tractor by using more human power.

B. This could be a combination of high-yielding variety, tractor and human power. Here too the use of tractor could be substituted by human power. However, the quantum of farm output (and its value) that could be produced more by one more worker (used to substitute tractor) in this case could be more than what is produced when the traditional seed is used.

Thus the growth in income per worker may reach a particular level when A is used. Similarly, the growth of income per worker under B would also reach a particular level. But these two levels are different—with the level under B greater than that under A. Similarly one can think about another technological regime, for which too, the growth of income per worker may reach a steady state, but this level would be higher than that under A or B.

Endogenous Models

The idea of technological process as noted in the neoclassical theory of growth has some loose ends. First, it does not tell us the source of such technological growth. Is it imported—like more developed economies transferring their technologies to less developed economies? How does the technology developed in one country/firm help the others? Can they simply copy it? Some of these issues are addressed in 'endogenous growth' theories developed in the eighties. A few basic ideas of such growth models are that technology, education or knowledge is taken as a factor that enhances productivity and so production depends on both efficient labour and capital invested. However, the efficiency of labour achieved by one firm does not depend only on the knowledge stock of that firm itself but the knowledge of all firms/actors or the knowledge base of the society. This is so since it may be difficult to keep such knowledge as a sole property of one firm and it may spread to the wider society through imitation, movement of labour from one firm to the other and also through the codification of knowledge through different means that may become accessible to others. Knowledge has a certain 'public good' character, which makes it costly to prevent somebody from knowing/using it when it is already there. This creates a positive externality in the sense that the efforts to be more efficient by one firm make even other firms similarly efficient over a period of time.

Under the endogenous model growth need not reach a stagnant state (unlike the neoclassical model). This is so since the stock of knowledge and capital together need not lead to any decreasing returns. Even population growth may lead to a positive outcome since it creates more people contributing to ideas and innovations. To some extent, endogenous models are something similar to the Harrod–Domar model where the growth rate is determined by the stock of knowledge and savings and is not affected by the decreasing returns to capital.

However, the technological process recognized in endogenous growth models should take place smoothly in an economy to achieve the growth envisaged. To some extent, this process is similar to the creative destruction outlined by Schumpeter. But this can take place only if there are some enabling entities. The economy encountered by Schumpeter had most of these entities. For example, exchange was taking place mainly through markets (and not through quotas decided by the officials as in the Soviet Union) and hence each producer had an incentive to come out with new products to gain monopoly advantage or to reduce the cost to increase the market share. The threat posed by this process to his competitors encourages them to learn from successful innovators/entrepreneurs. There is a risk to be taken by the new entrepreneur coming out with a new product. What if the product is not accepted by consumers? The risk is high and only a few will be able to take such risk if all the required capital is to be from one's own resources. But if banks or other financial intermediaries provide capital, then more entrepreneurs may be able to take such risks.

On the other hand, consider what happens if the government provides capital for a new product (as in the case of a public sector organization in India). The person producing/supplying the new product does not lose even if people reject it. It would mean that people may take excessive risks or they do not have the incentive to see that the new product should be the one demanded by consumers. Thus, financial intermediation by the market is needed for useful innovations.

Thus, we need institutional mechanisms to see that society creates a conducive environment for sustaining innovations and technological process. What are the different dimensions of this institutional mechanism? Financial intermediation, which provides appropriate incentives for risk taking, is one. The markets where suppliers and consumers exchange the goods and services form the core of this institutional mechanism. However, such markets alone are not sufficient. There should be a viable and effective state, which provides public goods and ensures that markets function well. There should also be some protection for certain kinds of innovations through patenting (even though it may not be the only way of protecting knowledge; and even with such a protection, knowledge may spill out from one firm to the other or to society). There should be protection of contracts enabling economic actors to get into long-run relationships. Such contracts have to be enforced through formal laws or strong social relationships.

There may be certain social contexts like Japan or Korea where pre-existing conditions may have created strong social and community relationships and here these may have helped the enforcement of contracts and economic relationships. On the other hand, Western developed economies rely on formal laws, evolved over a long period, to enforce such contracts. In countries like India, which has a much higher diversity in terms of culture and where there is a need for interaction between people belonging to multiple ethnic and cultural backgrounds, probably a 'formal' framework of disciplining economic relationships may be needed and this cannot be left to the social relationships and cultural norms of any one group or the other.

QUESTIONS/EXERCISES

1. Collect the economic growth rates of different states of India in a given year. Carry out a comparison.
2. Using the annual GDP growth rates of India from 1950 to 2010, list down your impressions.
3. What is the need for higher savings to achieve a faster rate of economic growth?
4. Why is it not advisable to focus only on savings rate or capital investments for attaining economic growth?
5. Neoclassical models and endogenous ones talk about technology but what is the difference in terms of conceptualizing technological change between these two sets of models?
6. What are facilitating conditions needed for endogenous technological change to take place?
7. The chief minister of your state reads some popular books in economics. He has read somewhere about endogenous growth theory. He asks you about the implications of this theory and what he could do in his own state based on the insights provided by this theoretical stream. What would be your advice?

NOTES

1. For those students who want a more detailed treatment of this part may see the book written by Hayami and Godo (1997).

2. However, there are some insights of Marx which are relevant even today in understanding the problems of developing economies. For example, the continuation of involuntary unemployment and an economic growth pattern which does not necessarily produce more jobs are some phenomenon which can be analysed with refined versions of Marxian insights.

⊰ TEN ⊱

ECONOMICS OF GROWTH: PART II

———◦•◉•◦———

It would be interesting to analyse the growth experience of India or many other countries, which had followed a socialist path inspired by the Soviet Union. Here, the economy was viewed as a system and investments were planned by the government or its designated agencies to determine the growth path and development outcomes. In the Soviet model almost all aspects of consumption (what people should buy and from where) and production, including those in small agricultural farms, were planned and carried out under the watchful eyes of the government. It spent a considerable amount of resources on education and research. The government mobilized the savings of the society (mainly through state ownership) and this was invested in capital-intensive industries. The Soviet Union witnessed rapid growth and the index of human development (in terms of enhancing educational opportunities and improving health care of the population) improved. However, the system could not be sustained politically. There were also some economic factors behind the collapse of the Soviet Union.

Though there were phases of economic growth, the 'residual' effect (or the role of technological progress in economic growth) mentioned in the previous chapter was not so substantial in the USSR compared with the developed nations like the US and Europe. The USSR was not the only country that reported a lower 'residual effect'. See Box 10.1 for details.

132

Box 10.1 Role of Technological Progress in the Economic Growth of Different Countries

Though technological progress could explain a large part of economic growth of the US and West European countries to some extent, the extent of the contribution of technological progress, the duration of its contribution varied between different countries. In some countries or regions, the contribution of technological progress (or what is called total factor productivity) was found to be lower than that in Western developed economies. This was found to be the case in the Soviet Union and also in the lately industrialized countries like South Korea and Taiwan. It meant that a greater part of the growth that had occurred in these regions was due to capital investments or increased labour use and only a smaller share was due to improvements in total factor productivity. There are many concerns in this regard. Depending mainly on capital investments and less on technological progress could be a costlier way of achieving growth. Moreover, further enhancements in growth had to depend on additional capital investments, which would be constrained by domestic savings or by the capital flow from elsewhere. If the capital investors from outside see other regions as more attractive (and labour cost could be an important consideration for such attraction), the inflow of foreign capital may get reduced. Thus a growth strategy dependent mainly on capital investment, without much technological progress, is not considered either desirable or sustainable. There is also an issue of possible inequality in capital investment-based growth. This is so since those sections in society, which do not belong to the capitalist class, usually achieve social mobility through education and participation in production that values their skills. When the role of technological progress is limited and growth depends mainly on capital investments, the avenues of social mobility for the non-capitalist class may get narrowed. We will take this up in the section on inequality.

Source: Author.

Soviet economic growth was driven primarily by capital investment and not much by technological progress. (But such capital-intensive growth did not lead to an enhanced inequality because of strong state control over distribution of

income.) This relatively less important role of technological progress in its economic growth was surprising since the Soviet Union was also known for its
educational and scientific achievements. But these achievements did not contribute much to the improvement in the productivity of the economy. The decreasing
returns inherent in a growth strategy mainly based on capital investments were
also found to be operating in the USSR.

However, India did not totally opt for the model of the Soviet Union. During
the first five-year plan, India adopted a slow growth model where there was more
emphasis on providing some support for employment and consumption and only
a smaller part of resources was set apart for industrial investments. When India
attained independence, our savings rate was around five per cent of the GDP
(which essentially would mean that if an income of ₹1,000 crores is generated
within the country in a year, then about ₹950 crores was used for consumption by
the people, companies and the government). What is the growth rate that can be
achieved with this small savings rate was a concern that was faced by the planners
then.[1] It is not that the savings rate was fixed. It could have been possible for the
state to intervene to 'extract' higher savings from the economy and push for a
higher growth path. Such extraction may lead to some social costs and the soci-
ety/politics may have to tolerate such costs. For example, were we then in a position to tax farmers (since agriculture was the main source of economic activity of
that time)? That would have been a major source of rural tension, which a newly
independent country like India could ill afford. The choice before the government
was either to use a greater part of taxes to meet the consumption needs of some
sections of society or to use it for capital investments (in say industry) so as to
have a higher growth rate. Though both the options were theoretically possible,
the first option may be politically more acceptable in a given time. These two
examples show that if the governments try to 'extract' a greater amount of savings
for investments (which is needed for growth), it may affect the current consumption of some people (like farmers who may then have to pay taxes). This is so
since the overall production of goods and services in an economy at a time is to
be used for consumption, for investment and also for government expenditure.
Increasing the amount under one item (say investment) would be at the cost of the
other two.

It is not that all the money for growth (or capital investments) has to come
from internal sources. There can be a more open-economic policy which allows

foreigners to invest in the country. Of course, this may also have some political implications. A country just free from colonial rule may not like to give a free hand to foreign investors and in the absence of such freedom many may not be willing to invest their money. What is important here is to note that there can be multiple ways of channelizing resources for the growth in an economy but each may have different social and political implications.

However, from the second five-year plan onwards, India focused on a heavy industrial growth path by mobilizing public resources and foreign aid and invested in specific projects. In order to be self-reliant the government invested heavily on commodities like steel. Most of such investments were made through public sector (or government owned companies). The government also imposed quantitative restrictions on imports and exports and made it mandatory for almost every entrepreneur to get license from the government to run a major production unit. In both these cases, individuals' incentives (a subject matter of microeconomics) were not a major concern.

But both the Soviet Union (and socialist countries in East Europe) and India have now rejected these models of planned development. India has moved out of what is called license raj and excessive control of exports and imports. Other socialist countries like China and Vietnam have not rejected the political monopoly of their communist parities but have reorganized their economies with greater emphasis on markets and private entrepreneurship.

WHAT ARE THE PROBLEMS WITH THESE MODELS OF PLANNED ECONOMIC DEVELOPMENT?

First, a large number of economic activities, especially in the USSR, needed to be coordinated by a centralized system and this was found to be very challenging. For example, each factory was given the task of producing a given quantity of one or more commodities; there were also incentives to produce more. The capital was also rationed out to each production unit. Under such a scheme, the only concern of the manager was to produce the specified quantity or more. He did not have to worry about its sale or to minimize the cost or to improve the quality (to see that it meets the taste/requirement of consumers). There was also a lack of incentive to come out with newer products. It was difficult to achieve efficiency in exchange when it was coordinated from above.

This may be compared with market coordination. Whether to produce or how much to produce are decisions taken by a multitude of producers depending on the signals received from different types of consumers in several markets. It is this process that was to be coordinated by the central agency. Information processing that is taking place in many decentralized markets cannot be replicated by a central planner. Second, even when signals exit, how those signals are used for changing one's decision depends on the incentives. For example, a private company selling soap may reduce its production if this product is not selling in the market. This would reduce the losses for the company. However, such a decision need not be taken by the manager of a public sector company—since his rewards might not depend on the profits/losses of the company. Similarly, if the owner of a private company sees that customers are moving away for poor-quality services, he has an incentive to make the service customer friendly, while such an incentive might not be available in the case of a public sector organization.

Giving a greater role for the state in India and also socialist countries was also based on the assumption that the government (or its decision-makers) was benevolent and their interest was to maximize social welfare. This turned out to be a very unrealistic assumption. Politicians and government officials, like others in the society, also have their own self interest and the strategies that maximize their rewards need not be the one that enhances social welfare. Though India spent a greater part of public resources on heavy industry and productivity-enhancing public projects, there were serious problems in their implementation (including delays) and the returns from such investments were lower than the expected levels. Thus license raj which may have originated with some ideas of protecting 'infant industries' in the newly independent India, may have later on become tools in the hands of some capitalists (who wish to retain their monopoly position) to reduce competition from others (by denying license to others) in collusion with the politicians and government officials. Thus, the monopoly rent got divided between the capitalists and politicians, while the consumers suffered due to a lack of competition.

The closed nature of the economy also prevented internal factors of production from capturing their global value. For example, if Indian labour was cheap due to the population and the level of economic development, that would be an attraction for foreign investors to come here since that would reduce their cost of production. But such an inflow of investments is possible only when the economy is open. When Indian investors are allowed to import technology from elsewhere and start factories here using relatively cheap Indian labour and then permit them to export their products, Indian resources would be used based on their global value. The realization of such value also needs a relatively open export and import regime. The absence of such a regime during most of the post-Independence period (when we were focused on 'planned economic development') had a negative impact on economic growth.

However, on hindsight, we should see that both the Soviet and Indian models of development have also resulted in some achievements.[2] Both these countries have used a major part of public investments for capital-intensive industries (even though the use of such capital-intensive technology may not have been in tune with the low wage rates prevailing in India then. Remember the discussion on the selection of technology and its relation to wage rate in an earlier chapter). There were also significant investments in science and technology. In India there were investments in higher education even though the benefits of that could reach only a small section of the population. (On the other hand, a lack of adequate investments in primary education and literacy created a situation where a substantial part of the population remained illiterate even 40 to 50 years after Independence.) In the case of most socialist countries, there were rapid improvements in primary education and health care and most of the society became literate. Such educational investments and those in S&T helped these countries especially those which were part of the USSR, the East European socialist bloc and India in reaping some benefits when they became open economies and started participating in the global production/exchange of goods and services. The roots of the Indian IT-service industry could also be traced to the investments India made in higher education during the early decades after Indian Independence.

We have mentioned that schooling or education is important for economic growth. However, this does not mean that capital investments are unimportant. What may be needed is an optimal balance. If a country encourages capital investments without enhancing/enabling access to education and technology, it may not benefit from productivity growth through technology. Similarly, if a country provided mainly schooling and education, but the situation is that the country does not enable capital investments that too may lead to an underproductive

situation. These educated people may not have adequate production systems/
companies/organizations where they can work. They may migrate elsewhere if
there are opportunities there. Such educated people may not like to work in
unskilled or less skilled jobs like that of an agricultural worker if there are some
other ways of subsistence. Thus when governments provide minimal social security, there may be an increase in unemployment among the educated people in
such contexts. There can also be some situations where people are 'excessively
educated' compared with the domestic capital investments and work opportunities and this can be a problem when there are limited opportunities for migration. This was visible in many ex-socialist countries where their governments
took many effective steps to enhance educational opportunities. Thus focusing
only on education and neglecting capital investments may not be desirable,
especially in closed economies.

Yet another important achievement of India during the period of planned
economy from the perspective of economic growth is the increase in food production in the seventies and eighties through what is called the Green Revolution.

THE ROLE OF THE GREEN REVOLUTION

The Green Revolution meant the use of high-yielding varieties, chemical fertilizers and pesticides to increase the yield per hectare of mainly food crops like
wheat and paddy. The severe food shortage in the fifties and sixties and the
dependence on food aid from the Western countries forced India to look for alternative strategies of enhancing food production. One can see the evidence of different theories of economic growth in the shaping of the Green Revolution. First
of all, it was possible through foreign financial support. Second, the research
originated from US universities but was tested in developing countries like
Mexico, which was another major input. But the Green Revolution succeeded in
India because of the technical and research personnel available within the country. Foreign technology was adapted to suit local conditions through research and
extension programmes carried out in our agricultural research stations. Our own
technical capability too played an important role here.

But the speed at which the Green Revolution spread and how its benefits got
distributed were not in the expected manner. For example, the initial phase of the
successful impact (in terms of yield growth) was visible in states like Punjab and

Haryana or some parts of Tamil Nadu, where controlled irrigation was available. Thus, controlled irrigation became a pre-requisite for the use of the Green Revolution package. It was not surprising that farmers with large sizes of land-holdings reaped more benefits than the small holders. This was because the well-to-do farmer could mobilize the required resources easily.

However, during and after the eighties, an increase in rice productivity could be seen in other areas as well. Thus, parts of West Bengal, Assam and other parts of the Ganges belt too started benefitting from the use of this tech-nological package. India could achieve near self-sufficiency in food grain pro-duction. This, however, did not mean that everybody got adequate food as it depended on the purchasing power of the people and the food distribution sys-tem. There is also a concern that the increase in food production has tapered off during the last decade.

The Green Revolution has been criticized from different perspectives, which are as follows:

- It has widened inequality in rural areas, especially that between large-size farm holders and small farmers and also between farmers and farm work-ers;
- It has increased the use of chemical fertilizers and pesticides, making a negative impact on the fragile ecosystem; and
- Because of excessive reliance on high-yielding varieties of seeds tradi-tional varieties are disappearing and this may have an impact on the bio-logical and genetic diversity.

It is not that economics as a discipline is indifferent to such impacts and focus only on growth (of crop productivity and economy). It has a particular way of looking at these issues and prescribing solutions. These are discussed in Chapter 16.

MOVING OUT OF A CLOSED ECONOMY FRAMEWORK BY INDIA

Considering the limitations of the growth strategy adopted till the eighties, India started opening up its economy in the mid-eighties. In the first few years of such open interaction with the outside world, many commodities were imported and credit available elsewhere was used for this purpose. But this created a crisis in the Indian economy in the beginning of the nineties—there was not enough foreign exchange to finance imports or pay back debts. This forced India to further relax government control over the economy and this process was called economic liberalization. Though the foreign exchange crisis was a major reason behind the liberalization of Indian economy, there were also other factors then. The collapse of the Soviet Union was one. There was a realization that international trade and globalization could be a source of economic growth for the developing economies. The contribution of trade and globalization to economic development is discussed briefly in the following section.

Trade as an Engine of Economic Growth

Globalization means many things. First, there could be an internationalization of production and consumption. Different goods/services are produced in different parts of the world. For example, an American may be consuming food produced in Latin America, using clothes made in China and East Asia, may be depending on certain services (like knowing the bank balance) being provided by Indian companies and use US universities for getting quality education. Goods produced in one country are being consumed in other parts of the world. Toys from China reach almost all continents. Production in one place depends on inputs from many parts of the world. Japan may be depending on fuel, metals and spare parts supplied from other parts of the world for its car production. An important input in production being labour the production of a commodity in one place may be depending on labour from different parts of the world, either aggregated at the site of production or located in different countries. The production of cars may depend on the designer in one country, worker at the site in another country and the marketing person located in yet another country and so on. Production and associated services in one place depends on the mobility of labour. Thus petroleum production and the development of the associated economy in West Asia depend on designers/managers from the US and Europe, clerks and workers from South Asia, house maids from the Philippines and nurses and entertainers from ex-Soviet countries. Capital is also moving from one place to another. The production of electronic goods gradually shifted from Japan to South Korea and other places in South

East Asia (as the cost of production is lower there) and then to China (where the cost of production is still cheaper).

This sort of internationalization of production and consumption is not all new. One can see different phases of such globalization in different periods of human history. Silk from China and spices from India were crossing the ocean even 2,000 years ago. Arab merchants were the main intermediaries in this trade. This was accompanied by the expansion of empires crossing the conventional national or ethnic boundaries. The Mongol rulers expanded their zone of influence to most of central Asia; the Roman kings like Alexander moved westwards. The next phase of intensive globalization came with the European colonization of other continents which started in the fourteenth century. The demand for natural resources from the colonies and the need for expansion of the markets of the products of colonizers were important drivers of European colonization.

The current phase of globalization may have to be seen in another context. The resistance towards colonization in the countries which became independent in the early part of the twentieth century and the availability of a socialist model at that time led many of these countries to adopt a closed economy framework. It laid greater emphasis on internal consumption and production or on self-reliance and such reliance was to be achieved through reduction of imports. Thus many countries, including more populous ones like India and China were by and large closed economies until the seventies. Different factors forced them to open up their economies. They wanted to export their goods to world markets. They were also interested in allowing foreign capital investments. When they sought soft loans the World Bank or the International Monetary Fund advised them to open up their economies. Some of the closed economic policies created macroeconomic distortions like the balance of payment crisis. This is a reflection of what the country can buy by paying in a major foreign currency like the US dollar. The stock of US dollars with the country can be an indication of this balance of payment issue. But the collapse of the Soviet Union and the shift towards export-orientation by China too have encouraged many which followed a 'middle path' (which adopted some socialist policies but were not fully socialist) countries like India to adopt an open economy model.

Technology too played an important role. If outsourcing is an important part of globalization today, where certain parts of the services in the US are carried out in a distant country like India, it is a direct contribution of technological change. Financial organizations in the US providing customer service to the citizens of the developed world started outsourcing some parts of book keeping and call centre services to India (which were earlier carried out in the US itself). The role of information technology here is obvious. This was mutually beneficial. The customers of the developed world would get and their financial organization could deliver these services cheaper since the cost of service has decreased due to outsourcing. It also enhanced the income and employment opportunities in countries like India. This could also broaden the avenues of economic growth in India.

As noted earlier, cheap labour alone may not be sufficient to attract foreign investment or to get outsourcing opportunities. The fact that a large number of educated Indians were available for this work helped that process. The importance of the rule of law also plays an important role. If a company taking up an outsourcing contract in a country could get away without delivering service because of poor law enforcement, this may discourage foreign companies going there. This was one reason why some poorer African countries could not gain much from globalization until recently. (Of late, a change in this regard is visible in some African countries.)

It is also not correct to view that the production of all goods and services are equally amenable to globalization. Goods that can be imported from elsewhere (say toys) or services that can be outsourced (say call centre services) are called tradable. However, there are non-tradable services too. Nursing care in a local hospital (say in London) cannot be outsourced to an agency abroad. Similar is the case of teachers, plumbers, cleaners and so on. If the commodities and services are tradable—or which can be sourced from a distance—then the incentive is to import or outsource them. Thus, cheaper toys can be imported from China or call centres can be outsourced to India (especially when the cost of long distance communication comes down). However, in the case of non-importable services for which the presence of the service provider in the locality is unavoidable like that of home maids, plumbers, nurses and so on, the incentive is to allow service providers to come in (as migrants). This may be true for teachers and university professors.

Thus, migration can also be viewed as an integral part of globalization. There are costs and benefits for the developing world from which most of the migration originates. Benefits include remittances, which not only add to the income of the people but also encourage certain kinds of economic activities in the country. Migrants can also be a major source of technologically and financially empowered capitalists in the source country. China is an important case in this regard. However, possibilities of migration may render certain economic activities costly in the source country. For example, the wages of farm workers may go up and this may have a dampening impact on agriculture. More precisely, the growth path of a country with outmigration could be different from the one without a strong outflow of people. One negative impact could be on the people who do not migrate. The specific path through which the economy grows with outmigration may not be the ideal one for the people who are left behind.

There are also different strands of critiques on globalization. We may consider a few of them. One major concern in India is that though globalization has benefitted some sections of Indian population, many others live in absolute poverty and they have not benefitted. This is related to what we have mentioned above. There may be certain other requirements like education to benefit from globalization and the fact that many Indians do not have adequate skills and education is one reason why they could not benefit from this process of globalization. Thus the inequality between those who benefit and those who do not benefit widens and this can be a major concern. We will consider the reasons for such poverty and inequality in detail in Chapters 13 and 14.

There can also be some impacts in the product market through globalization—a wider market competition. Products which were sold earlier within India may fetch a higher price today because of its demand elsewhere and this can have a negative impact on domestic consumers. Similarly, import of certain products from elsewhere may benefit domestic consumers where as it could be harmful for domestic producers. Thus there can be an opposition to the opening up of certain markets. However, this is to be seen as part of a distributional struggle between different sections of society within the country. For example, if exports of food grains from India are restricted, it may benefit consumers but may create losses for farmers. Thus there would be sections losing and benefiting from the process of globalization and hence a politically acceptable pace of globalization could be an issue of contested debate within a country. Similarly each country may benefit by certain open economy policies, whereas they may want to have some protection in other sectors. Thus different countries may have varied interest in opening up and protecting different activities depending on their production systems. Thus

a global debate on globalization may have to deal with these varied and sometimes conflicting interests. Thus, one cannot expect a unidirectional and smooth
passage towards a globalized economy.

Yet another critique of globalization is about its potential impact on the environment. However, such criticism has to be seen in the context of any expansion
of markets (and not only the global market). For example, the cutting of timber
(and associated deforestation) may increase if there is an expanded market for
timber within the country or elsewhere. This is so if there are no effective regulations controlling such extraction. One particular concern about globalization
versus pollution is that industries from the developed world may relocate themselves in the developing world, if they see environmental regulation stricter in
the former and not so strict in the latter. Thus, with the given difference in these
regulations between the developed and developing world, a faster pace of globalization may create more environmental pollution in the developing world.
However, whether this is harmful or not depends on the current level of environmental pollution and the preferences of people. This would be discussed in detail
in Chapter 16.

QUESTIONS

1. What are the central features of a planned economy model used in countries like India?
2. What could be the problems of such planned development?
3. What is globalization? How does it help the developing world? Which are
   the sections likely to suffer losses due to globalization in a country like
   India?
4. Write down some major criticisms on the process of globalization? How
   do you respond to these criticisms?
5. How does outmigration help developing world? Are there some costs due
   to this outmigration?

NOTES

1. A debate of this kind happened between the then Prime Minister of India,
   Jawaharlal Nehru and an economist of the planning commission namely

Dr K.N. Raj. For those who are interested in this debate, see Government of India (1952), *First Five Year Plan*, New Delhi: Planning Commission.

2. A good account of the history of India's economic growth can be seen in Balakrishnan (2010).

ELEVEN

ECONOMICS OF UNDERDEVELOPMENT: PART I

In the previous two chapters we have talked about the factors that enable economic or income growth of the country as a whole and the experience of India in this regard. However, as we have noted many times in this book, such growth need not lead to the development (in whatever way we assess) of many sections of society. This chapter deals with the reasons for underdevelopment. Underdevelopment manifests itself in a number of dimensions and the income level of some people not going up is one of them. This chapter focuses on such people.

Based on the growth theories described in Chapter 9, one can conclude that a country may report lower levels of economic development if it cannot mobilize enough savings for capital investments and/or cannot undergo technological progress (including the skill enhancement of the population). This is true even for different sections of the same society. Then the key question on under development would be: why do some sections within developing economies find it difficult to mobilize enough capital or attain technological progress to enhance their productivity, so as to achieve higher levels of income?

Nobel Laureate Arthur Lewis was the first who tried to explain the state of developing economies. He propounded the dual economy model. According to him there are two economies in developing societies—one is the subsistence agriculture in rural areas and the second is the industrialized or the modern economy.

Most villagers are involved in traditional agriculture in one way or the other—(even old men/women grazing the cattle). Their involvement is not determined by the additional product (marginal product) that they can produce. (You may remember the discussion in the 'Analytical Box of Economics' section regarding the efficiency in the decision to use one more worker as part of a production process.) Instead, everybody is involved and the gains are shared within families, kinships or even communities. Everybody should be getting something needed for sustenance (probably there would be a reduction in population if some people cannot survive in such a context). Thus, many people are engaged in agriculture even when there is no substantial additional gain.

In such a context, if the wage rate in industry is higher than the individual's gain from agriculture, there will be many people willing to be industrial workers. There will be supply of labour to industries without any increase in wage rate until all surplus labour from agriculture has migrated to the industry. Once there is no surplus labour in agriculture, wage rates in agriculture will increase. For Lewis, this is the process by which development takes place in less developed economies. This implies the need for a consistent process of industrialization to 'take out' the surplus labour used in agriculture.

There was also an idea that sections of population remain poor, since most people there are not 'rational' in the sense that they do not allocate resources in a manner that maximizes their gains. It is this view that was countered by another famous economist (another Nobel laureate) T.W. Shultz. He found that even marginal farmers respond well to technological and market opportunities. The way Indian farmers and other countries responded to the opportunities offered by Green Revolution too underscores this point. Thus the underdevelopment of poor countries or sections of society cannot be attributed to their irrationality.

Another view of underdevelopment looked at the possible vicious cycle in terms of population and income growth. Extreme poverty may encourage people to produce more children, which may reduce the natural resource base in the surrounding area, which in turn may encourage them to have some more children. This is so since the subsistence mode of living may require a greater number of workers to earn food and other materials (including water and fuel). This may need more 'hands' or people. Similarly, parents having nothing else to fall back on during their aged life, may consider children as their social security. All these may encourage people to have more children. In such cases, children are viewed as the main productive assets.

Underdevelopment may encourage parents to have more children for another reason too. There can be higher Infant Mortality Rates (IMR) in such contexts. Thus parents are not sure whether some of their children would survive as adults or not. Given their interest in having children (as to supplement their subsistence production process and to give them social security), higher IMR itself may encourage them to have more children. Even when societies could reduce IMR, there may be a phase of population growth. This is so due to the momentum created by the reproduction of people who could go through their adult life, compared with a situation in the past where only a part of the children born reach adulthood (due to higher IMR). This process is part of what is called the Demographic Transition.

DEMOGRAPHIC TRANSITION

The net increase in population is the difference between birth rate and death rate (if we ignore migration). Historically, both death and birth rates were higher. However, since both the rates are higher, the net population growth rate would be smaller. This is the first stage in demographic transition. However, death rates started declining first, partly due to the improvements in nutrition and improved public health infrastructure and health care (and the development of medical technologies). When the death rate falls without any reduction in birth rate, the net population size will grow faster. (Empirical evidence from developed economies shows that there could be an actual increase in fertility rates during this period. This could be due to an increase in the reproductive life of women enabled by the decline in death rates.) This can be taken as the second stage of demographic transition. Then there would be incentives and social efforts to reduce the birth rate. Gradually, this would reduce the net population growth rate. This is the third stage of demographic transition. Many developing countries in Asia and some states of India have already completed these different stages of demographic transition. However, many countries in sub-Saharan Africa and also some states in India are yet to see a significant decline in birth rate (even though their death rates have declined, barring African countries where it has gone up due to HIV infection).

People who benefit from economic and social development may have incentives to reduce the number of children. In societies where women take up jobs in the industrial and service sectors may find more children increasing their cost, considering the opportunity and the cost of time of women needed for childcare. Similarly, parents in such families may have access to other means of social security and they may not see children in this regard. Here, children are viewed as those who provide utility or satisfaction as part of the process of nurturing them. Under such a situation, there may not be an incentive to increase the number of children. To some extent, this is evident from the empirical reality too. Most of the developed economies have moved towards low birth rates, which is either close to the replacement rate of the population (and hence their population size may remain more or less stagnant) or less than the replacement rate (and hence the population size is declining).

Female education and participation in work in the industrial/service sector have played an important role in reducing the number of children. Education helps in other ways too in this regard. This enhances their awareness regarding different contraception methods. It also enhances their empowerment leading to asserting their rights in the reproductive process. In general, female education was found to be an important factor encouraging the decline of the number of children. Under such a situation, rather than population growth scuttling the opportunities of human development, the latter seems to provide strong inducements for reducing population size.

CURRENT UNDERSTANDING OF THE CAUSE OF UNDERDEVELOPMENT

Why do some people fail to increase their income? Since economists do not consider that some people are stupid or not smart enough (having less intelligence) to increase their incomes, they look for some other reasons. Similarly, economists do not take the view that poor people are ignorant. Yes there could be some ignorance but there are many sources of information in an open society. Some smarter people acquire that information fast and their personal growth may create a demonstration effect on others to catch up with them.

Economists know theoretically that a person's income goes up when his/her productivity goes up. Such an increase in productivity is possible when somebody works with the help of machines or better skills (or education) or with better technology. They have also seen that many poor people or those from lower middle class families become affluent or rich in many societies. Why do others flag behind?

This is a concern for economists. They cannot believe that some people remain poor because they do not have the money. Let us take the example of a carpenter. Assume that he is paid ₹200 when he cuts timber with a hand-operated saw. He knows that if he has an electrically operated tool, he can increase his productivity. If he takes a bank loan to buy the electric tool, he should be able to repay the loan from the increased income that he receives.

Think of a farm worker. He is paid ₹60 per day. He does not want his children to end up as farm workers. He knows that if they study until the tenth standard and acquire some vocational training, they may get some job in the town or city. Though he cannot afford to give such education, it should be possible, in an ideal sense for the farmer or their children to borrow money and acquire the required education and repay the loan from the increased income.

Theoretically, therefore, it should be possible for someone to acquire a higher income over a period of time. People who have become capitalists or owners of enterprises are not necessarily born rich. They borrowed money at reasonable rates from capital markets and with their labour (and ingenuity) produced a greater return, which enabled them to pay back the loan. Thus, our concern about why some people remain poor should lead us to another question: why can poor people not borrow or do not have access to capital markets? As mentioned in Chapter 4, the functioning of banks needs collaterals. Those who do not own assets cannot show collaterals and are denied loans. Thus, the argument that some people remain poor since they do not have money may be translated by economists as follows: some people remain poor since they do not have assets (to show as collaterals). This is a 'capital market problem' and the recent understanding of underdevelopment is closely linked to the problems of capital markets.

Hence the solutions for underdevelopment are discussed in this context. It should enhance the access to assets—like land, capital and human capital (education)—for the lower income groups. Thus, strategies like land reforms or those which provide them loans at subsidized interest rates or those which provide education to people who cannot acquire them are used to overcome underdevelopment. We will consider some of these strategies here.

ENHANCING ACCESS TO LAND

Redistribution of land by the state (or government) would have helped in improving the capital stock of the landless or those having small holdings; it would have enhanced their access to capital markets as they could show the land as collateral. Cultivating more land may increase worker productivity (that is, the income per worker). If a farmer supervises cultivation in two hectares of land instead of one, his income from farming may go up. This is because he may have unused labour while supervising cultivation in only one hectare and this unused labour could be used meaningfully when cultivation is carried out in two hectares. Such a land distribution was not implemented in many Indian states.

One possibility is for the state to distribute the land owned by it. For example, it is recorded that the state governments in India are yet to distribute the 16 lakh hectares of surplus land owned by them. A part of the waste land available with the various governments (63.85 million hectares) could also be given away to the landless. Even here states have encountered political, administrative and procedural difficulties in India.

It is easy to argue that the governments should take over land from the landed and distribute it among the landless. But landless does not constitute a politically or electorally powerful lobby in many parts of India. (Dictatorial regimes in some countries implemented such redistribution of land.) It was through political mobilization of the tenants and landless that land reforms could be taken up in states like Kerala and West Bengal.

Though land ceiling laws (which say that no household can own land-holding beyond, say, 15 acres) were passed in a number of states, these could not be effectively implemented in most of them. Even in states like Kerala, which implemented certain aspects of land reform, the implementation of the land ceiling rule was far from complete. The reasons for this are not merely administrative but more a reflection of the political and social factors impeding such an enforcement. These factors continue to operate in many states. There is also an issue of the appropriate form of acquiring land from the landowners. Compensation for acquiring land is one such issue. Even if compensation is provided at market price, it may upset the budget of most state governments. It may be very difficult politically to acquire whole surplus land without paying any compensation.

This is especially so in the changed socio-economic context in India. In 1947 a small section of the population owned most of the land. But due to the social and economic changes in the last 50 years, those who own surplus land in the country today need not belong to the richer class. It is possible that the upper class/caste sections might have sold some portion of their land-holdings to sections of middle class/castes. This may have enhanced the political difficulty in a democracy in taking over land for redistribution.

Hence, radical proposals of land reform, however laudable they may be, could not be implemented during the last 60 years in most parts of the country. Substantial social barriers against their implementation exist and these could not be overcome through democratic political processes.

Importance of Lease Markets

Even without redistribution of land, the landless should ideally be able to access land for cultivation through tenancy. It is likely that some large, medium and small farmers do not cultivate their land well. They may be involved in non-agricultural occupations and hence, they may not be able to use family labour to supervise farm operations. On the other hand, people who are willing to cultivate land may not own the land.

When X has some land and cannot cultivate it, she may want to lease it out to Y, who may have surplus farm labour. Such lease markets are important for facilitating social and economic change. The land-owning families may have greater opportunities to enter non-agricultural occupations or to invest in the industrial or service sector. Given the need for family labour for supervising farm operations (considering the principal agent problem),[1] many such families cannot devote quality time on agriculture. Such a trend is visible in areas where there are ample educational and migration opportunities. Even among farmers owning larger size farms, the younger generation opts for jobs or uses non-agricultural entrepreneurial opportunities; and this may have an impact on their investment in agriculture. If leasing is not possible, they may either cultivate the farm without much return or may keep it fallow. Even when these people do not use land efficiently, others who have surplus labour do not have access to land, the lease market does not function well. This creates social inefficiency. Thus, land should move from people who find it difficult to use it for maximum productivity to those who can do so.

Such transfer of land is seldom possible through land sale market. Even those who do not cultivate their land effectively may not sell it because land is perceived as a safe asset serving as a security or insurance mechanism. Land serves as capital investment and social security in India, and this is rational considering the inadequacies in capital and insurance markets. As a capital asset the value of land does not depreciate as in the case of house or machines; in fact its value appreciates over time beating inflation. When land is sold, its price is determined not on the basis of the agricultural income from it but by its value in asset market (and its future appreciation). Because of that there is a general preference for owning or keeping land, even among the non-cultivating sections. Thus the availability of land for cultivation may be reduced, if leasing is not practiced. Thus, well-functioning lease market is one option to see that land productivity does not decline due to the increasing dependence of landowners on non-agricultural sources of income in the same locality or elsewhere (associated with different levels of migration).

However, the lease market would function well only if the landowner and tenant have clear expectations and if each one of them is not subjected to ad hoc actions on the part of the other. Thus the landowner should get control over land without much difficulty on the expiry of the lease period. If not, it reduces the incentive of the landowners to lease out. The tenant also should not be subjected to eviction during the lease period in an ad hoc manner.

In a situation where tenants are subjected to ad hoc punishments (including evictions) and when there is uncertainty in the rent extracted, allocating full titles to the tenants can enhance productivity. This is so since any increase in certainty in this regard would enhance the incentives of the tenants to invest in enhancing productivity. This is the positive impact of giving full rights to tenants. Earlier, when tenancy was practised widely in India, landowners exploited the tenants. When poor people had no option other than tenant agriculture, landowners were in a position to extract maximum rent from tenants (leaving only a share just adequate for their subsistence). The situation today is a little better with rural employment schemes and relatively better non-agricultural work options even in rural areas. The ideal policy is to enhance the bargaining power of poorer families by providing other employment opportunities and also to allow tenancy so that people may not be accepting highly exploitative tenancy contracts. On the other hand, tenancy itself has been abolished in some states fearing exploitation of the tenants. This could lead to inefficiency.

In many parts of India where tenancy is legally prohibited, illegal leasing is still widely practised. But the operations are restricted. Thus, land may be available on lease only for certain crops (usually short-duration ones). The land may be leased out to people who can be controlled through informal means (since law cannot be used), and hence this limits the access of some people to lease markets. The landowners and the tenants participating in such illegal lease markets may have to incur greater transaction costs (including those psychic costs associated with the uncertainties). This may reduce the volume of lease transactions even though such transactions would enhance the social welfare.

A lack of clear legislation and institutional mechanism that allow tenancy, which can generate clear expectations on the part of the landowner and the tenant increases the inefficiency of land use. Lack of tenancy reform reduces access to land for the landless and others who have excess labour for cultivation.

Are Small Farms More Efficient?

An argument in favour of land distribution among the landless was that small farms were more productive (that is, producing more output for a given level of inputs). A number of studies from Sen (1962) onwards, show that there existed an inverse relationship between farm size and productivity—small farms are relatively more productive (with other factors like location, weather, inputs, farmer's education and so on being kept constant). However, according to later studies like Deolalikar (1981), the inverse relationship between yield and farm size is valid for traditional agriculture, and it need not exist in an agriculture which experiences rapid technical change. Even if productivity is higher, small farms are found to be technically inefficient as they use some inputs (supervisory labour) more than those used by large size farms. This is because some of the inputs available with small farms, including family labour, are not commercialized adequately and hence have low opportunity costs. This may change with increasing opportunities for non-agricultural employment. Even schemes like MGNREGA may have an impact on this situation. If the inverse relationship exists due to reasons of market imperfections, then the ideal development strategy is to correct those imperfections and to increase the opportunity costs of those inputs. Thus, the inverse relationship cannot be seen as a general picture and as agriculture undergoes a dynamic change, there is a greater possibility of the disappearance of this relationship. This could be partly because the inputs excessively used in small farms (due to their lower prices) become scarcer as rural economy undergoes transition.

What is an efficient size of the farm? There is no single answer for this. The size is likely to vary from place to place, depending on weather conditions, soil parameters, crops or crop mix, availability of labour or the optimal level of mechanization and so on. It is difficult to arrive at an efficient size of the farm and to ensure that land reforms aim at limiting the farm size to this 'efficient size'. It has been noted that land distribution in certain contexts have led to extreme fragmentation of landholdings and there has been a decline in productivity due to this reform. However, through tenancy reform, inefficiencies associated with ad hoc size fixation can be avoided.

When a large sized farm finds its productivity declining for different reasons, it might lease out a part to tenant families if it helps enhance the overall income. A higher productivity in small firms may be due to the incentives of family labour to supervise and monitor farm operations efficiently (whereas hiring supervisors to do the same job well in large farms costs a lot of money). In such cases, large farm owners may be interested in leasing out operations to a number of families and they may concentrate on operations in which there is some economy of scale (like marketing or processing of agricultural products). Currently this is not happening, since the legal provisions regarding tenancy are either prohibitive in nature or create uncertainties in the minds of the landowner and potential tenants.

There can also be a totally opposite process. When there are many small size farms, they may try to become part of a larger unit to seek the benefits of economies of scale and scope. This is contract farming. Thus, economies in input purchase, technology acquisition, processing, marketing, and so on, may become attractions for small farmers to get into a contract with an agriculture processing firm. The kind of fragmentation (tenancy) or integration (contract farming) mentioned here can take place based on what is the most rational thing to do in a given economic context. Moreover, people may change approaches if any one of them becomes less profitable in an emerging context. This will lead to the efficient size and scope of farm operations. Thus if there are diseconomies of scale (inverse relationship between farm size and productivity) in a context due to genuine economic reasons, then tenancy reform would lead to the emergence of more optimal farm size. On the other hand it is almost impossible to arrive at an efficient farm size through the implementation of legal land ceiling since such a size will vary from place to place and also from time to time.

We have considered those who do not have an adequate size of land. However, even those people with reasonable sizes of landholding face a number of challenges in India. This may prevent them from acquiring higher incomes through productivity-enhancing investments or from giving education to their children. This is taken up in Chapter 12.

However, we may note that subsistence agriculture or income from small-sized plots is not going to solve the livelihood problems of the marginalized and poorer sections. Their needs for education, health care and skill development are paramount to enable them to participate in a growing economy like India. Considering that India still has a large percentage of population dependent on agriculture, much greater than what is desirable, enabling a substantial part of them to move out of agriculture is the only way of sharing the benefits of economic prosperity with a larger section of the population.

Vulnerabilities Faced by Farmers in India

Enhancing access to land is one way of solving the difficulties encountered by the poor in their efforts to acquire higher levels of income. However, even farmers owning reasonable areas of land face serious problems in our country.

Before getting into the specific problems of developing countries like India, it may be noted that agriculture is a 'problem sector' even in the developed world. In these countries, less than five per cent of the population is involved in agriculture. A 100 years ago most of the working people were engaged in farm-related activities. People moved out of agriculture to industries and then to services (and also from rural areas to urban settings). Farmers in the developed world are also considered a vulnerable category. They may need many sops and concessions from the government to survive or to earn an income comparable to those who earn their livelihood in industrial and services sectors. There are some basic reasons. In general, productivity increase (income earned per worker) that can be achieved in agriculture is much less compared with that in industry or in services. (Even when the quantity of output per unit of land can be increased—and this is indeed possible as evidenced from the experience of the Green Revolution—revenue may not go up substantially.) This may be due to the demand for some agricultural commodities (like food grains) not going up drastically since people may not consume more of these commodities even when their incomes grow.

Agriculture is also an occupation in which many people acquire a proficiency early in their transition and hence many societies, including poorer ones, can produce farm products. The fact that they are poor also means that the cost of production of farm products is likely to be lower in such societies. Thus, if farm products are freely traded between the developed and developing countries, that would put pressure on the income of the farmers of rich countries. Thus, many rich countries are using some protection measures (basically to prevent the imports of farm products or to make such imports costly) and/or to provide a high level of subsidies to help their farmers.

However, the problems of farmers in the developing world are of different kinds. Productivity (income per worker) in agriculture can go up with the use of technology, better use of modern inputs like fertilizers, high-yielding seeds and irrigation and also by bringing more land under cultivation. Let us consider the last factor first, that is, the land. Even with better technology and other inputs, if the land size is small, what people may earn from a farm may be a meagre income. The average farm size in India is small for a large section of farmers. How does this situation change in other countries? When the development of the industrial and service sector takes place, a substantial section of the population moves out of agriculture. Thus those remaining in agriculture will be able to expand the farm size. This is carried through a number of means. Those remaining in agriculture may purchase more land. The other possibility is the development of the tenant market. Those who continue in cultivation can lease more land on payment of a rent to those who move out of cultivation. However, these two processes (sale and leasing) are not taking place smoothly in India, as we have discussed in the previous section.

Industrial growth (or the growth of the manufacturing sector) is not of an adequate level to absorb large chunks of the rural population in India. (It may be noted that a similar country, namely China, owes much of its economic growth to the development in the manufacturing sector.) In India, it is the service sector that predominantly drives its economic growth. There are inherent limitations for less educated rural people to gain from service sector growth, which benefits mostly those with higher education. The fact that the spread of education to rural areas in many Indian states took place at a much slower pace too has aggravated this problem. Even if the majority of the rural population has undergone schooling for about 8–10 years (with some skills), their skill sets match more with those of the manufacturing sector rather than the service sector. Thus, the lower levels of education of a majority of the rural population, combined with the not-so-impressive growth of the manufacturing sector led to a situation where even today nearly two-thirds of Indian population depend on agriculture.

Farmers with lower incomes have difficulty in accessing capital for financing their farm operations. This problem of capital market, especially for the small and marginal farmers and tenants, has led to what is called, interlocking of credit, input and other markets in agriculture. A person may be willing to give credit to a small farmer if the latter agrees (with some way of assuring it) that he would sell the produce to the former. Here, the buyer (or the intermediary trader of the agricultural produce) functions as a lender too. Similarly, those who sell inputs like fertilizers or seeds may provide them on loan to the farmers, with the understanding that the farmer sells the produce to this trader. Of course, the farmer may be getting a price for his produce lower than the market rates and this may become part of the cost of his loan. There can also be exploitative tendencies in these lending or interlocked relationships, depending on the bargaining capacity or the outside options of the farmer.

We will consider some more issues of underdevelopment in the following chapter.

QUESTIONS

1. Why did early development theorists consider the developing countries to have dual economies? How does it, according to them, affect the development process of these countries?
2. Explain the relationship between underdevelopment and the problems of capital market.
3. How does the access to land for the poorer sections help the overall development of a country?
4. What is the importance of tenancy reform in a country like India?
5. What are the underlying reasons for the challenges faced by farmers in an economy like ours?
6. What is an interlocked market in rural economy?

7. You heard an economist from a US Think Tank speaking in your university. He said that economic underdevelopment could be due to the imperfections in the capital market. What do you understand from this statement?

NOTE

1. The difficulty encountered by the principal (who hires somebody to a work for him) in making the agent (who is hired) work with the same objective as that of the principal. This may require the design of an appropriate reward system.

⊰ TWELVE ⊱

ECONOMICS OF UNDERDEVELOPMENT: PART II

---•◦•◦•---

W e have seen that the sections of people who do not benefit from the overall income growth of the economy include the following categories: landless marginal farmers, petty producers and the less educated. We have discussed the landless in the previous chapter (and how their access to land does not improve through possible legal and market routes in countries like India). We have also discussed the problems faced by farmers in general and in a developing country like ours specifically. One way to help farmers to improve their income is for the government to support them directly to enhance productivity. We will consider our experience in this regard in this chapter.

The remaining sections would consider the other strategies to help people to enhance their productivity. (This is so since income growth requires enhancement of productivity of individuals.) Provision of subsidized credit so that lower income groups can make productivity enhancing capital investments is one such strategy. Facilitating access to education (since skill development also helps increasing productivity) is another strategy. The issues involved in the implementation of these strategies, especially in the context of India, are also discussed in this chapter.

International organizations and the governments of the developed world also extend support to enhance the productivity of poor people of the developing world through financial and technical support. Some issues of this international aid are also discussed towards the end of this chapter.

GOVERNMENTAL EFFORTS TO ENHANCE PRODUCTIVITY IN AGRICULTURE

Governmental support to some sections of the people can be broadly categorized as follows:

1. Those which subsidize their current consumption or production.
2. Those which enhance productivity.

Support price for crop and fertilizers or electricity at subsidized rates belong to the first category. Interventions like subsidy for tube wells, construction of a rural road or an irrigation system help increase productivity. However, this categorization is not so neat.

When people get support for consumption/production, theoretically, they can use more of their own money for productivity enhancing investments and vice versa. Similarly, when recurring costs are subsidized (through subsidized fertilizers and electricity), it should make farming attractive and encourage farmers to make productivity enhancing investments. But in reality people who receive support for current consumption and production may not be doing enough productivity-enhancing investments (probably due to their increasing needs for consumption). On the other hand, if governments spend money for enhancing productivity, people cannot divert that support for consumption (and hence some impact on productivity is inevitable).

A major policy pursued by governments is the provision of public goods that help agriculture like canal irrigation, rural roads linking to district roads and agricultural research and extension. Such public goods helped in ushering the Green Revolution in India. Canal irrigation provided adequate moisture in fields and rural roads enhanced market connectivity and boosted sales. Research and extension too played an important role in enhancing access to and awareness of the farmers regarding high-yielding varieties and other related inputs.

But there are some problems associated with these public goods. Expansion of irrigation has exacerbated environmental problems like salinization of soil and waterlogging. (We will consider how economists take into account such environmental impacts in Chapter 16.) Irrigation projects are never completed on time and even when completed, the quality of work is poor reducing the returns from them. With even rich farmers not paying for water supplied, the resources available for maintaining irrigation canals are meagre. Thus, a greater part of irrigation development during the last three decades was based on tube wells constructed mostly by the individual farmer with or without capital subsidy from the government. Some states provided subsidized credit for boring tube wells and electricity for lifting water was either free or heavily subsidized. These encouraged competitive boring of tube wells leading to a decline of the water table in many areas and wastage of electricity and use of inefficient pump sets.

There are also government interventions in the output and input markets. In certain cases, the government buys farm products at a fixed price—higher than the market rate—and sells it at a lower price to the consumers. Thus, rice and wheat are procured at fixed support price and are sold through the PDS at subsidized prices as a social security measure (we will consider it in detail in the chapter on poverty). However, thanks to the loopholes in the PDS, there is a lot of wastage of public money.

There were commodity boards (for coffee and cardamom), which bought farm products and sold (or exported) them but such an intervention is less now. Governments also intervene in the input market through the subsidy of fertilizers and pesticides. This may encourage farmers to use excessive fertilizers. Moreover, there are problems in the way this subsidy is distributed. Since the government directly gives money to fertilizer companies, which sell fertilizer to farmers at pre-fixed prices, a part of the subsidy is to bear the inefficiency of these companies.

Then there is subsidized credit which operates at different levels. First, there are schemes that encourage government-controlled banks and cooperative organizations to extend soft loans to farmers. The subsidy involved here is finally borne by the government. Some farmers default on repaying even these soft loans either due to fluctuations in their income, due to crop losses or other factors or due to the diversion of part of the loans for consumption and other needs. Yet another set of farmers find it difficult to acquire enough loans from such formal or government-controlled organizations and depend on moneylenders who charge very high interest rates. Many such farmers have resorted to suicides. The government periodically announces debt waiver schemes and writes off loans taken by poor and not so poor farmers. This can affect the viability of the banking system, including cooperative organizations, if there is any delay in the refinancing of the loans written off by the government. Governments may face increased burden in terms of fiscal deficit (and it has all the negative consequences discussed in Chapter 7). Moreover such debt waivers encourage farmers to look forward to loan waivers and this may influence their repayment pattern.

There is also a growing political demand to increase the allocation for all these schemes (debt waiver, free power and subsidy to fertilizer). Farmers or political groups representing them want an increase in procurement prices and subsidies for inputs. All these have become easy strategies for attracting votes by the political parties during the elections. The effect of all these is that there is growing allocation for subsidizing the recurring costs of production and consumption in the agricultural sector. This leads to a situation where the most part of government money meant for agriculture is used for such recurring expenditure. This reduces the allocation for public goods in agriculture like surface irrigation or research and extension. These are investments required to enhance productivity in agriculture. Moreover, in the absence of such investments, the vulnerability of farmers (arising out of crop losses and other unpredictable events) increases. For example, lack of adequate investments in the supply chain (in terms of refrigerated storages and faster mobility) create a situation where farmers may not get a reasonable price at the place/season of production, whereas consumers pay higher prices in other localities in the country and in different seasons. This is one factor that enhances the difficulty of the farmers (and consumers). Even with subsidies, soft loans and debt waivers, such vulnerability may not decline. There is a slower growth of public investments in Indian agriculture (despite an increase in the burden of the government in terms of supporting farmers) and many people consider this a threat to the sustenance of growth in Indian agriculture. Thus, the productivity-enhancing role of government intervention in agriculture is not performed adequately in India.

FACILITATING ACCESS TO EDUCATION

Some people may not have adequate income because they have very little valuable assets. Landlessness is one such issue and we have discussed land reforms in the previous section. However, when the economy develops, the role of agriculture may decline and industry and services acquire prominence. To get adequate income from industry and services, people need education and skills (especially, if they do not belong to the capitalist class). Education is important for other reasons too: it inculcates habits, practices and values that change the behaviour of people towards the needs of development. The role of education in reducing infant mortality and facilitating demographic transition is discussed in Chapters 8 and 13. One can think about the role of education unrelated to development too. But these do not underplay the importance of education as a productivity enhancing investment.

What are the factors which prevent some children in developing countries from acquiring education? If education, provided by private firms, costs money, many people cannot afford it and therefore those who do not have the money cannot acquire education. Education is an investment and an educated person is likely to get higher income in the future and hence he/she should be able to borrow to pay for the cost of education. A part of the future income can be used to pay it back. But lenders ask for collaterals, like land, which the poor may not have. This may prevent them from acquiring educational loans.

Therefore, many societies have public or charity funded education systems especially for school education. Societies in general are unwilling to leave primary education to the discretion of parents and children. Some parents may not be aware of the need for educating their children. They may be forced to take children out of school for other pressing needs of sustenance—like child labour, the need to take care of younger siblings and so on. Most societies insist on primary education and encourage parents to send their kids to schools.

For higher education too public or charity financing is available mainly for the following reasons:

1. An educated person creates positive externalities. There is a social return also when one more person is educated, in addition to what he/she gets as private return. Thus there is a need for social investment.

2. We have seen that if educational investment is purely on the basis of private investment, people who cannot get educational loans may not acquire education. This may reduce the quantum and the quality of the set of skilled persons in a society. (If only 20 per cent of population has assets to pay for education—or get educational loans, then skilled persons in that society would come from this section of population. The more talented among the remaining 80 per cent cannot acquire skills. This may affect the overall quality and the number of skilled persons in a society.) This is inefficient in the sense that the productivity increase that can be achieved with this limited pool of skilled persons is lesser than what is possible there.

Thus there are publicly provided or financed education in most societies. However, there are a number of problems in countries like India in this regard. There can be supply- and demand-related problems which prevent many children from acquiring education. Let us consider supply-related problems first. Even though public-funded education is provided, it may not be adequate considering the requirement of society. For example, if there is no school in the neighbourhood, it may prevent many parents from sending their children to school. Thus distance to the nearby school can be an issue. This may be more so for girls in countries like India. Though a number of schools have come up even in backward states, there are locations where there is no school within a reasonable distance.

Even in presence of a school, the facilities provided may be inadequate like shortage of qualified teachers; or even if employed they may be irregular. This is especially so since the monitoring of the teachers' work in such public-funded schools can be very difficult, especially when the parents or local governments do not have a role in their performance evaluation. Even if present, many of them are not motivated enough to do their job well. Again, there are infrastructure problems like lack of class rooms, furniture and so on. If the attention is minimal and children are not showing any signs of learning, some parents may lose interest in sending their children to such schools. There is a cost to the parents in sending the kids to school even if the public education is free—parents incur opportunity costs. Those who cannot afford this employ children to do some household chores (like the elder girl child taking care of younger siblings), or working at own farm or as a wage earner.

The lack of resources on the part of the governments to provide adequate number of schools and facilities, and inherent problems of the government to ensure their performance create supply problems like non-availability of enough quality schools. It does not mean that privately funded schools are problem-free; nor the governments can take a hands-off approach in the case of those private schools. Quality control is a severe problem in education, and this is usually carried out by the separation of teaching and conduct of examination. The boards conducting examination are either controlled or regulated by the governments. The advantage of the private school is that it would try to meet the 'needs of the parents', even if such demands need not be appropriate for themselves or for the society as a whole. Thus many parents may send their children to private schools even if these do not have adequate building space or trained teachers, but if they can ensure children's passing of examinations or teaching of English.

However, the non-use of schools is not solely due to 'supply' factors. There can also be demand issues. The parents should feel that sending their children to school is important as a future investment. In fact in certain cases, when there is demand, many parents, including those from non-affluent backgrounds, may send their children to non-public or fee-paying schools either due to the non-availability of the government-financed schools or due the perception of their poor quality. An important determinant of this demand is that people should perceive benefits of education/schooling. In a village where unskilled agricultural work is the only occupation, many people may not see schooling or education as a valuable investment. Thus availability of better job opportunities for those with education either nearby (or in places where they see possibilities to migrate), is an important attraction for accessing schooling. Such demand factor too played an important role in states like Kerala where universal enrolment in schools was achieved decades ago. There are also cultural factors which discourage parents from seeing the value of sending girls to schools, and overcoming them is also important for enhancing enrolment.

Thus, there may be a need for coercion, persuasion and incentives to force some parents to send their children to schools. In the case of people who are extremely poor, and who take their children out of school for earning wages, there can be some incentives which may enhance their readiness to use the school. Mid-day meal programme which was introduced first in Tamil Nadu and adopted later throughout the country is one such incentive. There are cash-support schemes (or a lump sum grant) aimed at children belonging to scheduled caste and tribe families. There are also free-boarding schools for some specific sections (though some of the government-financed boarding schools have poor facilities in India). There is a scheme in Brazil to provide cash to mothers if their children are present in schools (as a strategy to enhance attendance). All these, if implemented well, may work as incentives to send children to schools. Demonstration and peer effects too work here. If many children from a settlement attend school, it may put some informal pressure on other parents to send their kids to school.

Thus, if access to education is to work as a strategy to enhance productivity (which in turn should facilitate development) we need to address the supply and demand problems in education. So far we have considered only the school education, but higher education is also important for enhancing worker productivity. However, there is some virtue in providing school education to all, whereas higher education may not be given to all. We will consider the issues in higher education in the chapter on inequality, since such education is emerging to be an important determinant of inequality in modern economies.

ACCESS TO CAPITAL FOR THE LOWER INCOME GROUPS—ROLE OF MICROFINANCE

We have seen that the lack of access to capital markets does not allow poor and other lower income groups (especially the petty producers) to take loans to improve their productivity. One strategy currently used in many parts of the developing world in this regard is microfinance. We have seen that collateral is needed for banks or for other formal financial organizations to ensure repayment of loans. This is addressed in microfinance in another way. It is expected that the community or network of such people (especially women) would do monitoring among themselves. Thus the strategy is peer monitoring (rather than bank monitoring each borrower). The banks do not lend to such individuals directly, but extend loans to the groups of such individuals. These groups in turn decide the allocation of loans to individuals. If a particular individual is defaulting, other members from the group can exert some pressure on the defaulting member to repay loan. This group consists of people living in one place for some time and facing similar conditions or work together in an occupation.

They may have reciprocity relationship even beyond microfinance and it is expected that peer monitoring may work. (The lessons of 'folk theorem' in strategic analysis discussed in Chapter 6 may be considered here. We have seen that cooperation in such community interactions sustains only under certain conditions. These are valid even in the case of peer monitoring of microfinance.)

Since banks extend loans only to the groups, and allocation and monitoring of loans are carried out by the groups, their transaction costs are low. So there will be no need to hike interest rate to offset transaction costs. In a situation where the bank does not get any subsidy, it has to recover an interest rate from the borrower which meets not only the interest rate to be paid to the depositor but also the cost of bank. The cost of bank per client will be higher if it has to spend more of its (staff) time and resources for monitoring individual borrowers regarding repayment. (Thus the transaction costs involved in extending say ₹1 million as loan to 10,000 individuals may be much higher than giving the same amount to one or two individuals/firms.) If all individuals who can be part of a microfinance group get loan directly from the bank, and if there is no peer monitoring then the transaction costs to extend such loans would be very high. Thus, microfinance can reduce interest rates compared with what would have been the rates if there were no group lending cum peer monitoring.

However, the effectiveness of microfinance may depend on several factors. (Self-help groups formed as part of microfinance are also used in certain circumstances to encourage saving habit among their members, and it is not considered here.) How effective is group-monitoring is an important issue. It is not possible in all situations for the members of a group (even if they live in same place in a similar situation) to exercise an effective control over its members. Secondly, if microfinance has to help development in a sustainable manner, it should enhance the productivity and incomes of the members. This is possible only when people make an effective use of loans for productive activities. The lack of adequate skills not only in production but also in marketing, accounting and so on, may reduce the viability of productive enterprises started with microfinance. Thus the role of an intermediary organization like the Self-Employed Women's Association (SEWA) is very important. There is a tendency among many microfinance borrowers to use a major part of loan for the consumption purposes. This works against any sustainable improvement in the living standards of people.

Many times the governments or international and national charitable organizations provide subsidies as part of microfinance. This has also accentuated the competition of different microfinance-facilitating organizations to extend loans to the same group. It may also encourage one individual to be part of different groups expecting loans from different funding agencies. If the borrowing is for consumption purposes, such competitive lending increases the indebtedness of these individuals. (On the other hand, competition by different microfinance facilitating agencies may be useful in doing a better and more efficient intermediation service. This, however, depends on whether the organization has an interest in repayment or whether some funding organization is writing off these loans.)

It may be noted that many people may not have an 'absolute' lack of access to capital market. There are money lenders in most villages and urban slums who charge very high interest rates. The rates are high partly because the repayment rates are low and there may be a need for costly mechanisms to ensure repayment. Most of these loans are taken for consumption purposes. The fact that these are poor people, taking loans for current consumption only means that their repayment ability is reduced further. Thus the crucial issue is providing them access to loans for productive purposes so as to enhance their income on a sustainable basis. Microfinance cannot be a sustainable strategy for enhancing access to loans for consumption. On the other hand, if poor people cannot meet certain important expenditures like that for health care, then enhancing access to loans may not be the appropriate strategy. This may require other strategies like public provision of health care or insurance mechanisms.

There could also be a long-term development issue here. Do we want to convert poor people into self-employed ones or workers of larger enterprises? (Of course in the case of those who have gone ahead of educational age, there may be limitations in acquiring new skills, and for some of them self-employment may be the only option. For such people microfinance could be an appropriate option. But here we are thinking about microfinance as a long-term development option.) There may be inevitable limits beyond which the group enterprises of poor people cannot enhance productivity and income. Skill sets of these people are an obvious limitation which can be overcome only when such group enterprises can hire qualified professionals and managers. Though this is theoretically possible, there may be reasons why we usually see managers hiring workers (and not workers hiring managers). The income of an enterprise may depend on the market share, and marketing is an important activity, for which small enterprises (even if these are federated) may have constraints. Federated enterprises (federations of these small group-based enterprises) may not have adequate incentives to be efficient and enterprising as private endeavours. If the scale of the activity is limited, and it cannot get the benefit of network externalities in marketing, the enterprises started by the poor may end up giving them a return much lesser than what they would have earned if they were working as a wage labour in a private enterprise. Thus even though the microfinance-enabled small enterprises may be an important strategy considering the percentage of the illiterate adult population in India, whether it is a long term viable development strategy needs critical analysis.

Microfinance is not the only way to enhance subsidized credit. There are other soft loan schemes used by the governments all over the world to enhance the access to credit for the people belonging to economically and socially backward sections. Housing loans extended to lower income groups in the US which have partly caused the sub-prime crisis and recession in the US is one such example. Subsidized credit extended to farmers (which are written off periodically) in India is another example. In general, there is a view that such soft-credit need not be an appropriate tool whether the objective is to help people in terms of their consumption or productivity enhancement. This is so since such soft-credit often creates undesirable complications in the economy as a system, and also leads to perverse incentives for the borrowers and the lenders. On the other hand, improving access to education is considered to be a better strategy to help lower income groups to enhance their productivity in the long run.

INTERNATIONAL/FOREIGN AID AND GRANTS

People who do not have access to capital market can benefit if they are helped with money or aid to enhance their productivity. To some extent, international aid has this objective. Let us consider this in detail in this section.

What could be the impact of 'international aid' in ushering in development of different parts of the world? Discussions on what the developed countries can do for the development of poorer countries started mainly after World War II. The experience of the US in facilitating the re-emergence of economies of Germany (and Europe in general), and to some extent Japan after World War II, influenced this thinking process. As a parallel process, the Soviet Union (which became more powerful after its decisive role in World War II) was also exporting its model of development and support to many poorer countries. US thinkers and the development machinery affiliated to the US government were also concerned about the spread of communism and also the influence of the Soviet Union. They were thinking about strategies to counter this influence.

The following ideas were prevalent then:

1. Poor nations remain poor since their labour productivity is not increasing because there is very little capital in their production process.
2. There is very little capital in these countries as a whole as the people there cannot save much money since what they earn is barely sufficient to meet their subsistence requirement.

Similarly, there were also equally convincing arguments for exporting technology to these poorer countries. The Green Revolution is a product of this thinking. The Soviet Union was also involved in the transfer of capital and technology and India was a destination for such help. (This transfer of capital or technology is different from setting up factories by the companies of the developed world in the third world—which is a phenomenon we discussed as part of globalization.) The transfer mentioned here was taking place between the public sector or the governmental (and sometimes non-profit, non-governmental) organizations.

Such an export of capital and technology from the developed world to poorer countries during the last 60–70 years has helped in general the development process of the developing countries. The contribution of the Green Revolution in enhancing food production is a shining example of the positive effect. There could also be several other specific cases where the infusion of foreign capital and technology may have aided the development of specific regions. Public sector steel production in India was an area where technology from the USSR was a helpful contribution.

However, such an infusion of foreign capital and technology, through government to government transfer, did not meet the expectations in many poor countries unlike the European experience. One reason could be that pre-war Europe had already built up human, social and institutional assets (which were not very different from that of the US) and thus the inflow of capital helped in rebuilding since such social infrastructure was already there. Such assets were missing in most of the developing world. Another reason could be that what was actually transferred was not very useful.

So what are the prospects and limitations of international aid in a general sense, considering the interests of the donors? Most people like to support, depending on their ability those who are in need as is evident from contributions to charitable organizations all over the world. Thus it is not surprising to see citizens of the developed world contributing for the removal of poverty and other problems affecting the developing world. This is the 'altruistic' component of international aid.

There are also some cases where poverty and problems of the developing world can be perceived harmful to the people of the developed world. In fact, the spread of communism was perceived to be a threat to democratic countries. Extreme poverty in some countries was seen promoting desperate migration to the developed world. The lack of hygienic practices in poor countries may be creating contagious diseases which could spread to the developed world. Of late, the high level of unemployment and domestic problems (like lack of democracy) were perceived to be creating terrorist networks and these are also seen as harmful to the developed world. In essence, all these perceptions encourage the developed world to help poorer countries so that they are not affected by these externalities. This is another reason for international aid.

The third but not the least important interest to give international aid is to expand the business of aid-giving developed country. For example, a main part of aid could be the goods and services produced by the aid giving country. This helps to sustain or expand certain business operations in that country. For example, a country which has invested heavily in creating hydroelectric projects may be interested in providing international aid to have such projects in poorer countries. Through this some products (say turbines) or some consultant services (like for planning, implementing and maintaining hydroelectric projects) can be exported to these countries. This is a cheaper way of helping the other country and also perhaps to sustain some jobs (in factories and in consultant business) in the donor country.

Thus, the interest with which a donor country pursues the development objectives of the recipient country depends on what motivates it to provide such aid. If altruism is the main factor, donors may get satisfaction from the process of giving it and they may not pursue it adequately to see that the money is used effectively. This is especially when a government organization in the donor country mobilizes altruistic donation from its citizens or when their government transfers a part of the public tax for international aid. (Of course private charitable organizations like the Melinda and Bill Gates Foundation are much more concerned about aid effectiveness). When the motivation is to see that the domestic problems of the recipient country do not create harm for the developed world, their interest is just limited to containing that externality, and not much more (for example, if the growth of terrorism in a country is the reason for supporting it by the developed world, its interest may decline if terrorism is contained). Third, if the expansion of the business is the motivation behind international aid, developed world may pursue strategies that may maximize their own interests (like transferring some technology or services) even if such strategies are not of much use to the recipient country.

International aid can create some incentive problems in the aid-receiving country too. First of all, aid comes to the government, non-profit or NGOs. People working in such organizations do not have adequate incentives to see that the aid is utilized in a manner most useful for the society as a whole. Sometimes personal or political interests, not in tune with social interests, may drive the use of such aid. Projects which are more visible as achievements of politicians (like buildings, dams and so on) may get priority, whereas not so visible ones like improvement in education or health care may be neglected if sufficient attention is not given by the funding agency. Such aid has also encouraged the use of more capital-intensive technology in contexts where labour is cheap (where ideally labour-intensive techniques have to be used). If aid brings in technology and consultant services from elsewhere, it is not rare to see the use of technologies which may not be the most appropriate to the natural and social conditions of the aid-receiving country. When the wage rates (and salaries) between the donor and recipient countries vary, it may bring in another set of problems. There may be a set of local officials showing extra interest in externally funded projects since that may give them benefits which are not available to them in internally funded projects. There can also be other goodies that may encourage domestic politicians and officials to favour a certain kind of external projects. Thus, the dependence on external funding may not be in tune with the actual requirements of the economy in question, but may be driven by the goodies that come with it for specific but powerful individuals in the recipient country.

In summary, due to the lack of adequate institutional set up in the recipient country or due to the perverse incentives created by international aid, the extent of the productivity enhancement which can be brought about by international aid can be limited.

QUESTIONS

1. 'Some features of Indian agriculture do not facilitate the development of an important section of the country's population'. Discuss.

2. Do you agree with the proposition that a substantial section of people currently involved in farming in India (as farmers and/or workers) need to move out of agriculture for development? Substantiate your answer.

3. What is microfinance? How is it different from the usual financing carried out by banks? What are the prospects of microfinance in terms of enhancing productivity of people who cannot access capital markets?

4. Why do banks insist on collateral in disbursing loans? In this context, how is it that self-help groups extend loans without collateral?

5. Do you have the experience of studying in or working with (or visiting) a government (or aided) school? Do you see some supply–demand problems mentioned in this chapter operating there? How do they address these issues?

6. Here is a family of three: Radha (40), her husband Ravi and their daughter Anupama (12) and two younger daughters. They are reckoned to be poor. Ravi, though was working as an auto-rickshaw driver, does not bring much income due to alcoholism. The rural development agency decided to support this family. They provided a small grant and a loan to Radha through the self-help group to start a 'papad' unit. She makes papads and sells to the nearby households. She needs the support of Anupama at home. Both together make 300–400 papads and a daily income of ₹60. What do you think about this development intervention?

7. You may do some (re)search to get the experience of any one project in India funded with international aid. How do you rate its effectiveness? What could be the reasons for its success or failure?

PART IV

ISSUES OF DISTRIBUTION AND SUSTAINABILITY

◄ THIRTEEN ►

THE POOR AND POVERTY

―――――◦•◉•◦―――――

Poverty is one manifestation of extreme underdevelopment. This chapter deals with the causes of poverty and the discussions on solutions to avoid it. The discussion here is limited to meeting the requirements of development practitioners.

Many people all over the world live on less than ₹45 a day at international prices. Though such poor people are there in all parts of the world, including North America, their number is high in South Asia (covering India, Bangladesh and Pakistan)—40 per cent and sub-Saharan Africa—46 per cent. In India, 41 per cent of people lived on less than ₹21 a day in urban areas and around ₹14 in rural areas in 2005. These numbers were higher than 60 per cent in 1981. In the rest of the world, this number is less than 20 per cent. There are many methods to assess poverty and so the figure can be anywhere between 40 and 27 per cent in India depending on the method employed. There is also large variation in poverty between different Indian states. Rural Odisha or rural Bihar may have a poverty rate comparable to sub-Saharan Africa (around 42–45 per cent), whereas rural Punjab, Haryana or Kerala may have much lower rates (around or less than 10 per cent).

Who is poor? The immediate definition is that a person who does not get adequate food is poor. A major part of the understanding of who is poor has depended on the consumption (of food). The accepted benchmark of food consumption, needed for sustenance of a human being (who can also carry out adequate physical work), is 2,100 kcal per day in urban areas and 2,400 kcal in rural areas (the difference due to the nature of work carried out by an average person in these two settings). Anyone who consumes less than this can be considered poor or those below poverty line (with the line being this minimum required consumption). Similarly, those who are not spending enough money to buy this required amount of food can also be classified as poor. This would be based on consumption surveys—which assess the quantity of, and the expenditure spent for, consumption of different items by households. The National Sample Survey Office of Government of India (and similar organizations in other countries) carries out consumption expenditure surveys periodically and these can help identify those below the poverty line according to consumption criterion. (In general it is difficult to conduct surveys to assess income in countries like India, since people may not give correct information. However, it is relatively easy to gather information on expenditure.)

It is not that this consumption-based definition of poor is perfect. First of all, people can live in unbearable conditions even when their consumption just meets the calorie requirement. (There is also some evidence that even some affluent people may not consume food to get this 2,400 kcal requirement and hence the use of this benchmark can lead to some overestimation in certain cases.) There have been efforts to broaden the conception of poverty. One attempt in this direction is to consider the amenities and facilities that households have. Thus a household without a proper house, access to safe drinking water and hygienic toilet could be considered poor. This list can be extended depending on the situations.

Even with these amenities and facilities there are problems. If the children cannot go to school, or if a sick person cannot get treatment (for want of money), these would have a significant bearing on the functioning of these individuals. There are different attempts to count poor or vulnerable sections based on these different conceptions. However, all these are based on two ideas: someone else is assessing the poverty of a person and the assessment is based on absolute criteria like whether somebody is consuming 2,400 kcal of food, whether a person has access to a hygienic toilet or whether the members of a household have access to primary health-care facility.

This is the starting point of two further variations in the conceptualization of poverty. There is a recent trend to assess poverty on the basis of the perception of people themselves. This is partly driven by the inadequacies of the previously mentioned third-party assessments of the poor. Moreover, such third-party quantitative assessments need not take into account certain qualitative dimensions of deprivation. There are efforts to make people articulate their own perceptions through qualitative methods of assessments (such as focus group discussions), and in this process some may identify themselves as poor (even when they live in conditions which cannot be objectively called poverty) or some may not consider themselves as poor (even when they live in poverty according to outsiders). Though such qualitative self-assessments cannot substitute for quantitative/objective assessments (for the implementation of poverty eradication schemes), the former can give insight to a neglected dimension of poverty.

A family living in a small two-room building with a tiled roof, in a posh area, may consider themselves as poor. Hence poverty can also be relative. Somebody who does not have a power connection in a village in Bihar or interior Assam may not consider it as an indication of poverty, where a household in Kerala without an electricity connection may feel so (since the state has 85–90 per cent of its households electrified). To some extent such relative poverty will reflect in the self-perceived poverty mentioned above. Beyond that there is merit in considering some sections as poor based on the local or regional living conditions. Thus, a definition of poverty that may be valid in Kerala need not be so in Chhattisgarh. (However, such differential definition of poverty may create a problem for the Government of India which has jurisdiction over both regions if it wants to allocate resources according to different definitions of poverty. An appropriate solution in this regard is for the Government of India to allocate resources on the basis of a uniform definition for both Kerala and Chhattisgarh, but for the state governments to spend additional resources for poverty eradication considering that part of the poverty within the state, which is based on local conditions.) Thus, poverty has to be seen in a relative context too.

A major part of the economic literature on poverty deals with identifying poor people on the basis of macro-level data. It covers the use of different ways of assessing the number of poor people and the possible pitfalls in using each macro data set or methodology. However, it is not very difficult for development practitioners to know whether a person is poor or not if they could interact with him/her for a while in his or her surroundings. Thus an elected representative for a local government does not need much data to identify who is poor in his constituency. Of course he/she may reckon some really non-poor as poor and extend public money used for poverty eradication to such a person. Or the representative may be treating a really poor person as non-poor so as not to extend the benefits of pro-poor schemes. Thus, macro-datasets are important for two reasons: it should help the planners at different levels of administration to decide the allocation of resources and also to see the trends in poverty (to know whether it is declining or increasing). Such an objective criteria of defining the poor is useful to monitor the implementation of poverty eradication schemes--to check if the funds under such schemes are being diverted or whether some poor people are intentionally deprived of these benefits. But it is not being dealt with here because this book is aimed at micro-level actions.

It is expected that a development professional focusing on micro-actions need not be told about how to identify a poor person. He or she may have seen many who do not get adequate food, are not adequately clothed (even during the harsh winters) of North India, do not have a minimum hygienic place to live nor access to safe drinking water, and are not used to hygienic toilets, exposed to indoor pollution causing respiratory illnesses, who cannot send their children to school and who may be suffering from many other illnesses without adequate health care. When we talk about development in India, it is the plight of these people that should matter most.

CAUSES OF POVERTY

To some extent the determinants of underdevelopment, discussed in the previous two chapters—some are unable to enhance income per person since they do not have assets (to borrow capital) or education, are valid in the case of poverty. However, poverty is not general underdevelopment but its extreme manifestation. That the income of some people is not adequate even to meet their basic needs of consumption can be due to several reasons. Their only asset is the ability to do physical labour and if the income earned from such physical (unskilled) labour is not adequate to meet the needs of basic consumption and amenities they may end up in poverty. This can happen if the number of jobs available and/or wage rate for unskilled work is very low and hence the total income that they can get in a year is inadequate to meet the basic consumption. This can happen to those who have small land-holdings, if their returns from agriculture, and also the income from working as a wage labour together are inadequate to cross the benchmark of minimum consumption for them and their non-working family members. This can occur if each working member (or unskilled worker) may have to support a large number of non-working members in the household. Thus household size could be a relevant factor.

It is also incorrect to think that all adult members of all households can work, even if such work is available in the locality. Aged members of the household cannot work, and hence they can be in poverty if they do not have adult children taking care of them. Even when they have children, the actual resources that they get could be minimal when their adult children are also struggling to make both ends meet. There could be some families headed by women (due to non-marriage and widowhood). There are many reasons why women may not be able to work even when work is available. During the periods of pregnancy and nurturing young kids, they may not be able to participate fully in unskilled physical labour. Thus, the income of such families may be minimal even when work is available in the locality.

So far we have focused on income factors that may cause poverty. There could also be expenditure-related issues. If for some reasons, the price of food goes up in the market, people with lower incomes may not be able to meet their basic consumption, even when they were doing so previously at lower prices. Thus even those people who are not poor (or who are just above the poverty line) may become poor under such situations of a temporary increase in food price. The expenditures on other unavoidable items can also make some people poor. For example, some health problems may force them to incur significant expenditures (probably by selling the small assets they may have) and this may have two negative effects. They may not be able to work during and immediately after the period of disease and this would reduce income. Health problems encountered by the main bread earners of the family can lead them to poverty. A similar effect can also be there due to the loss of limited assets they had for paying the unexpected health-care expenditure.

There could be vicious cycles that may lead to the persistent of poverty. We have already mentioned the possible linkage between population growth, natural resource use and poverty or underdevelopment in the previous chapter. The people in poverty who depend only on their physical labour to mobilize food, water and so on (either through paid work and market purchase or through collection/cultivation from/in surrounding land as in the case of people depending on degraded forests), may have an incentive to have a greater number of 'hands'. This may lead to a greater number of children. This may perpetuate poverty. Another vicious cycle could arise out of minimum nutritional needs. An undernourished person cannot generate adequate income for one's own nutrition. That would mean that malnutrition can persist, or the impact of malnutrition can worsen over a period of time. People in poverty may use the natural resources in the surrounding area in a more damaging manner—for example, by reducing the period of rotation for the burn and slash cultivation of forests. Thus the quality of the natural capital, they depend on, may decline over time and this too can lead to the persistence or worsening of poverty. Poor people may also have to use all their time for acquiring minimum earnings, and hence they may not be able to spare time (of their children) for schooling. The fact that many boys and girls from poor families may be working (and not studying) or the girls from such families remain at home to attend to their younger siblings, may reduce the human capital achievements of their next generation, and this can reduce the possibility of overcoming poverty in future.

POVERTY ERADICATION MEASURES AND THEIR EFFICIENCY

Measures to minimize poverty are formulated by studying the different causes mentioned in the previous section. One can identify the following specific schemes:

1. PDS: This is to ensure that everybody has an access to some basic food items (mainly food grains but also other commodities like sugar, oil and so on) and fuel (kerosene) for cooking them. This is provided at subsidized prices to people who are identified as poor, but with some subsidy to others. This is essentially meant to see that people's lower incomes should not affect their basic food consumption. We will consider some specific issues related to the efficiency of PDS in the later part of this chapter.

2. Rural employment schemes: In order to use PDS, people need some money. They will have it only if they have some wage earning work or

returns from self-employment. Thus, the wage rate and the number of days of work available are important. There are attempts to prescribe a minimum wage rate, but this may not work well in a country like India where 80 per cent of the people work in the informal sector. In the absence of enough jobs, people may be willing to work at rates less than the minimum wage. Hence the other option is to increase the number of work days. In the rural areas, the availability of work depends on farm operations, since there is not enough non-agricultural work in many villages. There are seasons where agricultural work may not be available, especially in non-irrigated regions, reducing the total number of work days even when people are ready to work. That is the rationale behind the employment guarantee scheme. The seasons where agricultural work is not available can be used for mobilizing rural labour for creating some public goods/services (for example, construction of roads, drainages, cleaning of channels) or for some water or soil conservation activities. This can be carried out as public investments (using government money). Such schemes should help create public assets on the one hand, and create employment opportunities for the underemployed on the other hand.

There are a number of issues related to efficiency here. Theoretically such Employment Guarantee Schemes (EGS) should help people when there is no job in the vicinity. When the jobs are available, people should not be encouraged to take up EGS jobs. This would reduce the supply of labour for normal productive activities within villages and can enhance the cost of operations (which may have a negative impact on the economy). There are instances where the implementation of EGS has affected the supply of labour for agriculture in many parts of the country. This is usually addressed by not having EGS job creation when agricultural operations are going on in the village. Another strategy is to give a wage rate for EGS which is slightly lower than the normal wage rate in the locality. This would discourage people from taking EGS jobs when normal work is available. Since the normal wage rate in many parts is very low (and can be lower than the minimum wage rate prescribed by the government) reducing the EGS wage rate below the prevailing wage could be a difficult decision. There is already a demand to enhance EGS wage rates. One advantage of giving a higher wage rate in EGS is that it may force rural employers (mainly farmers) too to enhance the wage rate, whereas a minimum wage rate cannot be enforced easily through the enforcement of law. This could be a distributional strategy (but what would be its impact on agriculture and whether this would lead to a reduction in farming operations reducing further the number of days of work for agricultural workers needs to be analysed).

3. Social security for those who cannot work: To use the PDS requires money. But this may not be available for those people who cannot work for several reasons. Aged people, women heads of families who cannot work due to some reason, mentally and physically challenged people and those people who are sick for a longer duration may not have a regular money income. Thus it is desirable that such sections get some social security (normally in the form of a cash transfer as pension). This is especially since pension in countries like India is received only by people who have worked in the government or formal sector private companies, and 85–90 per cent of the people in our country have been working in the informal sector (without such post-employment social security schemes).

4. Enhancing access to health care, safe water and other amenities by the state: We have seen that an unexpected expenditure on health care can push some not-so-poor families into poverty. Hence schemes that provide health care to poor and lower income groups without making a dent on their income/assets have to be an important poverty eradication strategy. This is usually addressed through the provision of subsidized or free health care in publicly owned hospitals and health-care centres. However, due to the inadequate allocation of public resources for this purpose (and the lack of resource mobilization from those who can afford to pay) and also general issues of inefficiency in public systems, the services provided by public hospitals may not meet the requirements of even poorer or lower income groups forcing them to use costly private hospitals. These days government-subsidized insurance schemes are also being tried out with the government paying part or full premium for those below the poverty line (and with incentives for others also to join in) and these insurance schemes may enable people to use health-care services from both public

and private hospitals. However, it is doubtful whether a model fully based on insurance and private health care would meet the requirements of a large section of people in a country like India. (There are issues of increasing costs of health care for both the government and the people in countries like the US where the financing is carried out mainly through insurance.) Thus, having an accessible network of public health-care centres and enhancing the quality of services provided in them have to be part of an important strategy here.

In addition to the provision of health care, the public provision of safe drinking water and subsidies granted for construction of toilets, houses and so on to poor people are also the needed strategies to address poverty. However, there could be alternative policy options for each of these strategies, and the criteria to evaluate them would be discussed in a later chapter.

There have been several other efforts too to eradicate poverty. But there is a perception that many of these programmes do not give the desired results. Thus there is a felt need to improve the effectiveness and efficiency of poverty eradication efforts and many experiments are going on in this regard.

One problem of poverty eradication is that only a fraction of the money spent reaches the beneficiaries. The rest is gobbled up by the intermediaries or other non-poor sections of the population. There are a number of reasons for this. For example, for some poverty-eradication programmes identifying the poor is difficult. This is especially so when data on income are almost non-available as most people are unwilling to state their exact income. Thus when identification is difficult, the tendency is to a cover a wider set of population or to give a particular support to all (and it is called universal coverage).

There is also some theoretical justification for this wider/universal coverage. There are two possible errors that may happen if help is extended only to the poor. The first error is that some of the people who are actually poor may be excluded, when the delivery machinery reckon them mistakenly as non-poor. Let us call this 'A' type error. In the 'B' type error some non-poor sections are included when the delivery machinery mistakenly groups them as poor. The social cost of 'A' type error is much higher than 'B' type because when some poor are denied benefits, their life itself can be in danger, whereas in a 'B' type error the cost is only some wastage of money. Thus if identification is indeed difficult, then there is some virtue in giving help (especially of the life saving kind like food) to a wider set of population.

Even if something is given free to a wider set of population, everyone need not use it. For example, in primary health-care centres everybody can get most of the services free. But a substantial section of population does not use this facility because one may have to wait longer to see a doctor. The government cannot appoint more doctors to cut down the waiting time. Again, rooms cannot be provided to all patients and they may have to use general wards which is not an attractive proposition to some (relatively well to do) patients even if the services are free. They go to a private hospital. This is called self-selection. Such self-selection happens in the case of PDS too. People from relatively affluent sections may not like the quality of food grains provided there. Nor do they like to stand in a queue for the ration. Thus even if something is provided to all or a wider section of people (including non-poor), many among the non-poor may not use it due to this self-selection process.

However, the lack of targeting is still a problem. Let us take another example. If water supply is provided free of charge (or with a high level of subsidy) through piped water supply to homes, both the poor and non-poor may use it. It may be possible that the affluent sections may use such 'free' supply of water for gardening too. Thus, instead of self-selection happening here, there could be an increase in the consumption as the affordability goes up. So finding some way of targeting is important.

But this targeting need not be based always on technical considerations. This can be determined very well by political considerations. For example, when politicians decide to supply power free to all farmers, it is the not the difficulty in targeting the really needy that encourages such a decision. Politicians expect 'all farmers' getting free power to be a support base for their re-election. Similarly, one can see politicians offering rice at ₹2 a kilo or ₹1 a kilo and so on to 60 or 70 per cent of the population. This wider coverage too is due to political interests and not much due to any technical difficulty in targeting. (In this case, the correction of any inefficiency due to such wider coverage needs to be discussed in the context of the political economy problems which have a bearing on development and not merely in the domain of poverty eradication. We will take some of these issues in Chapter 20.)

We restrict our discussion here to those technical difficulties of identification. It may be noted that these difficulties are not that static. These may change as technology changes or when the systems of governance change. For example, if the relevant information related to the income/assets of all people is available easily and accessible quickly, then targeting may not be so difficult. There is hope that the Universal Identity Number currently being tried out may facilitate such information sharing. But there are also concerns whether all the diverse set of populations (landless, permanently mobile, migrants and those who may have lost their finger marks due to hard work) could be covered under such a number-ing system and whether information stored about them could be updated fre-quently. (There are also concerns about possible discrimination facilitated by such information sharing, since caste/religious/ethnic based discrimination in the provision of public services is not that unknown in the hinterlands of countries like ours.)

Of late, there is an advocacy for cash transfer schemes instead of kind trans-fer as in the case of PDS. Cash transfer may give freedom to people regarding consumption. On the other hand, kind transfer may force them to use the items whatever be their quality. Second, kind transfer requires a large machinery to procure and distribute them. Since this is public or governmental machinery, there can be several levels of inefficiency. Thus, the transaction costs involved in kind transfer are high. Cash transfer does not require huge machinery (and it can be distributed even through postal money orders). Since people getting cash can go to any shop to buy the consumption items that they prefer the traders will be responsive since they have to compete for customers. On the other hand, retail outlets providing kind transfer (like ration shops) are monopoly, and they may adopt a 'take or leave' attitude to the customers.

However, there are many problems with cash transfer too. There can be inflation reducing the purchasing power of consumers, especially if the trans-ferred amount is not indexed to inflation. There can also be local factors that may increase prices (like hoarding in a village where there are only one or a few traders). Such local price rise may not get recorded in inflation figures, and thus even if cash transfer is indexed to inflation, it may not be adequate to address all such price rises. Who gets money within the family can also be a major concern in India. If it goes to men, they may squander it on alcohol. (We will consider some of these issues in the chapter on gender discrimination.) There can be leakages in cash transfer too; the middle men, including the postman, trying to take a cut. Many people in India do not have adequate financial liter-acy or bank account facilities, so as to make direct bank transfer (which could be done without leakage) a reality. Thus cash transfer schemes should take into account all these limitations.

A SPECIFIC ISSUE ON URBAN POVERTY

A major part of the urban poor lives in slums. These are people who may have migrated from the rural interiors to urban settings. There is an economic argument that improving the living conditions in urban slums may actually increase the growth of such settlements rather than reducing them. The logic behind the argument is that the people decide to migrate to cities in the hope of getting a higher income. Assume that the wage rate of the unskilled worker in the village is ₹50 and that in the urban area it is ₹100. The expected wage rate in an urban area is the product of the wage rate and the probability of getting a job there. Thus even if only 55 per cent of the people going to the urban area get a job there, the expected wage of the urban area $(0.55 \times 100 = 55)$ is higher than that received in the rural area (50). Thus, there would be migration to urban areas even if 45 per cent of people who do so become unemployed. Thus, migration can coexist with unemployment in urban areas even though the reason for migration is to seek employment. A similar effect can happen if there is an increase in the amenities for the urban poor or a reduction in the cost of living for them. This may encourage more migration, and hence the number of urban poor may increase. Thus, a desirable strategy is to improve the living standards and employment opportunities in rural areas so as to discourage them from migrating to the urban slums.

IMPACT OF POVERTY ON GROWTH AND DEVELOPMENT

In general economic growth reduces poverty, but this reduction may not be adequate considering the high levels of poverty that exist in many parts of the developing world. (Thus there is not much point in debating whether economic growth reduces poverty or not. Even when some people remain poor, we need supplementary policies, and in that sense it is very clear that economic growth per se is inadequate to avoid poverty in a country.) But sustained poverty reduction will be difficult without economic growth (or without a flow of income from elsewhere in the form aid or remittances). This is so since money is needed to implement the supplementary policies needed to reduce/avoid poverty. Thus there should be economic growth, even if that is not adequate to eliminate poverty.

Poverty per se is unacceptable for social and moral reasons. This is especially so since much of the poverty is avoidable with the resources that the growing economies like India has. However, the presence of poverty is not an issue mainly for the poor. It can also affect the prospects of economic growth negatively. This does not mean that an economy with many poor people does not grow. It may be growing, but it may not reach its full potential of growth for a number of reasons. First of all, when a large number of people do not acquire skills, the pool of skilled labour is very limited (compared with what would have been the situation if most people can acquire skills and supply labour). Similarly, if only those people who have their own capital can become entrepreneurs (since the capital market is not accessible to a large section as they do not have adequate collaterals), the pool of entrepreneurs would also be smaller. Such narrow sets of skilled labour and entrepreneurs may have a limiting impact on growth of an economy in the long run (compared with what would have been the potential, if the pool set was wider).

Yet another cost of poverty is the need to use a significant part of the resources for poverty eradication. This may have opportunity costs in terms of reduced availability of public goods and other governmental services. Moreover, poverty eradication expenditure usually has higher 'transmission losses'—out of the ₹100 spent for that purpose, only a small part may reach the poor and serve the purpose of poverty eradication. There may be some incentive costs, since all types of expenditure for poverty eradication need not create incentives for people to come out of poverty. There may be some perverse incentives that may encourage people not to develop self-reliance.

QUESTIONS

1. A young politician with a degree from Harvard Business School is making the following proposition for eradicating poverty in India: use the Unique Identification Number (Adhaar) to identify 40 per cent of the Indian population who are poor or economically vulnerable and transfer money to their bank accounts using mobile money transfer. Then the country can scrap its PDS. What would be your response?

2. 'The design of a poverty eradication programme should take into account the gender discrimination that may exist in that particular context'. Explain.

3. What is self-selection? How does it impact the PDS?

4. 'Accessible health care for non-poor could be considered as a poverty eradication measure'. Discuss.

5. Compare the merits and demerits of universal versus targeted PDS.

6. Why do we need a social security measure beyond PDS and EGS?

7. What is the rationale in keeping the wage rates of employment guarantee schemes lower than those prevailing in the labour market?

FOURTEEN

INEQUALITY

———◦•◦———

Poverty is deprivation in an absolute sense. Poor people may not have enough money even for basic food consumption. On the other hand, it is obvious that inequality is relative. It may be possible that everybody in a society may have enough food and basic goods, but even that society can have a very high level of inequality. There can also be a counter case. Almost everybody in a society can be poor or near poor, but it can be more equal—there is no great difference between the rich and the poor. This chapter discusses some dimensions of inequality. How do economists measure inequality? What are the factors that determine inequality as discussed in economics? How does inequality affect economic growth and development? What are the feasible strategies that societies can adopt to address or reduce inequality? These are some of the questions taken up in this chapter.

MEASUREMENT OF INEQUALITY

There are many ways of measuring inequality but all of them would assess the distance between people who have the highest level of wealth (income) and those having the lowest. The ratio between the maximum and minimum salary in the government or company is a measure of the inequality in that variable. We will consider one such measure of inequality often used in economics.

Measurement of Inequality Using Gini Coefficient

As in the case of poverty, it is reasonable to measure the inequality between the households in a society rather than the individuals. Children in richer households may not have any direct income. Thus, an easy measure of inequality would be to measure what percentage of the national income is held by the richest, say 10 or 20 per cent of the households in a country. There can be a ratio of this figure, with the corresponding value of the poorest (10 or 20 per cent, respectively) households. However, there can also be other measurements which take into account not only the richest and poorest but also those who are in the middle. Let us consider Table 14.1, which gives the share of income going to 20 per cent each of the whole population in three countries/regions namely A, B and C.

Table 14.1:
An Example to Calculate Gini Coefficient

1/5th blocks of population from rich- est to poorest	Share per- centage of total income held by each block in A	Share per- centage of total income held by each block in B	Share per- centage of total income held by each block in C	Cumula- tive per- centages for A	Cumula- tive per- centages for B	Cumula- tive per- centages for C
5	20	30	50	100	100	100
4	20	25	20	80	70	50
3	20	20	15	60	45	30
2	20	15	10	40	20	15
1	20	10	5	20	10	5

SOURCE: Author.

The graph in Figure 14.1 gives the cumulative percentages of the income in the *y* axis for A, B and C, with the cumulative percentage of the households in the *x* axis. We can see that A shows perfect equality, with each one-fifth block holding one-fifth income. However, B is an unequal society compared with A, and C is much more unequal. The line representing A is a diagonal of the graph, whereas the curves representing B and C create an area with the diagonal. The

Figure 14.1

Calculation of a Measure of Inequality: An Example

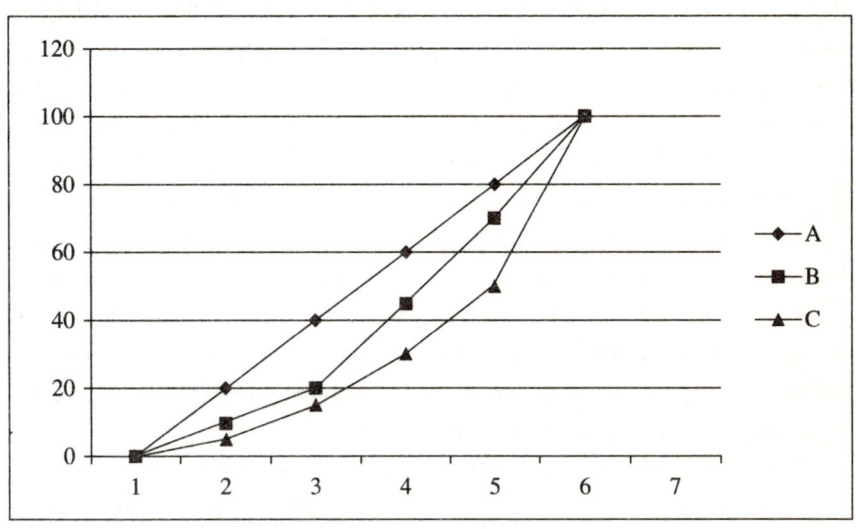

SOURCE: Author.

area between the diagonal and the curve of B can be taken as the level of inequality of B (how much B deviates from the equal society). Similarly, the area between the diagonal and the curve representing C is the level of inequality there. Assume that there is another country where all the income (100) is held by the upper 20 per cent. Which area would represent the level of inequality here? (The answer to this question will help you to understand better why we call C more unequal than B.)

> The area of the triangle below the diagonal represents the inequality of a highly unequal society. Let us call it Max Area. Gini Coefficient of a particular society (say B) is the ratio between the area between the diagonal and the cumulative income distribution curve representing it (B), and Max Area. It is easy to see that the Gini Coefficient of C would be greater than that of B.

Determinants of Inequality

There are different factors which may lead to higher levels of inequality. If the distribution of land in a country is skewed, this can lead to inequality. Such inequality in income could be the outcome when land is the main non-labour input into the production process and when it is unequally distributed. If the capital is distributed unequally, a similar outcome can be expected. When economic growth takes place mainly based on capital investments (note the discussions in the chapter on the economics of growth), and if the majority of workers have no capital assets and what they have is only their labour force, there can be a higher level of inequality. To some extent this is what troubled Karl Marx. This situation of inequality was created since there was a competition of many such workers to get a job, and what they earn may be only slightly above the subsistence income. Hence they were not able to save any income. Thus they could not make any capital investments on their own. The major part of the gains from production (or surplus) was distributed to the limited number of members of the capitalist class, and the working class could only hope to earn an income just adequate for subsistence. Such a situation could be highly iniquitous.

When different people start with unequal levels of capital assets, there may be a reproduction or perpetuation of inequality. In general market economy enhances efficiency, but it cannot do much to reduce the inequality created by these initial conditions. If inequality is perceived to be a serious problem, there will be a demand for the redistribution of assets in many societies. One such tangible asset is land. (People who have money can make it invisible in many ways.) This is the reason for the demand for land reforms (though such reforms may be beneficial in other ways too, which we have discussed earlier). Those countries which have implemented land reforms in the past could address the problem of inequality to some extent. It is generally noted that East Asian economies like South Korea or Japan could implement land reforms well, and this has helped their long-term economic transition. On the other hand, land distribution was skewed in the (post-colonial) Latin American countries, and it had also created high levels of inequality there.

However, we have seen from the discussions on economic growth that a major driver of growth in developed economies was technological progress which included schooling, other forms of education, skills and knowledge base in addition to technological and managerial innovations. When economic growth is based on such technological change, initial capital endowment need not matter much (provided that is not a major constraint in acquiring education and skills to use or work with technological and managerial innovations). In those economies where technology became the driver of growth, inequality has moderated later on compared to the situation when the growth was mainly driven by capital investments. This has led to a generalization that economic growth at initial stages may enhance inequality (probably due to capital-investment-driven growth) but such inequality may decline gradually (as technological progress becomes the main engine of growth). This is called Kuznets's hypothesis, following the economist namely Simon Kuznets. Here the relationship between economic growth (growth of per-capita income) and inequality is hypothesized to be like an inverted U. There is lower level of inequality when per-capita income is lower and also when it is sufficiently high, whereas inequality is higher in between. The empirical evidence for this hypothesis is not that straight forward though it provides insights into the historical factors accelerating growth and inequality.

In fact this is one reason (along with social and political actions) that had led Western developed economies to deviate from a path predicted by Karl Marx. He postulated that capital investment-based economic growth (or capitalism) in these countries would increase inequality drastically, and this would catalyse social transformation towards socialism (where the working class would take over the ownership of assets used for production). However, we know that such transition to socialism did not occur in these countries (though it has taken place in less developed economies of East Europe and China). This could be due to the fact that Western economies could then follow a technology-based growth trajectory. The technology/knowledge-based growth has a clear difference. Here along with capital, education or knowledge too becomes an input into the production process. Some part of the surplus has to be set apart for the contributors of knowledge/skills (in addition to what they contribute as mere labour). It has created different layers of workers. Well-educated workers could get much more than the subsistence wages received by unskilled workers enhancing the hopes of the former of making some capital investments in the future (probably as small shareholders of some big companies, which may enable them to claim parts of profit as dividends). Hence the polarization in society between capitalists on the one hand, and workers on the other hand got blurred. Many people started occupying the position in the middle or the middle class could emerge. They did not share the same concerns and interests of those who continued as the 'pure working class'. Some among the middle class emerged later as part of the owners of firms or could become part of the richer sections of the society. In fact when knowl-edge/creativity become the main component of production or source of income as in the case of software industry, one could see people with education but without much capital asset, becoming successful entrepreneurs even in countries like India.

In modern economies, the most rewarding form of capital is education (human capital). Thus newer levels of inequality are growing in developed economies caused mainly by the differences in higher education. The return from higher education (college education) is much greater than that derived by those who could not reach college. Moreover the impact of higher education persists across generations. A person with 16 years of education with parents having higher education may have more of an upper hand (in terms of income) compared with another person with the same years of education but with par-ents having only minimal education. Thus enhancing access to education has become the most appropriate way of reducing inequality, even though it may take time to see the fruits of such education especially for those who currently do not have access to it.

INEQUALITY VERSUS POVERTY

The relationship between poverty and inequality is also interesting. There can be a high level of inequality even when there is very little poverty. Some of the developed economies like that of the US has higher levels of inequality but the share of people living below poverty is lower. There can also be countries where inequality may be insignificant but poverty can be high. Some of the communist countries like North Korea could be an example. There, almost everybody bar-ring the family of the ruler and his close associates may be leading a subsist-ence life. The level of consumption of most people in countries like Cuba is also at a lower level and here too inequality may be low. However, such a situation of the less unequal but poor may not be sustainable as evident from the experi-ence of many socialist countries in the past. (Even Cuba is currently undergoing a process of transformation.) Many people may see prospects for enhancing their personal consumption in an open market economy, and this may encour-age them to pursue changes in the economic system, even if such a change may lead to increased inequality.

POSSIBLE SOLUTIONS TO ADDRESS INEQUALITY

One way of minimizing inequality is the redistribution of assets. Land redistribution could be an important strategy if land is the main reason for inequality and an asset in the generation of income (see Chapter 11 for details). Access to capital is also important and we have already considered some strategies aimed at enhancing access to capital markets used by different governments. However, a well-developed capital market may come out with instruments (even without the support of governments) to see that people who have enterprising ideas get enough capital to translate them into reality. Venture capital is one such instrument. Here people or a company may decide to fund the set-up of a company based on the idea of a person who does not have adequate capital of his/her own. Of course this decision to fund would be based on a detailed examination of the viability and the likely success of the proposed business plan. A venture capital firm funding the business may take an appropriate share of the ownership of the new firm. Once the company is set up and is ready to stand on its own, the funding company may withdraw support and get back its capital with profits probably by transferring the shares it held to another investor or through offloading in the stock market (if the new firm could be listed in the share market by then). Of course some of the newly set-up firms may fail, and this is taken into account by the venture capital firms, and they may make substantial benefits from those which succeed. Since it is the private entrepreneurs who take such decisions to fund other firms (and not the government), they have appropriate interest to evaluate the viability of new business proposals. On the other hand, there are many government schemes to help new entrepreneurs. It is not uncommon to see such schemes leading to the support of unviable firms, or such government funding agencies finding it difficult to get back their money. The government may use taxation as an instrument to address inequality in society, and the details are discussed in a later chapter while discussing governments and taxes in general.

ACCESS TO HIGHER EDUCATION: A STRATEGY TO ADDRESS INEQUALITY

In a modern economy, the most important asset that creates inequality is higher education. This is so since technological growth is the important driver of economic growth here and education plays an important role in facilitating and assimilating the benefits of technological growth.

Higher education is an important determinant of the income status of individuals and hence inequality in society. Meritorious students coming from poorer financial backgrounds should not be deprived of higher education just because they do not have money. This is a problem not only for the 'equality of opportunity', but also for economic growth (since there would be a limited pool of educated persons if talented among the poor or lower income groups cannot access higher education).

Is it not possible for those students, who have aptitude and interest, to acquire higher education with educational loans? As in the case of other loans, the lender want to ensure that the loans are paid back with interest. This makes them seek collaterals from the borrowers. Students from poorer backgrounds may not have adequate property or close relatives with salaried jobs to ensure the banks that they can repay the loans. Most students from poorer financial backgrounds, who get admission in higher education institutes, may be unable to demonstrate beforehand that they can indeed complete the course successfully, take up paying jobs, and repay the loan in time. Getting educational loans may be relatively easy (even without collaterals) for some of these students, if they get into (by doing remarkably well in competitive entrance examinations) very prestigious institutes or in those courses for which well-paying jobs are ensured after the completion. Thus job-assured courses, and those who enter such courses through taxing entrance examinations (like those for the Indian Institutes of Management) can benefit from educational loans. However, such courses and institutes form only a minor part of whole higher education scene. Thus, education loans may not solve this problem and social intervention is needed to see that meritorious students from poor families have access to avenues of higher education. If governments insist on public sector banks to provide such loans without collateral, this can lead to an inefficient/ risky allocation of resources in banking sector.

This does not mean that there should be universal access to higher education. Creating educated persons is not possible simply by 'supplying' education. Only those persons who internalize supplied education become educated. Internalization requires a certain level of ability and willingness to devote time. Thus it may not be desirable to provide higher education to all, since acquiring it may require a certain ability and preparedness on the part of the student, and in the absence of these, what is provided may be wasted. This is especially so if the user of higher education is not bearing the full cost. If the student is bearing the cost, he/she has an incentive to be careful in choosing whether to pursue higher education in general or a particular course depending on ability/interest. If the society decides to provide free/subsidized education, then there will be a demand problem. If something is freely provided (or with subsidy), there will be an excessive demand— excessive considering the social benefits and costs. Thus rationing is needed and stringent entry qualifications should be set in the case of those students who get public funding or social support for higher education. Everybody cannot be provided with higher education. However, this does not mean that the provision can be based on the willingness to pay.

How does one provide meritorious students from poorer backgrounds access to higher education? Historically this could be a reason for governments and charity organizations, including religious bodies, starting educational institutions which charge a nominal fee. There are also scholarships and fee waivers offered directly by charitable organizations which can be used in government/private/ charity managed colleges. Thus, the two effective interventions which can be used to solve the issue of access to higher education for students from poor financial backgrounds are:

1. Government/community/charity organizations starting colleges to provide free/subsidized education.
2. Provide financial support to these students to pursue education in colleges of their choice (run by any type of agency like public or private).

However, countries like India have not succeeded much in this regard. This is not the failure of merely government but of society as a whole. First, middle class and richer sections are yet to show a willingness to pay the cost of education in government institutions, even though they may be spending more to get (through entrance examinations) into such institutions. There is not enough charity-based education in countries like India. Management of colleges belonging to even religious and charitable organizations do not (or are unable to) mobilize as many endowments and charitable resources as possible to run their educational institutions as good-quality organizations. Mobilizing such resources would have enabled them to give admission to meritorious candidates from all backgrounds, give fellowships to some poorer students with merit, and invest in faculty for good-quality training and teaching/research. Though there is a growing affluence in India, charity is not catching up adequately among Indians. (On the other hand one can see charity or altruism playing an important role in education in countries like the US.)

In addition to the subsidized provision, another strategy used in different parts of the world to enhance access to higher education for the socially and economically backward is positive discrimination or what is called reservation of seats (as in India). This strategy is used if economic backwardness can be seen among some socially (or geographically) definable groups of people in terms of caste/race, religion, gender, parental education, place of stay and so on. However, such a reservation can be implemented in a very mechanical manner so that some among those sections make use of them forever, whereas those who are really backward economically may not get the benefits of such a system. Though the rationale for the reservation of seats in higher education for socially backward sections is sound, its implementation in countries like India requires critical analysis. (The procedure used in the Azim Premji University to use the socio-economic criteria in admissions is an innovation in this regard.)

IMPACT OF INEQUALITY ON ECONOMIC GROWTH

If a large number of people are in poverty as part of inequality, then such poverty will have a direct negative impact on development. However, one can analyse the impact of inequality per se, even if many people are not poor. There are a few ways of analysing the impact of inequality. Is inequality bad in itself? At the conceptual level, it is reasonable to think so about inequality. Then the issue is how to address inequality. One may argue that even if inequality is unacceptable, the ways of addressing it should not lead to outcomes that are more unacceptable. One way inequality was addressed in communist societies was to dampen individual initiatives. This led to a drastic decline in wealth creation. The ultimate result was that a large number of people in a number of communist countries like Laos, North Korea and Cuba were forced to live in near subsistence levels (or in poverty as in the case of North Korea). Hence when inequality is not acceptable, we may have to think about ways of addressing it without creating more harmful consequences.

Is inequality bad for economic growth itself? If inequality and poverty are combined, and a substantial part of the population is in a deplorable condition and only a small part of the population is wealthy, it can have a negative impact on economic growth. There are a number of channels through which such inequality affects growth. If the majority of the population perceives themselves as poor, democratically elected governments will be forced to spend a greater part of the public resources for 'redistribution'. This may reduce the availability of money for public goods needed for facilitating economic growth. The fact that a large section of the population lives in deplorable conditions may manifest in increased crimes and violence. The experience of many Latin American countries, which have a majority of the population living in urban areas, and the poor among them in slums, indicates this possibility. Thus, extreme inequality may be 'bad' and costly even for the well-to-do sections. This is not to deny that addressing poverty and inequality are desirable on their own (and that need not be due to the negative impacts of them on economic growth or on well-to-do sections).

IMPACT OF INEQUALITY ON DEVELOPMENT

There is a strong argument that the reduction of inequality should be an objective of development itself. This could be the view of the victims of unequal income distribution. It can also be a moral or rights-based stand point about which economics may not have much to contribute. However, recent literature on development has brought out the importance of reducing inequality. It is here that economics has something to say and this is about the relationship between economic growth and happiness.

As noted already, the human development index is a minimal concept of development. There are several criticisms of such an approach. One strand of criticism came from what can be called happiness studies or measures of the Global Happiness Index. It is noted that the happiness index based on reported perceptions of many societies does not show much improvement despite the fact that their economies undergo reasonable economic growth or the same people witness an increase in their incomes. (One can ask the question whether the reported happiness is a reasonable measure of real well-being but that we will not discuss here.) This gives an impression that income growth does not matter much for happiness. There have been different responses from the discipline of economics to this debate. Though we are not touching all these responses, one stream of thought may be important for development practitioners.

Economic Understanding of the Divergence between Growth and Happiness

There is a general recognition that income growth or the increased consumption associated with income growth may not create additional satisfaction due to what can be called the 'benchmark effect'. It is recognized that people consume for two major reasons: first, is an innate need satisfaction and second, is it to achieve some status among peers (who could be neighbours, community and so on). This distinction in consumption is different from the categorization into basic consumption (for example, food, medicines) and luxurious consumption (for example, cars and expensive clothing). There can be some luxurious items even for innate need satisfaction. Somebody may be spending substantial amounts of money to visit some forests or to attend music concerts, without being concerned about what peers do or without making these expenditures known to others.

When a part of consumption is for achieving or maintaining status, a general increase in income to all may not lead to much additional satisfaction. If some-body struggles to acquire more income to buy a scooter, seeing that a few others in the community have scooters, then his level of satisfaction may not go up substantially when he finally purchases it, if by that time many others in the com-munity have bought a car. There may not be any fulfilment of satisfaction of status consumption if others' consumption goes up perennially. On the other hand, there may be temporary fulfilment of satisfaction when the objective of consumption is to meet innate needs. Thus there is a view that too much focus on status consumption need not be a desirable trait. In fact it may be desirable for individuals to develop habits (or internalize norms) that enable them to concen-trate on innate need consumption rather than status, which is more like a mirage. To some extent, the demand for powerful positions in society is also a part of the need for status. Such a demand for power can also be undesirable in terms of achieving happiness as in the case of status consumption. (Someone trying to acquire more power to become happy can become unhappy while knowing that there are others who are more powerful.)

However, we should not underestimate the importance of status consumption in a poor country where a large number of people live in poverty and do not consume even the basic needs. People learn to use (and hence struggle to acquire) certain commodities or services when they see others in the community using them. Such demonstration effect works in the use of electricity, clean toilets, hygienic houses, vaccination, healthy food, education and so on. Certain desirable practices like limiting the number of children are also seen to be driven by the demonstration effect, as was evident from the demographic transition of societies which did not have any coercive population policy. Thus, status consumption has an important role in poorer societies.

The idea to emulate others may also have some socially desirable effects. Those who make money through industrial enterprises may have the option of spending it wholly for one's own, including that of his/her own future generations' consumption (in addition to reinvestments in their own enterprises). They can also spare a part of the resources for some public needs. Not bequeathing all wealth for one's own children, and providing some part for public causes like endowments to universities, are common in developed countries like the US. But such a habit is yet to take root in India. If some billionaires, like Bill Gates, Warren Buffet or Azim Premji, spending a substantial part of their own wealth on public needs encourage some other billionaires to emulate them, then it can have a socially beneficial outcome. Thus emulation need not always be seen in poor light.

If inequality results in the deceleration of the achievement of development, then that is to be reckoned as a negative outcome. To some extent, such a problem arises when unequal wealth held by some also leads to public expression of opulent consumption. This may encourage the not-so-wealthy or normal people to emulate the consumption of the rich. They may struggle to earn more income, but a greater part of that would be used to emulate the consumption of the wealthy, and this can become a constantly moving target. Thus, for many people, there may not be a tangible improvement in satisfaction or happiness despite an increase in consumption and income.

There are two possible solutions to this issue. One issue is to develop a 'culture' or norm that encourages people to focus more on innate consumption rather than on status-based consumption. Second, the fact that some people are wealthy (whereas others are not) need not always encourage opulent consumption. The wealthy can also be spending money in ways that need not encourage too much consumption by others. These days a number of billionaires all over the world spend a part of their money on charity, nature conservation, preservation of culture or for promoting socially relevant research and so on. Azim Premji University itself is part of such an effort.

Bibliographical Note: An interesting book on inequality is Bowles, Gintis and Osborne (2005). A description of the economist's response to the happiness debate can be seen in Frey and Alois (2002).

QUESTIONS/EXERCISES

1. Get the estimates of the Gini Coefficient of all Indian states (the latest figure). Any surprises?
2. Get the inequality estimates of 50–70 major countries (including those from Asia, Africa, Latin America and North America). Draw major inferences.
3. All talented students should have access to higher education irrespective of their ability to pay, but universal access to higher education need not be desirable. Discuss.
4. How is inequality related to happiness?
5. What is your view of the future of society in terms of inequality and income growth of individuals?
6. The following are the values of the Gini Coefficients for two states in India calculated with comparable data:

   (a) Bihar (Rural)—20.8
   (b) Kerala (Rural)—29.0

   How would you interpret these figures given your knowledge of the relative human development status of these two states?

FIFTEEN

AN ECONOMIC UNDERSTANDING OF SOCIAL AND GENDER DISCRIMINATION

UNDERDEVELOPMENT OF SPECIFIC SOCIAL GROUPS

We can see underdevelopment manifested in more acute forms among certain social sections in different countries. For example, poverty is prevalent more among scheduled castes and tribes (even though there are poor among other caste groups) in India. If we do a disaggregated analysis of some development indicators, like literacy, school enrolment rate or infant mortality, we could see the status much lower among some social groups. Even in a state like Kerala with a high human development index, the achievements in this regard among the scheduled tribes are much lower compared with others. Poverty in the US is concentrated among the blacks. Poverty is correlated with social identity in India—with a greater share of poor people from specific social groups.

But why?

Underdevelopment depends on (the lack of) access to assets like land, capital or education. Historically some social groups were deprived of these assets. The fact that they were poor and underdeveloped for long durations may have also created vicious cycles perpetuating their status. Given that the advantages of education persist over generations, the lack of education among many people belonging to these groups perpetuates disadvantages.

Land redistribution is a remedial measure but has not been effectively done in many parts of India. Even where it is implemented, people belonging to the middle castes (and not those belonging to poorest and the scheduled castes and tribes) have benefited more from land reforms. This was because reforms were aimed mainly at entrusting titles of land with the cultivating tenants, and mostly it was the farmers belonging to the middle castes who were tenants in most cases depriving social groups which were landless and/or agricultural workers.

Efforts to improve literacy did not yield the desired results for a long time. So the route of education has not helped these social groups to get out of their poverty. The benefits of reservation for seats in higher education and government jobs, in place over the last 50 years, have reached only a small section of these communities. A substantial section of these people do not reach the level of higher education at which they can aspire for government jobs. This deprives them the benefits of reservation. They have not benefited much from the recent rapid growth of economy. Though they get jobs in unskilled or less-skilled activities in the informal sector, their participation in the formal private sector has been limited. Since the growth of the manufacturing sector has not been impressive, it has limited the job options of people who have completed seven–eight years of schooling or some vocational education. On the other hand, the developments in the service sector, including software industry, have benefitted those social groups which have been in the forefront in education for decades (and they belonged to the so called upper-caste groups). Hence improving access to education for the under-privileged sections seems the most important strategy required to remedy the situation.

This sort of a situation is not unique to India. Even in the US, though policies of positive discrimination or affirmative action are in place, the gap between the economic status of the blacks and others has not narrowed much. But some countries like China have overcome such ethnic or race-based underdevelopment although the rural–urban divide is widening faster there. This is partly because of their socialist revolution. In general, if ethnic or other social exclusions continue over a long period of time, it may lead to some such groups doing badly in terms of development.

In addition to the economic underdevelopment of specific social groups like the scheduled castes and tribes, cultural practices that exclude them in social interactions still prevail in India. Not allowing these people to participate in social forums (including entering tea shops) is not uncommon even today in some parts of India despite such groups enjoying political representation in elected governments (mostly through the reservation of seats). It is documented that the heads of village-level governments coming from such social groups (thanks to reservation of seats) face insurmountable difficulties in performing their role. The continuation of such social exclusion accentuates economic underdevelopment of these specific social groups.

There have been some recent attempts within economics to explain the persistence of the caste system. The central argument is that for certain groups (or individuals within such groups) it is rational not to break the caste norms and hence they follow them. This could be due to formal or informal ways by which caste groups punish those individuals who break the norms. This is reflected to a great extent in marriages. In some Indian villages we hear khap panchayats punishing boys and girls who marry against caste norms. Honour killings are not that uncommon in India (Turkey also has such incidents). However, even without such khap panchayats and honour killings, marriages against caste norms are not that frequent even among the urban middle class in India. This is true to some extent even among the educated workers who are benefitting from the growth of the service sector as part of the growing Indian economy. Such exclusionary practices may be beneficial for some members of these groups (but not to all among them—and we will consider one such group, namely women, as part of the next section), but it may not be beneficial for all. Though the caste system may be 'beneficial' for some, it can lead to socially inefficient equilibriums. As a response to the exclusionary practices of the so-called upper-caste groups, and also due to the opportunities provided by caste-based reservations and politics, the so-called lower-caste groups too practice exclusionary strategies. All these lead to the persistence of the caste system in India.

However, it is not that the evolution of a social practice or norm always follows a rational approach. This could also be more like a habit. Even if it is known to many that a particular habit is not desirable, it may take a long time to change it. The phenomenon of what is called path dependency is pervasive in the case of such norms. (We will take some of these issues in a little more detail in Chapter 19.) Whether it is due to rational reasons or habituation that takes time to disappear, exclusionary social practices, including the caste system, prevails in India.

Can economic or social policy do something to mitigate the situation? India has taken several legal and political measures. Discrimination on the basis of caste itself is reckoned as a crime. Reservation on the basis of caste in educational and governmental organizations (both for elected representatives and officials) has also enhanced the social and economic status of (small) sections belonging to underprivileged groups. However, these legal and political measures could not really alleviate the deprivation suffered by the majority of people belonging to these groups. It also shows that there may be many more fundamental reasons that make these legal and political measures against caste discrimination less effective in India.

Are there better policies which may address these fundamental issues that lead to the continuation of such discrimination? Probably this is an area requiring more focused attention of the development practitioners/researchers and activists. Efforts made to enhance the access to schooling and higher education for students belonging to the scheduled castes and tribes and the other less-privileged population needs to be analysed. Successful experiments in this regard can be replicated. Social policies that encourage inter-caste marriages may have to be strengthened. Effective steps to control khap panchayats, honour killings and such enforcement of traditional backward-looking norms may have to be put in place. Probably encouraging migration of rural boys and girls (especially the latter) to urban and newly industrialized areas where they can get jobs in the manufacturing sector (a practice that worked in China, Indonesia and some other Asian countries) could be one strategy to loosen their connections with the restrictive social norms of the villages.

Another form of systematic deprivation that is evident in India manifests in certain regions. Some states or regions continue to be underdeveloped for various reasons. Northeastern states, some eastern states, and those which are called BIMARU (Bihar, MP, Rajasthan, UP and Jharkhand and Chhattisgarh) face specific problems. On the other hand, south Indian states (Tamil Nadu, Kerala, Andhra Pradesh and Karnataka) are ahead in terms of educational and economic development (even though there are some zones of underdevelopment in these states). The ethnic tensions and political instability that prevailed for a long period have negatively influenced the development outcomes of Northeastern states (even though sections of educated people from these places move to other parts of India for education and jobs). The regional backwardness could be due to the differences in social, educational and political features of these regions and some of these will be discussed in Chapter 20.

The fact that some sections of society (certain social groups or regions) do not benefit from economic growth and continue to live in underdevelopment is undesirable. But it is also costly for others and the economy in general. There is a greater demand for redistribution of resources to schemes which may not make any visible impact on the life of these people (since these schemes do not address the fundamental issues sustaining social discrimination) but only add to the fiscal deficits of governments. The money available for public goods and infrastructure for the growth of the economy and the welfare of society in general is not growing up adequately due to this pressure to spend money on redistribution. The political scene of India is also getting divided according to caste lines. The democratization of less-privileged groups and their assertion of political and economic rights are important, but when the political process gets fragmented according to caste groups, it may lead to socially and economically undesirable outcomes. When certain specific social sections see themselves not benefitting much from the development process, the social negotiation over productive activities may get communal and caste coloured and this can create deadlocks in such negotiations. Thus, whether it is for the welfare of these sections, or for addressing the overall challenges of the society and the economy, we need to confront the caste-based discrimination prevalent in India. This is true for other societies (like the US where most of the underdeveloped population comprises the blacks) which too have such social cleavages in terms of development outcomes. This could be evident in the problems of integration of indigenous communities in some parts of Latin America or meeting the aspirations of some ethnic groups in China and so on.

One form of discrimination on which economics as a discipline has devoted substantial energy is that based on gender. (To some extent this could be due to the fact that such discrimination was prevalent in almost all parts of the world in varying degrees.) Feminist economics has developed into an important sub-discipline. We will draw some important insights from it in the following sections.

GENDER DISCRIMINATION IN INDIA

There are differences between men and women in terms of certain development outcomes. Literacy and school enrolment are part of these categories. However, the most notable manifestation of gender discrimination in India is that of sex ratio. In most developed societies, and in states like Kerala with a higher Human Development Index, the sex ratio is invariably in favour of women. A ratio of 1,050 women to 1,000 men is very common there. This could be due to the fact that the biological survival rate is generally higher for women, and in the absence of any discrimination against them, a sex ratio in favour of women is to be expected. However, there are states in India where the sex ratio is 910–920 women for 1,000 men. There are also anecdotal and other evidences from different parts of India that such sex ratios unfavourable to women are the product of intentional discrimination against the girl child. Medical developments that help sex identification of the foetus are misused for this purpose. Cases or stories of female infanticide are not very uncommon in some parts of the country. Though there are regulations banning the misuse (or restricting the use) of such medical technology, these are not very effective.

There is also discrimination in the resource allocation within the household. This may manifest in extreme forms even in the allocation of food. However, there is bias in the use of resources for education against girls even among the non-poor or well-to-do families. Conventional marriage and inheritance systems do not grant property rights to daughters in the family. The absence of such property rights negatively affects bargaining power in their marital relationships. This may force them to tolerate domestic violence and other harassment.

The dowry and the harassment related to it are another manifestation of the gender discrimination in India. This system is catching up even among those communities which were not practicing it earlier. The legal prohibition on dowry has not made any significant impact. On the one hand, dowry becomes a source of harassment in post-marriage contexts when there is continuing demand to get money and resources from the girls' family. Suicides or murders related to dowry are not very infrequent. On the other hand, inability to mobilize adequate money for paying dowry (to 'procure' a husband) is a source of frustration for many girls and their parents.

There are also an increasing number of cases of sexual violence and harassment reportedly occurring in public spaces and work places. One can view this in two ways. This increase could be partly because these days a greater number of cases are reported in the media, and people show a higher willingness to report such cases for police action. In the past, only a few such cases would have reached the media or the law and order machinery. Hence this increase in the reported incidence of sexual violence against women does not mean that such incidents were rare in the past. It is also possible to see an increase in the actual number of such incidents of sexual violence today. It could be the case that women were not moving out freely for jobs or other work in the past, and they were 'protected' by the families, kinships and communities. (There could be other forms of violence when women were 'protected' too much by their families and communities.) There could be an increase in sexual violence in public space as more and more women are participating in work outside the home and also going out (to live outside the home) for different purposes including education. Thus the challenge for society is to encourage women to go out for education and work on the one hand, and also to see that they are not subjected to sexual violence.

Though the educational opportunities for women have increased in the recent past (from a position of a very low literacy rate for them in many states until recently), their participation in the political sphere is very limited. This has created demands for the reservation of elected positions for women, which has been implemented already in the case of local governments, whereas adequate political support is yet to be mobilized for women's reservation in the state legislature and the parliament. Even when women are elected to local governments (as chairpersons) it is not rare (in some parts of India) that they do not come out freely to public spaces, and most of their powers are exercised actually by their husbands or sons. Even in states like Kerala where women are as good as men in terms of educational achievements, their participation in political sphere and civil society is very limited. It is not easy to overcome gender discrimination in public/political space, even when women acquire empowerment through education and employment.

FACTORS DETERMINING GENDER DISCRIMINATION

The discrimination against women and girls prevailing in some societies including India is partly due to non-economic factors such as social or cultural norms. Though economists will not write off such cultural or social norms, they have the urge to look for, what they call, more fundamental, 'objective' factors that cause such discrimination.

A common sense approach (of men but also internalized by women) is to think that men and women are biologically different, and women cannot do some tasks that men do, and hence they have an inferior position. There are many nuanced responses to such a common sense approach. We will consider a few of them. Though it cannot be denied that men and women are different biologically, feminist literature these days talks about a much greater diversity in terms of sexuality beyond a binary categorization of female and male. What is constituted as man and woman socially need not follow strictly a biological division. Economics is not the appropriate discipline to talk about this issue, and you may hear more about it from an interdisciplinary perspective of gender studies.

Even if we start with the point that men and women are biologically very different, why should that lead to an inferior social/economic position for women? There is historical evidence to indicate that women's social/economic position was not so inferior throughout human history or all over the world in a similar manner. An important argument in this regard was given by Marxists (based on the writings of Frederick Engels) that the position of women got subjugated along with the emergence of private property rights. When households came to possess properties (or when they consider the property as that owned by the marital family), the problem of transferring this property to younger generations came up. The urge to transfer the property to one's own biological children required a certain control for men over the reproductive powers of women.

There is also anecdotal evidence to indicate that the position of women based on some indicators (like the ownership of property) was different in different societies. For example, many groups in Asia, Africa and indigenous America practised a matrilineal property relationship—whereby ownership of landed properties moved from one generation to the other through women (or mothers transferring the rights to daughters). This was very different from patriarchal societies where the ownership of properties was moved from fathers to sons. There are also indications that matrilineal property rights existed in societies where food collection was made through gathering and non-irrigated farming, whereas other modes of subsistence like irrigated cultivation or cattle rearing (where people travel long distance nurturing livestock) encouraged patriarchal property rights.

Even the contemporary world shows much diversity in terms of the position of women and also their entitlements. Though dowry is prevalent in India, bride price is the most common form of exchange in many parts of Africa today. (Here the bridegroom has to pay money or kind—sometimes in the form of cattle—to the girls' family). The practice of dowry has declined in Western countries. Thus, one can see changes in gender relations across space and time. All these indicate that gender discrimination is not a biologically determined phenomenon, but is constructed according to social, economic and cultural contexts.

If primitive production systems had influenced the shaping of gender relationships in the past, then it is possible to think about changing these relationships as production systems evolve. Technology may be playing an important role. Thus production relations that existed when human power is an important input need not remain when other sources of power and technology dominate production systems. Thus even when there is a rationale for certain relations at some time in the past, these need not serve any legitimate purpose today.

Even when people are of different abilities (and different men also have different abilities), societies' approach to development need not give importance to those different abilities. Everybody, irrespective of different abilities, can be given 'equality of opportunities'. Thus based on the actual empirical evidence, and also the accepted views of modern societies, one need not give any credence to the argument that gender discrimination is due to biological difference.

Coming back to the contemporary situation of India, the continuation of gender discrimination here is, to some extent, similar to the one faced by the people belonging to the scheduled castes and tribes (or in some cases backward castes). The latter remain poor because they were systematically deprived of assets that matter in the economy. More among them were landless in the past, and as discussed in the section of poverty, asset-less households could not improve their livelihoods, and hence their backwardness may persist over a period of time. This is true with women too. For social or cultural reasons, women were systematically denied economic assets. This was initially land, and later education. Hence the livelihood and the social security of women were sought within the family, and not through income-earning through paid work (which is the way men are supposed to earn their livelihood). In addition to this, there was also a gender division of work, setting norms on what women should (or should not) do. They were burdened with the household work of taking care of children, housekeeping and also the care of the aged, and these works were not considered work in the traditional sense and is also unpaid. This too has limited their participation in the markets and gainful employment.

Thus, marrying girls to a 'better bridegroom' became an aspiration. When a number of girls or their families seek an alliance with a 'better bridegroom', his bidding price goes up. This has led to an increase in dowry payments. Though dowry is legally prohibited, the practice not only exists but is also getting wider acceptance socially. (Thus, societies which were not practicing dowry in the past have accepted it in recent history.) Thus, girls whose parents cannot mobilize enough dowry (or do not have attractive features determined by a patriarchal notion of femininity) are sidelined in the marriage market. This puts excessive pressure on the parents of a girl child. Thus the birth of a girl child is seen with a lot of caution, and if some couple has a greater number of girl children, then they are viewed to be doomed. Thus there is a social pressure to avoid the girl child.

Even if the social and economic conditions for some sections of society have changed with the education of women, and the increased possibility of getting jobs and their own income, the impact of past practices may persist for some more time. Social and cultural practices take a longer time to change and these are like habits. It is not rare to see employed women not having any right over their salary (and are forced to hand it over to the husbands). They may have to face the double burden—carry out the household chores single-handedly and then have to meet the demands of paid work. It is also not uncommon to see women themselves internalizing the prevailing gender norms against women, perpetuating these norms through the way children are brought up. Hence, even when economy and society change at a faster pace, certain norms including those guiding gender relations, may take longer time to change.

However, individuals, households, society and the state can take certain steps to minimize the impact of discriminatory gender practices that exist in society. Some of these are briefly touched upon in the following section.

STRATEGIES TO MINIMIZE THE IMPACT OF GENDER DISCRIMINATION

1. Inheritance of capital assets including land by women.

   There are a number of advantages in women having property rights. It was observed that such women have enhanced bargaining power within the marital family. The ownership of a house may make them relatively more empowered to resist excessive domestic violence. The assets and income stream that come to the hands of women may lead to a resource distribution within the family that would enhance family welfare. This is the reason why women are taken as the targeted groups when cash transfer schemes are implemented by different governments for poverty reduction.

2. Not seeing marriage as the only means of social security, and gainful employment is to be seen as the main source of income for women just like men.

   If employment is not viewed as the most important source of livelihood for women, then they would be forced to secure it from the marriages. This may reduce their bargaining power in marital relationships. They would be forced to continue within the marriage even if domestic violence and other forms of harassment become unbearable. Moreover, as mentioned earlier, it is this practice of considering marriage as the sole livelihood for women that drives up dowry payments. This can create social and human problems before and after the marriage.

3. A conducive environment which enables women to take up jobs considering their role in reproduction and early child care.

   Employment opportunities for women are growing as a part of the growth of the economy and also as part of the globalization/liberalization policies. There is an argument that liberalization has led to what is called feminization of the work force. This was partly because there has been a reduction in the rigidity of labour markets (formal and informal rules imposed by the government on what employers shall or shall not do with regard to employment), and this has encouraged employers to hire more women. The growth of employment could also be in an informal sector which also may have facilitated the entry of more women into the work force. However, conditions of employment have not improved much here. The lack of adequate measures to help women to carry out their reproductive roles (pregnancy and infant care) discourages women from utilizing these employment opportunities. Thus, making jobs appropriate for the requirements of women may be needed to encourage their work participation.

4. Urgent steps to mitigate the backwardness of girls in terms of access to education.

   The literacy rates among girls was significantly lower than that of male in many states of India nearly 20 years ago. However, this situation has changed since then. But one can see such a situation among specific social groups. Moreover, barring some states like Kerala, educational achievements (the number of years of schooling, enrolment in higher education) of women in general is lower than those of men. This may put them in an unfavourable situation in terms of the employment and wages. Jobs and one's own income are one way of empowering the position of women (albeit partially). Thus, special efforts should be made to improve the access to and the retention rate in education for women.

5. Acceptance of a practice where men share a major part of the household chores.

   If women have to continue with the task of carrying out the same level of household chores even when they have jobs, there could be a double burden. Thus, there is a need to reduce their burden of household duties. This may require the education of boys on the need to share household work. This could be part of a general gender education aimed at both boys and girls. One can see a gradual change in this regard in urban India, but more intentional efforts need to be made in this regard.

6. Institutionalization of care of young children and the aged.

   Many services carried out within the family, like the care of the aged or very young children, need to move towards public organizations provided by the government or the market. In the absence of such institutionalized provision of services, these may have to be carried out within households, and their burden may fall on women given our social and cultural conditioning. Though one can see a gradual process of institutionalization happening in this regard in urban areas, its pace has to become faster. It was through this process that socialist countries have brought out their women to participate in formal employment on a massive basis.

7. Making public spaces women friendly.

   One more factor that would facilitate the participation of women in employment and in public space is the safety of these spaces. Though there have been some improvements (including stricter enforcement of rules against sexual harassment in work places these days), much more needs to be done. There have to be stricter and quicker enforcement of laws against sexual violence in public and work places. Speedier mechanisms of law enforcement (including judicial systems), women friendly trial process and so on are important here. Women friendly infrastructure—well lit roads and public places like bus stands, markets, theatres, public toilets, extensive provision of public toilets, rest rooms, overnight stay hostels, a toll free number to report violence and extensive information about violence redressal mechanisms—is also important.

8. Making public projects/programmes gender sensitive.

Some of the strategies mentioned above require action at the level of individuals or households. However, public policy too plays an important role. There are many public projects like drinking water supply, or the health-care system, which can have a direct bearing on the welfare of women. The specific requirements of women may have to be kept in mind while designing such public projects. An enhanced gender sensitivity can improve even other public projects (which apparently may not have any direct impact on women). The design of a road or a bus stand can also be made to serve the purposes of women, if their issues are taken on board at the designing stage. The gender situation of a context can be taken into account while planning many other governmental schemes. For example, a consideration of the property right of women could be very useful while extending subsidies or support for constructing houses. Gender budgeting—an assessment of the government budget to see how much of the public money is spent on projects that may benefit women directly or indirectly or to address gender discrimination—has become an accepted practice these days. There is also a counter tendency. Since women are known to be taking care of the children better than men, there is a tendency to consider women as the sole intermediaries of poverty eradication schemes. This would only enhance their work burden (and probably encourage indirectly those irresponsible male members of the family.) Thus, care should be exercised in the design of such poverty eradication schemes, and these should not strengthen the gender stereotyping that prevails in society.

We have only mentioned a few strategies to reduce the impact of gender discrimination, and there can be many more such steps required.

Bibliographical Note: The importance of property rights in addressing gender issues in countries like India is discussed in Agarwal (1994). An economist's interpretation of the caste system can be seen in Akerlof (1976).

QUESTIONS

1. Can you search for the data on people below the poverty line in India according to social group? Do you see any relationship between the incidence of poverty and social identity in the country?

2. Which could be the most important strategy, according to you, to address the discrimination against specific social groups that is yet to disappear from India?

3. Which indicator of development captures well the gender discrimination that exists in India? Use the data on this indicator to give us the current picture in this regard.

4. Many people are surprised that dowry exists in the country despite making it illegal. What is your response in this regard?

5. Can you recall the most telling experience of gender discrimination that you have encountered or witnessed? What can public policy do in this regard?

6. We are concerned about the increasing incidence of domestic violence in the country. Politicians and lawyers are asking for a stringent law against domestic violence. What would be your suggestion as someone who has studied economics?

7. Even in a state like Kerala with higher levels of human development, some social sections like Scheduled Tribes have not progressed significantly in terms of development. Scheduled Castes have not benefitted much from the employment opportunities in the West Asian countries. How would you analyse this situation?

SIXTEEN

ECONOMICS OF ENVIRONMENTAL IMPACT

—◦•◦•◦—

It is known that economic activities of production and consumption create an environmental impact. These reduce the overall welfare of the society. However, it is an issue of distribution too since a major part of the cost of such environmental impact is going to be borne by future generations. Environmental impact poses a serious threat to the sustainability of development. Hence, a discussion on environmental issues has to be part of any course of development. But the purpose of this chapter is limited. It talks about the economists' understanding of environmental problems or the depletion of natural resources and their solutions. Such an understanding may not provide a complete picture of the nature of environmental impact and how we can meet the challenge in this regard.

NATURAL RESOURCES AND ECONOMIC GROWTH

The idea that the scarcity of natural resources may apply a break on economic growth was there in the nineteenth century itself and was discussed by classical economists like Malthus and Ricardo. It also attracted attention during the second half of the twentieth century when the limits to growth (it was also the title of a report prepared by a group of thinkers called the Club of Rome) were a major concern. This idea is very much there in the minds of many environmental activists today. Will the absolute reduction in the availability of any specific natural resource (say timber or petroleum fuels) reduce the opportunities for global economic growth?

Economic growth is the increase in the value of the economic activities carried out in a region every year. The price of a natural resource, which has become scarce due to its use, increases if its market is reasonably well developed and also when its price is determined, by and large, in a competitive market. Such an increase will reflect in the economic valuation of the resource. If it is an output, the production of the same amount of the output becomes more valuable. If the resource is used as an input, it will reflect in the cost of production and hence the profits.

An increase in the relative price of a natural resource will make it costlier as an input to production and consumption. This may encourage the substitution of this input by other cheaper inputs. When fuel prices went up, demand for smaller cars increased. Moreover, the increased cost of one input can also encourage the technical progress which tries to save or reduce its use. Such instances of saving energy were noticed when its prices shot up. As a specific natural resource becomes scarcer and scarcer, its value in the economic production/consumption process goes up, and it is likely to induce response strategies including the reduced use of it, or a technical change trying to save such a scarce resource.

This is visible in the case of land too. Land is a fixed resource. Thus if we use the same technology and there is population growth, land per capita (or food production per capita) would decline. This may lead to technological changes which would increase food from a given parcel of land. This may be possible by substituting capital or energy in the place of land in agricultural production. The Green Revolution is an example in this regard. Here more energy or intermediate inputs like fertilizers along with science-based knowledge are used to increase grain production in a given unit of land. If agricultural productivity in conventional rice cultivation (traditional varieties with manure with little or no use of machines and irrigation) is around two tons per hectare, it may go up to four tons per hectare with high-yielding varieties, chemical fertilizers, irrigation, tractors and so on. It may be noted that in the case of modern farming, though more is produced from the same area of land, more of other inputs (like more energy in the production of fertilizers and the use of tractors, more capital in the creation and maintenance of irrigation projects, and more human capital for the creation of newer varieties and extension services) are used.

However, there are many reasons why such market-driven adjustment of price may not take place in the case of some natural resources. First, in many countries, the prices of such natural resources like petroleum fuels are determined by the government (through the provision of indirect subsidies). This would mean that even if the actual price of natural resources goes up, users may not feel the pinch. Hence, they may continue to use it at the same level and they do not have adequate incentive to substitute it with other inputs.

There is not much competition in the case of some other resources. It may be that only a few countries are producing it and production can also be under a government-owned company. Even when a number of countries are involved in production, there can also be 'cartels' of them deciding the quantity of production so as to see that prices do not come down drastically. The most well-known cartel in this regard is the Organization of Petroleum Exporting Countries (OPEC). When production is carried out by a monopoly, the pricing/production need not reflect the actual demand. (Remember the discussion on monopoly as part of the 'Analytical Box of Economics'.)

ECONOMICS OF ENVIRONMENTAL POLLUTION

Some economic activities or the use of some natural resources cause environmental pollution. This may include the discharge of waste water into rivers, the emission of carbon dioxide into the atmosphere, too much use of fertilizer polluting soils and water bodies and so on. This is taken as a negative externality in economics (and it is defined in Chapter 5). Pollution imposes costs on others, but these costs are not borne by the person creating pollution or the person who uses the specific natural resource. That the polluter does not have to pay for the damages created by pollution is viewed as a fundamental problem. If the person polluting has to pay for (or suffer) damages, he/she has an incentive to pollute only up to the level where the benefits of additional pollution outweighs the costs due to it. What are these benefits of pollution? See the discussion next.

Costs of Controlling Pollution and Optimal Pollution

We all know that there are costs due to pollution. For example, if a local stream is polluted by the discharge from a factory, it may create costs of several kinds: people cannot use water for washing (or they may need more amount of soap for a clean wash) or bathing, fish and other organisms in the river may die, the health of animals or cattle using stream water may be affected, and in certain cases, pollution may cause diseases to the people who use water for washing or agricultural purposes and hence they have to incur costs due to ill health. However, there are also costs to avoiding pollution. The factory which discharges waste into the river may have to install and operate pollution control equipment and/or they may have to reduce the production in the factory. When production of a commodity/service is reduced, it may affect not only the producer, but also the consumers. (See the discussion on producer and consumer surplus.) In a situation where people are unemployed or underemployed, the reduction in production in some factories may create losses for workers too. All these can be counted as losses due to controlling pollution. These need to be considered for judging the 'desirable' level of pollution.

We can look at this issue in another way too. Assume that there is only one small production unit (say a diary farm) in a village. Part of the waste from this unit (cattle dung and urine) reaches the local water body. If this water body is sufficiently large, and the amount of waste reaching it is small, it may not create any significant environmental problem because the water body has a cleansing ability. But as the discharge goes up, the level of damage can also go up. Let us now consider the cost of controlling this pollution. If the purpose is to see that not even a small amount of waste particles reach the water body, very sophisticated equipment is needed. On the other hand, if pollution is already high with most of the dung/urine of the cattle farm reaching the water body, a relatively simple measure of separating out the solid waste (dung) would reduce the pollution significantly. Thus the relationship between the extent of pollution control and the cost of controlling it may follow a pattern where the costs shoot up as you want to reduce the pollution to a near-zero level. On the other hand, the cost of controlling some level of pollution when it is very high may not be that much.

Let us consider these two points together. When pollution levels are too low, the social costs of pollution are not high; the cost of pollution control is very high when we want to reduce pollution further when it is already lower. In such a situation, the cost of pollution is lower than the costs of controlling pollution and hence, allowing some pollution is socially desirable. Thus, there can be, what is called, an optimal level of pollution, beyond which the additional damage caused by pollution crosses the additional cost of controlling it. It is socially desirable to control pollution when it is greater than this optimal level, and it is not socially desirable to control it when it is lesser than the optimal point. So if a producer has to bear the whole cost of damage caused by pollution, then he/she has the incentive to control pollution to optimal levels.

How does one make the polluter 'internalize' the damages caused by the polluting activity (externality)? This problem becomes a little more complicated when the damage due to pollution is suffered by a large number of people. This is usually the case when a factory pollutes the river or atmosphere and when there are many units of pollution (say like poor-quality motor vehicles) causing damage to the ambient atmosphere. All the 'victims' of pollution may have to come together to restrain the polluter. But there can be coordination problems. (Remember the discussion of public goods here. Controlling pollution becomes a public good.) That would be another reason for the need of social intervention in the case of environmental pollution.

There is also another way of looking at environmental problems in economics. A factory discharges waste into a river which is not owned by anybody. A factory dumping waste on a private property has to get permission from the property owner (on payment or otherwise). This property owner can stop the dumping of waste in her property, if she desires to do so, as per law. However, such a control is not possible in the case of a river or atmosphere since these are not owned by anybody. Thus, there should be ownership of common resources and it is desirable to vest the ownership with some public authorities like the government which can then take action against the polluter.

Ideally, it is for the government/society to see that the party which pollutes (producer) internalizes the social cost of pollution (reflecting the damages that pollution imposes on society), so that the producer has an incentive to take into account these social costs too in his decision on the use of environment/natural resources. If a tax rate on each unit of pollution equal to the additional social damage caused by it can be imposed on the polluter, this should help internalizing the externality fully. This can also be a tax on the use of certain natural resources. Petroleum fuel is one example. Its use results in the emission of many harmful substances, including carbon dioxide (which causes global warming). Anybody using petrol/diesel can be taxed (not only to charge its price reflecting its scarcity) but also to reflect the additional pollution (in the form of carbon dioxide) caused by its use.

When a tax is levied on each unit of pollution, the polluting firm has two options: (a) pollute and pay tax or (b) control or avoid pollution and not pay tax. If controlling is cheaper than tax (per unit of pollution), the firm would opt for (b). Otherwise, option (a) would be taken. Through this, a socially optimal level of pollution can be reached. However, such taxation requires information on the damage imposed by pollution. That takes us to the issue of assessing damages due to pollution.

Assessment of Environmental Damages/Benefits[1]

Impacts have to be measured first in physical terms. Such physical impacts may include the area of burnt forest or of eroded soil, the length of beach damaged, the reduction in the volume of fishery catch, the reduced flow of water, the amount of a specific pollutant in the water, the number of individual members of a species killed and so on. It is usually the scientists and technologists who can provide this information. Economists depend on them for such information. This is followed by a step where such physical quantities are converted into money values. This is to be done by trained economists. Usually they use one or more of the following methods.

Use of Market Prices

Environmental or indirect changes can be valued on the basis of market prices, if available. For example, if the destruction of forest has led to the damage of timber, the market value of timber lost can be assessed. This can be done if such market prices are not distorted, and there exist competitive well-developed markets for timber.

Use of Restoration Costs

In certain cases, the cost of restoring or remediating a lost/damaged environmental asset may give a lower bound estimate of the loss due to environmental impact.

The loss due to the unhygienic disposal of waste can be estimated by the cost of having a proper waste disposal system. However, it should be noted that the loss already suffered (say increased levels of diseases) is not taken into account when we estimate the losses using restoration costs.

Use of Signals from Indirect (Surrogate) Markets

This is an indirect estimate of the goods/services for which there is no direct market by measuring the market prices of related economic goods (surrogate markets). The value of viewing a beach can be assessed by looking at the market for houses, that is, differential prices for houses with and without beach access/view (by controlling for other factors that determine the price of a house).

Direct Assessment of Willingness to Pay

Here, users are consulted through structured questionnaires about the value that they ascribe to the goods/services for which there is no market. However, the time and effort required for using such a method to give reliable results are substantial.

Value-transfer Method

This is a process by which the value of an attribute or of a group of such attributes obtained in one context is used to estimate the values in another context. It is common and accepted in the field of economic valuation. For example, the value of safe drinking water in a village can be assessed by using the values known from studies conducted in similar contexts. The appropriateness of previous studies has to be assessed judiciously. The context of this existing study and that of the new one should be as close as possible, in terms of the magnitude of change, baseline conditions and also the socio-economic features of the population.

We can take some specific examples:

1. Impact on water resources:

    • Damages can be estimated as the value of the project needed to restore the quality and quantity of water to pre-damage levels.

- Losses as the value of production that will not be obtained during the period of damage.
- Cost incurred to provide alternative sources of water since the current source cannot be used.

2. Impact on land:

- Losses can be estimated as the market value of the land (both urban and agricultural), provided these are not distorted by other factors.
- The value of agricultural production that will not be obtained over a long time period (that is, 10 years).
- If the land can be recovered, losses may be estimated as the revenue (urban land) and production (agriculture land) that will not accrue until it fully recovers.

3. Impact on forests:

- 'Losses' estimated as the market value of wood and other related goods (less their production costs).
- In the case of destruction of natural forests, damages may be indirectly estimated as the value of the environmental services (carbon sequestration) that will not be rendered by the forest over a long time period.
- Estimates of willingness to accept compensation for some changes in the quality/quantity of forests.

Such environmental valuation may be useful in some contexts—like cost–benefit analysis of a project (having significant environmental impact) or in cases where compensation for environmental damage is to be determined. But it is very difficult to quantify the environmental damage to determine the tax rate to be imposed on the polluter. Hence such taxation is rarely done.

Another way of making the polluter control pollution is to use certain command and control measures. The government might bring in a law which says that a factory or production unit cannot discharge a specific substance (like sulphuric acid) beyond a particular limit. This is called emission standards. The pollution control laws of India are mostly of this kind. There can also be another kind of standard. This is to insist that any production system should have a pollution control equipment of a particular kind. This may take the form of prescribing the nature (including the technology) of the pollution control system to be established as part of each factory. To some extent, this is the method used in the regulation of pollution from motor vehicles. The advantage of standards is that they are relatively easy to legislate and enforce.

But in countries like India such legislation is poorly enforced due to a number of reasons. Pollution control boards (PCB), which are supposed to take action, do not have adequate resources and manpower. Corruption may also prevent effective action. There is also not much public demand for effective action against polluting units in many parts of India (though once in a while one can see people agitating against some visible polluters). Pollution is carried out not only by the big factories, but large number of motor vehicles and also millions of households which discharge sewage, solid waste, and so on, are also contributing to environmental pollution in countries like India.

Since public enforcement is weak, one can see people taking direct action against polluters like filing public interest litigations or 'civil disobedience' actions like a sit-in strike in front of the polluting factory. Such actions are beneficial in light of the poor enforcement of law. However, institutional deficiencies of the country may make citizens' actions ineffective as polluters use these deficiencies to their advantage.

In an ideal context existing firms would expect enforcement of pollution/emission standards by a public authority or court, without delay, and would therefore impose enforcement on their own. New firms expecting enforcement of standards without delay try to start with pollution at an optimal or standard level. Citizens can expect only the enforcements of standards and thus have to become content with optimal pollution. Citizens are unlikely to take physical action against a polluter because the cost of those actions will be high due to proper law and order enforcement (and probably due to a high opportunity cost of time). On the other hand, institutional weaknesses such as a long delay in court decisions and the low cost of actions of civil disobedience are likely to create a situation in which new firms may find it difficult to establish, if citizens are vigilant to act. This outcome, too, creates social losses, like pollution at higher than optimal levels by existing firms.

Hence citizens' actions (in the form of citizens' suits and actions of civil disobedience) may not be that effective in avoiding the social loss associated with pollution, and may aggravate it under some conditions. Thus such citizens' action

may not compensate for the laxity in public enforcement and hence there is a
need for getting public enforcement right.

SUSTAINABLE DEVELOPMENT

Sustainable development is an overused term these days. Different people interpret it differently. It was first used in 1987 in the report of the World Commission
for Environment and Development (WCED) presided by Gro Harlem Brundtland.
Sustainable development, as defined then, was meeting the needs of the present
without compromising on the needs of future generations. It can be interpreted as
a development path which does not reduce the consumption possibilities of future
generations. It simply means there should not be any reduction in the consumption of future generations due to our use of resources (or they should have at least
the same consumption as that of the current generation). There should be non-
decreasing consumption over time.

Let us consider a family which has some assets from which it gets a regular
income. Its consumption is based on this income. How does it ensure that its
future consumption is not reduced? It should ensure an income in the future that
will at least be sufficient to meet the current level of consumption taking into
consideration inflationary trends. (What we talk about here is the 'real' income
and not the one whose value changes on the basis of inflation.) However, the asset
that gives them the income can 'deteriorate' in quality and this may reduce their
future income. For example, if their assets include a building rented out, its quality may decline; or if their assets included a factory, then the machines there may
depreciate, and so on. Thus if the assets have to yield an income to meet the same
level of consumption in the future, they need to make investments to compensate
for the depreciation in assets. If their asset is knowledge, this knowledge base
may also 'depreciate' and they need to make adequate investment to 'build back
the knowledge base' so that the income that it generates is not declining. This
may require updating knowledge on current developments, possibly through
additional trainings and other efforts. Hence a part of the future income is to be
reinvested to maintain the quality of the assets. Thus there is a need to have a
future income not just to meet the same level of consumption in the future, but
also to maintain the quality of the assets. This is important to ensure that the
asset base is intact.

Let us consider the assets in some more detail to understand another concept. Assume that a family has a building and some land. Two members of the family are educated. This family is thinking about their 'sustainable development'. There is a young girl in the family, and an income earning member who is nearing retirement. Their consumption will come down, if the earning member retires, and if the girl is not educated enough to take up a job. Therefore, the sustenance of the level of consumption of this family depends on the education of this girl. This may require some investment and thus they are planning to sell a part of the land to meet her cost of education. If this works out well, what they have done is to 'liquidate' (lose) one asset (part of land) to create another asset; that is, the education for the girl. If education enhances her income earning capacity, and if this additional income is more than what they would have received from the land sold, then such a liquidation of one asset will not affect their future consumption. What they have done here is to substitute one form of capital asset (land) with another asset (education of the child).

With this analogy we can think about the sustainable development of the world. If we want that our future generations as a whole should not have lesser consumption (compared to what we have today), what is important for us is to maintain the assets. All the natural resources, physical capital, financial capital, human capital and social and cultural capital are part of these assets. But here there can be two views on sustainability. Some view that some substitution of one capital by the other is possible within the framework of sustainable development. It is known as a 'weak sustainability' argument. This would mean that even if some natural resource assets are lost, there could be an increase in human or other forms of capital in order to see that consumption in the future is not declined— like the selling of land to give education for the child. In this view, the total capital asset is more important than their specific components.

There is another view called 'strong sustainability'. Some economists opine that such a substitution of natural capital (say forests) by other forms (like human or physical capital) is not fully possible and hence not desirable. The destruction of some natural assets can have negative impacts on the consumption of future generations and this cannot be compensated by improvements in other capital assets. Hence they argue that protection of some natural assets is unavoidable. They argue that if a specific natural asset (say a part of the forest) is to be destroyed for a development project then there should be an effort to rebuild a similar natural asset elsewhere. The ideas of compensatory afforestation are relevant here.

What is my view on sustainability? Like many other world views, the truth lies somewhere between two opposite ideas. For many capital assets, the idea of substitutability is a relevant one. There may be some natural assets for which a non-compromising position on their conservation may be useful, given our current level of (inadequate) information on their relevance for the future.

ACCOUNTING FOR THE REDUCTION OF NATURAL CAPITAL IN ECONOMIC GROWTH

Another concern is whether we are accounting for the reduction of the natural resources in our estimation of economic growth. For example, a firm may have produced ₹5 lakh as annual profit (revenue minus loss) but has it accounted for the depreciation of its machines? If the machine which costs ₹10 lakh needs to be replaced in 10 years, one should account for about ₹1 lakh per year as depreciation. This will bring down its profit from ₹5 lakh to ₹4 lakh.

One can have the same concern about the natural capital too. When a country achieves a growth rate of 5 per cent, but records a population growth rate of 2 per cent per annum, the real growth rate of per-capita income is only 3 per cent. If this 3 per cent growth rate is achieved in a year with a 2 per cent reduction in its natural capital, the real growth rate of per-capita income is only 1 per cent. For example, a country whose major part of income comes from the timber industry may be cutting down its forests heavily. There is a reduction in the (natural) capital base here and that has to be accounted for to give a measure of real growth. This is where GNP rates need to be adjusted for reductions in natural capital base.

LONG-RUN TRENDS IN ECONOMIC GROWTH VERSUS ENVIRONMENTAL IMPACT

Is the relationship between economic growth and environmental impact a linear one, with negative environmental impact increasing with higher levels of economic growth or development? Economists have hypothesized that this relationship could be one of an inverted U-shape. This implies that if some measure of environmental impact (say the presence of dust particles in the atmosphere) is plotted on the *x* axis and GDP per capita is plotted on the *y* axis, the relationship can be represented with an inverted U. This is called the Environmental Kuznets's Curve, following a similar hypothesis between growth and inequality postulated by Simon Kuznets. (We have mentioned the latter in the chapter on inequality.) It would mean that environmental impact is lower at the early stages of economic development and also at much higher stages. On the other hand, the impact on environment is higher somewhere in between. Thus the environmental impact which is lower at lower levels of GDP increases gradually and reaches a peak, and then comes down as the GDP per capita increases beyond the peak.

What are the reasons for such an expected trend? It is obvious that environmental impact is limited at lower levels of GDP since economic/production activities are also minimal. As growth picks up, there is a consequent increase in the negative impact on environment. However, when GDP per capita is high, there are multiple factors that may encourage more actions to control environmental pollution. The willingness to protect the environment may go up. The environment can be reckoned as another amenity. Just like any other amenity, demand for it or willingness to pay for it, is expected to go up as the incomes of people increase. Thus societies can afford to spend more money to control environmental pollution. They would also be expected to have better technologies or a better technical capacity and knowledge base for this purpose.

However, the actual evidence for this hypothesis is mixed. There is evidence confirming such a relationship for some environmental variables. These include dust particles in the atmosphere, sulphur dioxide and water pollution. Thus societies/countries take efforts to control these environmental problems as their economies grow. To some extent, this is evident from the fact that the cities of the developed world could improve their local environmental status compared with the situation nearly 30–40 years ago. The problem of acid rain, which was once an important environmental issue, could be brought under control in the developed world. Most of the highly polluted cities are currently located in the developing world.

However, no such relationship was found existing between the emission of carbon dioxide and economic growth. The use of motor vehicles increases as per-capita income goes up and the developed world continues to be a major contributor to global warming created by the emission of carbon dioxide. International collaboration worked to some extent in controlling substances like Chloro-Fluro Carbons (CFC), which have created another global environmental problem—depletion of the ozone layer in the atmosphere.

There is a view that developed countries can reduce environmental pollution in their own territory by 'exporting' their pollution to the developing world. This 'export' can take place in different forms. First, certain highly polluting industries can shift their production to developing countries. Second, developed countries depend on poorer countries for their requirement of natural resources. Thus, European countries may reduce the extraction of timber in their territories but may import it from Indonesia or Latin American countries. Third, urban solid waste from the developed world may reach the shores of a few poorer countries or damaged ships with hazardous materials may reach the shores of countries like India for decommissioning and dismantling, and so on.

We should not underestimate some of the domestic factors of developing countries like India which encourage the import of such waste and dirty industries. We need to create employment and so people are deployed to work even in such hazardous and polluting production systems. The enforcement of environmental laws here is weaker (despite having strong laws), and that facilitates the establishment of polluting industries here. Not many people demand stricter enforcement of environmental legislation, indicating the willingness to tolerate pollution to some extent. Thus these internal factors may encourage 'import of pollution'. A way out is the economic development of these countries making substantial sections of their population to demand effective pollution control.

Bibliographical note: There are many accessible books giving the ideas of economics on environmental and natural resource management. One book that this author found useful is Russell (2001). Some of the applications of the theory in Indian context can be seen in Santhakumar and Chakraborty (2003) and Santhakumar (2003).

QUESTIONS/EXERCISES

1. Gather information on the actual price of LPG in India. What is the price at which it is supplied to Indian consumers? Which sections of Indian consumers use LPG? Are they poor? Discuss.

2. Think about a case of pollution which you know directly. Use the economics framework to understand it.

3. Read any one law used by India to control pollution of water or air. Comment on the law based on what you have read in this chapter.

4. What are the advantages in using standards instead of taxes to control pollution?

5. What are the prospects and limitations of citizens' actions used to control pollution in India?

NOTE

1. This part is taken from a manual prepared by the author for the post-conflict/ disaster unit of the United Nations Environment Programme.

PART V

BEYOND INDIVIDUALS AND HOUSEHOLDS

≈ SEVENTEEN ≈

THE ROLE OF GOVERNMENT

———•◆•———

We have seen in Chapter 4 that there are some circumstances where iso-
lated actions of individuals need not lead to the most desirable outcomes
for society. The case of bringing electricity to a village, cleaning public places,
the need to certify that a particular commodity or service meets the requirement
of a standard, are examples. Thus we need an agency, something beyond individuals, to coordinate the provision of such goods and services. A village council or the local government, residents' association, a state or a national
government or even an international organization like the United Nations (UN)
are performing some of these functions. For each of these goods and services,
there may be an appropriate form of government (or meta-individual agency)
which may be most suited. Thus, the cleaning of the rural market may be
arranged by the village council or local government; the provision of policing
may be carried out by the district or state government; the protection of national
boundaries is to be performed by the national government; and it may be the
UN which is appropriate to see that fishermen from different countries do not
indulge in competitive fishing that leads to the depletion of fish stock in different seas.

In general, any government has to play three important roles. These can be
broadly listed as follows:

1.   Addressing market failure (see Chapter 4)
2.   Redistribution
3.   Maintaining the rule of law.

We will consider (2) and (3) here in some detail.

DISTRIBUTIONAL ROLE OF GOVERNMENT

There are different ways of viewing the distributional role of the government. One way is to consider that the government plays a benevolent role while trying to enhance what can be called social welfare. In that sense, there will be some sections in any society who may fail to meet (on their own) certain basic standards of consumption set by the society and the role of the redistribution is to help these sections. Thus poverty eradication can be an element of such redistribution. But giving food to a hungry person (or meeting the basic day-to-day consumption) is not sufficient. For some people like the aged, disabled or mentally challenged, continuous support may be unavoidable. But there are many people who cannot meet their basic consumption needs even when they do not have any such disability. A better way to help such people is to enable them to meet their consumption on their own. It may be needed to give them work in the short run but probably they may have to be enabled to acquire work in the long run (by helping them to acquire necessary skills).

There can also be another way to see the redistribution. Governments can take shape or sustain themselves only when there is some wider acceptance of its power. How does it derive its power? One can think about a cruel dictator ruling a society solely with the help of guns and army. But he may have to distribute some resources to his army and otherwise they can train their gun on the dictator. Thus even for the dictator to survive, there is a need for redistribution. This is much more obvious in a democracy. It requires majority support in elections. This support may be achieved through direct or indirect redistribution to some sections of society. It could be the reduction of taxes to the rich or middle class, if they are giving the majority support. On the other hand, if these sections are in the minority and winning elections would require the support of the workers, poor and the 'underclass', there can be more taxes for the rich. A part of this revenue may be used for redistribution to the former. There can be some specific groups (and they

can be from anywhere in the income spectrum) whose support may be more crucial to get majority support for specific political parties in a multi-party competitive democracy. There would be redistribution to these groups. However,
competition in a democracy determines or sets the limits or outer boundaries of
such redistribution. If one group feels that too much is taken from them to give
too much to the other, there can be efforts that may tilt the balance in power. Thus,
the party which is concerned about redistribution to a specific group is also
restrained by the discomfort that it imposes on others. However, if the society is
clearly divided by a minority of the rich and the majority of the poor, a democratically elected government has the incentive to tax the rich heavily and redis-
tribute these resources to the poor.

Whether it is due to social welfare considerations or for reasons of
political legitimacy, redistribution is likely to be an important function of any
government.

RULE OF LAW

The third function of the government is to maintain the rule of law. This can also
be seen as a public good which cannot be provided by individuals at socially
desirable levels. However, law and order is a higher order public good, since
almost everything that is needed for development would depend on it. Even a
view of politics, which sees only a minimal role for the government, would consider the provision of rule of law as a fundamental role of the government. Thus,
individuals cannot purse their freedom or private action without such a rule of
law. Protection of private property rights is an important part of this rule of law.
Without private property rights, individuals cannot derive the benefits of their
efforts and hence they may not be interested in pursuing wealth creation. This can
have negative impacts on economic growth. To a great extent, it is the lack of the
rule of law that makes many African countries backward in terms of economic
and social development.

APPROPRIATE NATURE OF THE GOVERNMENT

What is the appropriate role of the government, is a hotly contested issue (not
much among economists) but mostly among political parties, civil society and

also among social scientists. One can see some areas of agreement. I do not think that anybody today envisages an all encompassing state like that of the old socialist countries. There is also a general acceptance of the need for democracy. Even if democracy may not lead to desirable development outcomes quickly, democracy is valuable in itself. Moreover, democracy may have greater in-built strengths to correct the mistakes of the dictatorial rulers. The consensus view on the government is that it should allow sufficient freedom for individuals and private entrepreneurs and it should enable markets to function to meet the demands of most of the private goods and services needed by the people. The role of the government is to regulate markets, wherever such regulation is needed for rational reasons, and where government regulation does not worsen the situation. Governments have to take the main role in providing public goods, even though there can be some private or non-governmental action in this regard. It is also expected that governments will play a redistributive role. The degree of focus on such redistribution may vary between different political parties and this can determine whether a party is left of centre, centrist or right of centre. Even the most leftist party may not think about a government which has complete control over the economy, and a situation where market exchange is absent. The existing socialist countries, like China and Vietnam too, have moved substantially towards a market economy. Cuba has started transition in this direction. North Korea is the only country where the economy is under full government control, and it is hardly a model for other countries.

How Do Governments Get Money for Their Functions?

All forms of government (and its primitive form can be a mafia protecting commercial activities in an area) 'tax' people or beneficiaries of their protection as a reward for the services offered to them. In many cases, people would be willing to pay taxes and have some protection, since anarchy can be very costly. Thus, taxes are the main source of income for governments. In certain cases, government collects user charges to meet the full or part of the cost of providing a service directly. For example, we pay a fee to get a passport from the government (and it is a real government service—giving you national identification). There can be some assets owned by the government like land, mines, public sector companies, some money deposited in banks or bonds and the returns from such assets could also be another source of income.

Thinking about taxes itself is an important sub-discipline in economics. This is an area where specialized knowledge is needed for practice. Hence, this book does not intend to cover this area in detail. But some important issues are touched upon here. Taxes are of two kinds. Income tax is considered a direct tax, whereas the tax that we pay to the government while buying a commodity or service in addition to its price is part of indirect taxes. It is easy to assess who takes the burden of direct taxes (and who is the payee). But it is not clear who shares the burden of the indirect taxes, because in some circumstances, the consumers need not bear the cost of such taxes. The burden may fall on producers or suppliers of such services.

This is based on the nature of the supply and demand conditions. Take an item whose consumption is not reduced, or cannot be reduced, even when the price goes up. Here the burden of full tax may fall on the consumer. On the other hand, think of a commodity with a higher price elasticity. In this case, a greater part of the burden may have to be borne by the producer. This is so since the increase in the price may encourage the consumers to reduce consumption of that commodity, and this may reduce the surplus enjoyed by the producer. Thus, the actual incidence of the indirect tax may depend on the market condition, that is, the elasticity of supply and demand curves.

Imposing a tax on society has costs and benefits. The benefit is that it can be used for providing useful governmental services and other public goods. The cost has different dimensions. The tax has to be collected, and there should be record keeping and monitoring. There should be some system of verifying whether all tax payers have paid the tax due. There should be cost/effort to trace the defaulters and to punish them if they do not pay tax even after repeated notifications. However, there is another important cost of taxing. This is so since people may change the behaviour in such a way that they do not have to pay the expected tax. This may reduce the tax revenue from the expected levels. However, we may note that under certain conditions, the objective of tax itself is to reduce the consumption of a specific commodity. For example, the taxes on cigarettes or alcohol are generally high to see that their consumption is reduced. Such reduction is the purpose of pollution taxes too. Hence the change in behaviour is not that undesirable in all contexts.

However, unexpected changes in behaviour can upset tax calculations of the government. What if higher rates of income tax encourage people not to increase (or to reduce) their income-earning work? For example, professionals may reduce the number of hours of work. Entrepreneurs may not invest in new projects. This may reduce not only the tax income for the government but also the economic activity and employment in a locality. There is a trade-off between leisure and work in employment. More work would mean less leisure. Hence some people may reduce (the number of hours of) work if their income from work goes up. (They may not be willing to toil 13 or 15 hours a day.) Under such a condition, a tax on wage can be equivalent to a reduction in their wage and then such people may be willing to do more work.

Thus if revenue increase is the main objective, then the tax should be designed in such a way that a change in behaviour reducing the tax payment does not take place. Such a change in behaviour is called distortion. It is generally considered that lump-sum taxes (like the one which says that every adult should pay a fixed amount per year as tax) are the least distorting ones. This is so since there is nothing that the tax payer can do to avoid paying such a tax. There are also other problems with income tax. Why should income be taxed, since higher income would also mean higher savings and that would help more investments or growth of the economy (which would benefit others in terms of jobs)? Some would argue for taxing consumption, but that is much more difficult (if we are not using indirect taxes). Thus, there are a number of issues of administration and these may determine the choice of the tax system even if that creates certain distortions.

In countries like India, there are also enforcement issues. People may not pay tax, and it may be too difficult to trace them. Even if tax officials locate such defaulters, there may be corruption and other such malpractices which may enable them to get away by not paying the due tax. Thus improving the enforcement of tax collection is an important issue in countries like ours. Only a smaller share of the population pays income tax in developing countries. Increasing the tax-base may not be socially acceptable due to the perception that a majority belongs to poorer or vulnerable sections. There is reluctance among politicians to tax agricultural income based on the perception that farmers constitute another set of the vulnerable population (and because of that farmers with large farm sizes are also exempted from taxation). However, governments need money, and given the difficulty in imposing direct taxes, the tendency is to depend heavily on indirect taxes. In general almost the whole population may have to bear the burden of indirect taxes, even though there are attempts to avoid taxes on basic goods like food grains.

How Do Governments Assess the Needs of the People?

In the case of private goods (like a soap or ready-made shirt), the market itself communicates the information on the demand of consumers to the producers. If a particular suppliers' good is not liked by the consumers, they will stop buying that product. (This is called an exit option.) Such an exit of consumers sends signals to the producers. However, such a process is not feasible for many governmental services. There can be market surveys. These may include questions such as the following: are you willing to pay a given amount to buy a new product (for example, soap)? They will not get the soap if they are not willing to pay for it and hence they have an incentive to reveal their actual willingness to pay.

Consider the nature of public goods. They are non-excludable and indivisible. Hence if a street light is provided, many people may use it and one person's use may not make it unavailable to the other. It is difficult to exclude somebody from using the street light. Thus it is costly to collect a user charge. Thus people may get the benefit of a street light without paying for it. They know that they can get the benefit even without paying for it once it is provided. Thus, if somebody is surveying the demand for a public good like street lights, people may have an interest in saying that they want them without considering their actual willingness to pay. This is so since they know that once it is provided, they can enjoy it without paying for it, and hence they may not take into account their future cost in expressing the desire to have such a good.

There are occasions where such surveys are required (and are advocated) to assess the demand for public goods. If there is a plan for a new major road, it is useful to do a survey of the existing traffic (and factors that may enhance traffic in the future) and then to extrapolate the traffic for the next 50 years or so, and this may be useful to judge whether the benefits in terms of reduction in distance or traffic jams justify the investments required for the road. This is also true for some other services provided by the government like piped water supply.

However, in the real world and especially in a rural setting, information on the demand for governmental services usually passes through the political route. There is an elected representative to whom people may inform their needs, and he/she in turn communicates it to the officials or ministers formally or informally. The ministers and/or officials may allocate public resources based on the demands made or the influence wielded by a particular representative. Since not all demands are met, many demands are raised hoping that at least some of them would be fulfilled.

Even if a government official is not doing what he/she is supposed to do, people may approach the elected representative or other politicians. (Some people may bribe the officials without approaching the politicians. But the bribe can be for speeding up the work if an official is intentionally delaying the action; or for encouraging him to do what he is not supposed to do like issuing a driving license without a proper test. Thus, we will not consider corruption here.) What if an elected representative or a political party is indifferent to the demands of a section of people? Here there are two potential strategies: one short term and the other long term. The short-term strategy is to raise the 'voice'—conduct processions, marches and sit-in strikes to make the government listen to their demands. The long-term strategy is to vote against such a government, for which people have to wait till the end of its term. (In not so democratic situations, it is not so uncommon to see people resorting to civil disobedience or violent actions to throw out an existing government.)

Thus voting is an important way of communicating people's demands. Political parties compete with a wider set of agenda and the vote is for or against this set of issues, and here one particular demand cannot get much attention. In some countries, there may be a referendum on some major policy issues—whether to have a nuclear power station or not—but it is not common in countries like India. The costs may be too high; and many people may not have adequate information. Therefore, it is obvious that generating actual information on the demand for public services is not that easy.

DIFFERENT LEVELS OF GOVERNMENT

There are different tiers of government—starting from local, then at the state level and finally at the central or national level. Town or city areas are governed by municipalities or corporations. Why should there be different levels of government? What should be the function of each tier of government? Economics provide some insights into these questions.

For its functioning, a government should know the demands or the needs of the people (which we have discussed earlier) and also ensure that a particular need is met at a minimum cost. This assures efficiency and enhances social welfare because when the government is efficient, people need to pay only less tax and there will be more money left with them to pursue other wants. Given the difficulties in assessing the needs of the people, there is a perception that governments which are closer to the people acquire correct information on the actual needs. This is an important reason for decentralization or the formation of local governments. There are two dimensions to the cost issue. First, the government needs to know what is the best way of meeting the demand of the people. For example, if people in a village need an additional source of water supply and if there is a local source of water, the development of this source may be the best way of solving their water problem. Thus local information is needed to know about the alternative ways of meeting the demand of the people. This is yet another rationale for decentralization.

However, there is also a scale issue. Certain goods and services can be supplied cheaper if these are produced or distributed on a large scale. Think about a drought-prone area. Here solving the drinking water problem may require the construction of a large reservoir and laying of pipes to build a distribution network covering the whole district or a number of districts. This may work out to be the cheaper way of solving the water problem. On the other hand, if each village attempts to solve it through the development of a local source, it may not be a fully reliable source during the summer and needs supplementary sources like water distribution by tankers. Thus, the total cost of supplying water to all these villages may become higher than what would have been the cost for a centralized system. This is the manifestation of the economy of scale. The implication is that the water problem in this case should be solved by the district or state government and not by the village or local government.

In general, a particular governmental service is to be provided at the level at which it can be provided cheaply. This should be the basic principle in allocating different government services to different tiers of the government. In fact, one can consider this as a principle for individuals and households too. Thus, if something can be carried out efficiently at the individual level, it should be done at that level. The same logic applies for the households too. Only those activities which cannot be carried out efficiently at the level of individuals or households need to be brought to the public domain. This is called the principle of subsidiarity.

It may be possible for some people to locate their residence based on local governments. There was an idea that local governments can be disciplined by the people who 'vote by feet'. If a particular government has a combination of taxes and public goods, not liked by a voter (say according to him more tax and/or less amount of public goods), he may choose another territory where that combination is closer to his choice. This may be possible in contexts where people are willing to relocate their residences (to some extent this is visible in the US), but such relocation may not be that common in countries like India. Thus voting by feet may not be relevant for many of us.

PROBLEMS OF LOCAL GOVERNMENTS IN COUNTRIES LIKE INDIA

Governance in a context depends on democratization. For example, if there is one landlord and most people in a village depend on him for survival, the level of democratization in that village council is limited. People may support (or may not oppose) the landlord, as the head of the village council. There can be several situations where such a small section of the elite enjoys greater economic and social power (say as the upper caste or as priests), and this may translate into political power.

The implication is that governance in such a context can be captured by the elites. The public resource allocation in such a context may be determined by the interests of these elite. It is not that they will not give anything to the ruled. But who among the ruled would get, and how much they would get and so on, are determined by the elites. It may be necessary for the ruled to be visibly supporting the elites to get a share of the public resources. There are many villages in countries like India with such a social context. On the other hand, politics at the national level or at the state level have shown a greater degree of democratization and competition. This is so since there is a sizable section of the articulate middle class, and they are not heavily dependent on any particular section of elites there.

Thus there was a concern that if the powers of the central or state governments were decentralized up to the village level, the elite would capture public resources. Uttar Pradesh was an example in this regard. But even such states are now witnessing rapid changes in terms of democratization with middle and lower caste groups asserting their political rights. It is, however, a slow process. Elites need not be seen merely in terms of social or economic groups. There can also be a gender issue. For example, even when a woman gets the benefit of reservation for the position of village-council head, there are cases where she cannot exercise powers and most of the decisions are taken by her husband or sons. Similarly, elites can also be people belonging to a particular religion or caste, so that resources for people from other castes/religions may depend on the benevolence of the former. If a particular political party is very powerful, people who do not align with it openly may not get enough public resources. There was some evidence of this kind from the state of West Bengal.

Thus development outcomes may depend on the extent of democratization. If negotiation for political power and public resources works against the poor in certain contexts, the development outcomes may be biased against them. Similarly, decentralization may have an impact on inequality. The elite capturing power itself may lead to enhanced inequality to the extent that it depends on the allocation of public resources at the local level. Moreover, different outcomes in different villages in a state, depending on the level of the elite capture in each village, would mean that there can be unequal development across different villages.

Local governments have to generate some taxes locally. But it is necessary to collect some taxes like income tax or even indirect taxes at the central or state levels. This minimizes the possibility of territorial shifting of an economic activity to avoid the payment of taxes. Moreover, there may be some economy of scale in tax collection and enforcement machinery. It may be cheaper (for a given amount of taxes) to collect when there is networked state-wide or nation-wide tax collection machinery. That is why local governments usually tax buildings or employment, on which they have better information. Here, scale economy in tax enforcement may not be relevant. However, for other taxes, collection by the state and central government is needed.

This would imply that higher tiers of the government have to transfer some of the taxes that they have collected to local governments. That is why we have state-level finance commissions to fix the allocation rule for sharing such resources. (We have a Central Finance Commission to decide the allocation between the central and state governments.) This would mean that some money for local activities come from the 'above'. In fact, for most local governments in India, a major part of the money comes from higher levels of governments as a transfer. This creates complex issues. If most of the money that a government spends comes from its own voters, there is a greater incentive to be disciplined in terms of expenditure—to see that money is spent to meet the real needs of the people. When money comes from somewhere else, there may not be adequate incentives among the voters to see that it is spent for really useful ends.

At one level, if the local governments are more prone (compared with state and national governments) to be captured by the interest groups, it may have a bearing on the effectiveness of poverty eradication programmes. If local governments have the power to set the criteria and identify the poor, they may spend resources thinly on many individuals including on some non-poor. There may be an incentive under some situations to spend excessively on such individual-oriented schemes and less than adequately on public goods. In that case, it may be desirable for the higher levels of government to set the criteria for identifying the poor and only the actual implementation is left to the local governments. In essence, the crucial insight from economics is that one should not view decentralization in a moralistic framework as a desirable one in each and every context. It may or may not enhance efficiency and effectiveness depending on a number of contextual factors.

Bibliographical Note: An accessible book on the role of government and its incentive problems is Stiglitz (2000).

QUESTIONS

1. Why do we need a government? Do you have a more informed answer to this question after reading this chapter? Describe.
2. What is the role of redistribution in democratic societies?
3. What makes the producers share the burden of certain commodity taxes even when it is charged at the time of its sale?
4. Certain taxes may not bring in the revenues expected by the government. Why?
5. What are the difficulties for the government to get the information on the demand for public goods?
6. What is the principle of subsidiarity? What is the justification for decentralization of governance?

7. A company producing biscuits has a method of understanding the demand for its product. A government providing water supply may have to use other means to assess the demand for the services it provides. What are these other means and how do these have an impact on the efficiency of provision of water supply?

8. Local governments collect tax from the buildings and organizations located within its territory. It does not collect tax on the income of the people living there. Is there any economic logic behind such tax collection? Explain.

⊰ EIGHTEEN ⊱

GOVERNMENT FAILURE AND
NON-GOVERNMENT ACTIONS

———•◦•———

We have discussed in the previous chapter that there are certain activities for which voluntary exchange or the market is not adequate to maximize social welfare, and hence a meta-individual agency like the government needs to intervene. However, the basic assumption here is that the government has an interest to intervene with the objective of enhancing social welfare. In fact, a substantial part of economics which deals with the provision of public goods and so on, has viewed government as a benevolent dictator whose sole objective is the maximization of social welfare. But in reality such benevolent dictators are rarely seen. What is visible in most circumstances (and desirable to some extent) is democracy. There are some checks and balances in a democracy and unsatisfied citizens can vote against a government at the end of its term. We have seen the difficulties in assessing the real demands of citizens and also the possibility of capture of governments by elites or some other groups. Thus, in reality, one can see many governments failing to do what they are supposed to do. These failures may manifest in providing inefficient public services (at costs greater than what is required, and hence putting too much tax or debt burden on the people) or not providing public services adequately or by pursuing policies that may reduce incomes or private consumption.

POSSIBILITY OF GOVERNMENT FAILURE

Why do governments fail? Those who are in the government are also individuals. They may have their self-interest. Their main concern may be to maximize their own gains. Maximizing own gains for these officials and politicians need not go hand-in-hand with the maximization of social gains. For example, a typical objective of an elected politician is to get re-elected to the legislature/parliament. He may take actions that may help re-election. The election result can be influenced by some sections and hence he/she may have to focus on their interest. Such a focus need not always be in the interest of the society as a whole.

The relationship between citizens and elected representatives is like the one between a principal and an agent, which we have mentioned in Chapter 6. Any principal–agent relationship has a challenge—how to make the agent act in a way desired by the principal. However, the principal–agent relationship in politics is much more complex and here the challenge gets magnified. A politician can reach a position to deliver a public service only when a large number of people hire (vote for) him. Thus his interest in one voter may be insignificant, and one voter's ability to discipline the politician by voting for or against him is also very small. There are multiple principal–agent relationships here. The politician is an agent of citizens and ministers become the agents of elected representatives, and officials become the agents of ministers and there are multiple levels of officialdom. The divergence, if any, between the objective of a principal and that of an agent gets widened because of these multiple principal–agent relationships. Thus, what a section of citizens want and what is delivered by a government official could be very different.

Another problem of inefficiency encountered in the government can be understood while comparing it with private companies. In a private company, if a commodity or service is produced with lower cost (without compromising on quality—since if quality is poor due to cost savings, then people may not buy it and hence the owner may incur losses), the owner(s) of the company can take the unspent money. This will increase their net profit. In the case of an employee in a private company, if his/her action has led to a reduction of cost, the owner has an incentive to give him/her bonuses (as the owner gains directly from such actions of employees). However, in the case of government/public officials, even if their actions lead to cost reduction, they will not gain from such savings. They are not 'residual claimants'. Thus, their incentive to achieve efficiency is minimal and they need not be very careful in their decisions on how to use inputs or how to make investments and so on, as part of supplying public services.

This problem is well known. In order to avoid efficiency losses due to such a problem in government/public organizations, elaborate rules are made to make officials cost conscious. This can sometimes be counterproductive. If a private company has to have a small refrigerator for its operations, it may buy one from the nearby shop; all that the owner wants is a reasonably good fridge at the cheapest price. On the other hand, a government official would go in for a fridge that gives him the maximum commission. Even if the fridge develops a problem after a few months, the official does not lose much under normal circumstances. Thus there will be an elaborate rule which says that tenders have to be invited, quotes of price have to be obtained from a number of sellers, screening should be done on the basis of quality and the one which costs the least among the screened has to be selected. This can be a cumbersome procedure and may take time. Thus there can be an additional cost due to the non-availability of a fridge in time. Such a cumbersome procedure is needed for hiring all inputs including labour.

If a private company tries to sell a product which is not bought by many clients, it will incur losses. This may lead to its closing down, if corrective actions are not taken. On the other hand, a government organization need not close down, even if its products lose customers. This is so since the government may be providing budget provisions for meeting the cost of this organization. Thus, the market disciplining of closing down inefficient firms does not operate in the case of public organizations. This is called soft budget constraint. The persistent operation of bankrupt organizations of the public sector can increase inefficiency. It is not that every government/public organization should make revenues greater than costs. There can be such organizations providing a service free of cost (due to some well articulated and genuine social concerns). However, such organizations should get money from the government directly (through budgetary support). But this can become a reason for not reviewing the contemporary relevance of an organization, and hence even if its current form is inappropriate, the reshaping of the organization may become difficult. For example, the number of children going to the government or government-aided schools in Kerala (which has a wide network of schools providing access to almost all villages) has been coming down during the last decade due to the demographic change (absolute reduction in the number of children in the population) and also the flow of children towards fee-paying private schools. Despite this, any change in the government or government-financed schools (including the closing down of some) is politically very difficult to implement. All these factors may increase the cost of government intervention (beyond what is really needed) and enhance inefficiency.

In certain cases, the issue may not be the inefficiency of government intervention but the lack of adequate government action. There are many cases where the government fails to provide adequate public facilities like roads, bridges, airports, harbours, water supply, waste cleaning and so on. This is primarily because either enough tax is not collected (somebody benefits when tax is not collected) or a greater part of whatever is collected is spent on (or redistributed to) some specific sections. Thus governments do not have adequate money to provide public utilities. But there is also a view that the main role of a government is to give food, clothes, TV, laptop and so on to all sections of people. But an economist may view these as private goods and feel that the role of the government in this regard is to be limited to ensure that everybody can afford to buy basic goods like food.

When governments do not have adequate money for the provision of public services, there is a tendency to depend on private companies (with or without the participation by the government) even for services such as roads, airports and so on. Though such private provision of public goods is useful, in a context where adequate public goods are not provided (due to the governments' incapacity), there can be long-term problems such as the emergence of monopoly power for these private companies (which cannot be restrained easily even by public partnership in such private investments. We will take up some of these issues in Chapter 19). There can be some economic losses too. For example, consider toll roads. Once a road is built, the marginal cost of using this road by one more vehicle is near zero, especially if there is no congestion. But a toll road has to collect toll even if only one vehicle is using the road. Let us assume that the toll is ₹100. When there is no congestion, a vehicle willing to pay ₹45 will not be allowed to use the toll road, even though the additional social cost of that vehicle's use of the road is near zero. Thus there is a social loss. Toll roads can be inefficient in many ways. But when the governments do not have money to build roads, and when such needed roads are not built, there is a much greater social loss. Even though toll roads create social loss, the absence of adequate roads is costlier to society. Thus toll roads can be seen as a not-so-desirable alternative to a situation where governments are unable to construct enough roads using tax money.

On the other hand, a toll to avoid or minimize congestion is desirable. In this case, the toll is a tax imposed on the vehicle which creates congestion on the road. Congestion becomes costly for all vehicles or there is a social cost due to congestion. Thus toll can be an instrument to minimize congestion. There are technical mechanisms which assess congestion in a road on a real-time basis and by using them, an appropriate amount of toll can be imposed. Here toll serves a socially useful purpose.

In summary, even though there is a genuine rationale for the government intervention, its failure is also very common. It may fail to provide public services efficiently or adequately.

RESPONSES TO GOVERNMENT FAILURE

The awareness about government failure is widespread these days. There are two types of responses to this failure. First is the attempt to reform the government or governance. However, such governance reforms have not been very successful in many developing countries. There is a greater realization today that governance reforms cannot be analysed separately from the political economy. Hence these issues will be discussed in a later chapter.

The other response is to depend on non-governmental actions for the provision of goods/services which are supposed to be provided by the government. Such non-governmental actors, communities, altruistic individuals and organizations (like religious foundations) and private companies have been providing a certain level of public goods and services even before the establishment of formal governments in most parts of the world. They continue to play an important role even today when formal governments are in place almost all over the world.

Possibilities and Limits of Collective/Community Action

While discussing the role of the government, we have noted that any meta-individual organization, including residential associations or village councils, may perform a part of this role. However, for all such services, these 'collective' actions may not be efficient. For example, the security or protection from robbers is a service that can be performed by the community or a residential association or a village council. But it may be cheaper if the state government improves its policing rather than each and every village appointing its own police or security guards. It is only when a government fails to do so that communities are forced to act on their own.

We have also seen that there can be the problem of free-riding in the case of public services. Thus, the community association should be in a position to control free-riding (by persuading every user to bear a part of the cost of the public service). Such control is easy for the government since it has coercive powers (to put a person in jail). Community organizations cannot exercise such coercive powers (though some may be using some coercive strategies illegally). There should be some other way of punishing those who do not cooperate. This depends on how cooperation can be sustained in community organizations. (Remember the discussion on analysing strategies in relationships as part of the 'Analytical Box of Economics'.)

When the arms of the government had not reached each and every village or settlement of a country, the collective action of local people played an important role in providing some public services—like controlling overgrazing in community forests, use of water in tanks or small irrigation systems, use of trees and plants from forests, regulating fishing in coastal waters, and in many such contexts. To understand the economics of collective action, let us take a specific case of fishing as given in Box 18.1.

Box 18.1: An Economic Problem of Community/Collective Action

Assume that there is a fishing lake in a location inhabited by a community. The people can either fish in the lake or take up some job in the nearby town. Those who go to the town get ₹100 a day. Let us assume that no one owns the lake, and hence anybody wanting to fish can do so freely. We presume that the only cost of fishing is the time devoted to fishing. The following table (Table 18.1) gives the values of income from fishing as more and more people do it.

(Box 18.1 contd.)

(Box 18.1 contd.)

Table 18.1
Marginal verses Average Income from Fishing: An Example

Number of people doing fishing (A)	Total income from fishing (B)	Marginal income (increase in income from fishing us one more person enters fishing) (C)	Average income for the fishers D = B/A	Rent, if there is an owner (total income minus wages for the fishers) E = B – A × 100
1	300	300	300	200
2	700	400	350	500
3	1,050	350	350	750
4	1,320	270	330	920
5	1,500	180	300	1,000
6	1,620	120	270	1,020
7	1,680	60	240	980
8	1,600	–80	200	800
9	1,440	–160	160	540
10	1,200	–240	120	200
11	770	–430	70	–330

SOURCE: Author.

As more and more people fish, there is an increase in income initially, but it decreases afterwards. This is due to an externality—one more person's fishing reduces everybody's productivity due to crowding, killing of young fish and so on. Since the lake is not owned by anyone, people will enter fishing as long as their income from fishing (average income) is greater than what they may earn by working outside. Thus, nearly 10 local people will be involved in fishing (since at this stage, the average income is ₹120 which is slightly above ₹100—the outside income), producing a total income of ₹1,200. Assume that this lake is owned by someone, and he employs local people for fishing. Let us assume that the wage rate is the same as that of outside work. Then the profit he earns from fishing is given at the last column of the above table. It is clear that he will not employ more than six workers, since adding one more worker would reduce his profit. This corresponds to a total income

(Box 18.1 contd.)

(Box 18.1 contd.)

of ₹1,620. Thus the lack of ownership encourages more people to take up fishing and produce a much lesser amount of total income.

An outcome similar to that of the private ownership can be obtained if there is a community of the people there managing the access to lake. For example, it should allow only six people to do fishing, and encourage others to do outside work. The profit (or extra income) that can be earned by this regulation can be used for activities that enhance community welfare. However, this can happen only if the community has some control over the members (so that it can punish the non-cooperating members). We have seen that this cooperative outcome is possible only under some conditions.

Source: Author.

The initial understanding in economics was somewhat pessimistic about the efficiency and effectiveness of collective action. The numerical exercise given in the box was part of that understanding. Similarly, a more famous article titled 'Tragedy of Commons' in *Nature* magazine too projected such a bleak picture. However, a number of empirical studies (and some of them were done by the political scientist, Elinor Ostrom, a Nobel laureate in economics) have showed that community management worked reasonably well in many parts of the world. This was followed by theoretical developments in economics trying to understand the situations where cooperation can be sustained. This was based on infinitely repeated prisoners' dilemma games mentioned in the 'Strategic Analysis' part of the 'Analytical Box of Economics'. The insights are that people can cooperate on a sustainable basis through different kinds of threat strategies (and thus agree to some norms which avoid the inefficiency problem mentioned in the case of fishing in the box) under two conditions. The parties should not see their cooperation ending in the near future. They are not discounting their future gains heavily. This would imply that such cooperation may not be forthcoming if people are very poor or crisis-ridden (since they may discount the future heavily because for them current consumption may be more important). Similarly, if the parties interacting are not that familiar with each other (maybe because of in and out migration, and also the expansion of markets), they may not perceive their cooperation as infinite, and this too can lead to a break up. Thus in a rapidly changing social context, where people go out in search of better opportunities, and people interact with 'outsiders' for buying and selling goods and services, sustaining cooperation in a community context may be difficult. Otherwise, there should be strong social or civic norms that encourage people to stick to cooperative strategies and to avoid free-riding.

Second-best Market Options

Since government intervention is not forthcoming adequately or appropriately for the provision of public goods, environmental management or for addressing issues of asymmetric information, there can be 'market alternatives' to such government intervention. On the one hand, these are cases of market failure. But government intervention to solve such market failure can be costly or unreliable. Thus market alternatives may emerge to solve such cases of market failure. Let us take one simple case. We know that it is difficult for a firm to convey credibly to the customers that their product is of good quality (even if it is really of good quality). Thus the government intervention, for establishing a standard for the product, testing and certifying whether the product meets the standard or not, is useful. The firm itself may advertise that their product meets the government set standard (like BIS certification).

However, some firms may not depend on this government-set standard, even though they have to use it as part of regulation. They may sell the product with a quality which may be better than the standard. The consumers who use this product over a period of time may develop a positive experience, and they may go back to the same firm due to such experience. They become loyal customers of the firm. The firm develops a reputation among the customers and its name becomes a brand. Thus, the company's name itself may communicate a certain level of quality. (In fact, this brand name itself may become a product. Another investor may want to buy this company and/or give a price for the brand name due to its reputation value.) This is an example where a market solution is attempted to solve a problem of market failure. However, it may be noted that a new firm does not get the benefit of reputation.

Environmental problems can also be viewed as those arising out of missing markets, and the reason for this absence of markets could be the lack of well defined property rights. For example, conservation of soil (by using vegetation) in the upper catchment area of a reservoir may increase the water retention capacity of the soil, which may increase the water availability during the summer months. However, people conserving water in catchment areas need not benefit from increased water storage. (They are not selling the water retained in the soil to the electricity board owning the reservoir.) In such cases, a clearer definition of property rights and hypothetical markets can help. For example, an electricity utility in Costa Rica paid money to the upstream farmers to practice water-conserving agriculture. Through this way, the benefits that the company reaps in through increased water storage are shared with the farmers. This can also be termed as an example of a market-based instrument to conserve environment. Yet another example could be that of wild-life viewing/hunting in sanctuaries in Africa. There are private or community-owned forests there, and the owners develop an interest in protecting forests since it provides them revenue from controlled hunting or wild-life viewing without harming the ecological quality of the sanctuary.

There are market-based options for the provision of public goods or those with the feature of natural monopoly. In the section on natural monopoly (Chapter 5), we have mentioned regulated private utilities or regulated competition to serve as the monopoly providing a commodity or a service having natural monopoly. (Some more details in this regard will be given in Chapter 19.) The bidding to serve as a natural monopoly can also be taken as a market-based instrument. A substantial part of the public–private partnerships for the provision of public goods like harbour, container terminals, airports, roads and so on are examples of market-based or semi-private provisions of public goods. However, there are some serious contracting problems here which may create social losses and these are discussed in the following chapter.

NGOs Providing Public Service

We have discussed community action which is a form of non-governmental action. But there are also formal NGOs which are playing an important role in the provisions of services such as education and health care. In most societies religious organizations play an important role in this regard. Scholarship in many societies was traditionally linked to religion or theology, and thus it was not surprising to see such organizations having had a dominant role in education then.

The rulers or the kings supported such initiatives, but the urge to spread the 'ideas' of a particular kind was the main motivation for such an intervention in education. Christian missionaries played an important role in spreading education and health care to the colonized countries, including India, in the last 500 years. This was also partly driven by religious ideals (like helping the others) and the urge to spread the message of the specific religion. During the last 50–60 years, there was more intense action by secular NGOs. Some of them draw a part of the resources of international aid.

At the conceptual level, these organizations are driven by some ideals. Thus increasing profits is not the obvious objective, and hence some public concerns which are neglected in market exchange can be taken up through such NGO action. However, providing such services like education or health care need not be the prime objective of such action, and hence it can be the case that the provision of such service becomes an incidental benefit or by-product. Thus the social priorities in terms of education or health care need not be fully taken into account in the provision of these services by the NGOs. Moreover, the content or the priorities in the provision of these services may be driven by the 'ideals' of the organization. Thus, there may be more 'religious content' of one or the other type in the education provided by them than what may be desired by the wider society. This is not to belittle the services provided by the NGOs. However, due to the nature of the services provided by them, these have to be seen complementary to what is to be done by the state, and not as a substitute of the governmental provision.

There is one aspect of such NGOs that may reduce their cost of provision. First of all there is likely to be a self-selection in the employees of these organizations. They are more likely to be those who share the organizational objectives. (Such NGOs may create a workforce which is somewhat indoctrinated by the ideals of the organization as in the case of nuns and priests who may serve as nurses or teachers.) Thus maximization of income may not be an explicit objective of these people, and hence they may be willing to work for the organization at wages much lower than the opportunity costs. Moreover, the internalization of organizational ideals would also mean that these people may give less importance to 'material (monetary) incentives' and may have attuned to work with non-material incentives. Thus there may not be a great need to give more money to motivate them. Or this solves the principal–agent problem (discussed in economics) in a relatively cheaper manner. In addition, the employees of such organization may see a part of their work as altruism, and thus may be motivated in giving a part of their services free of cost. All these may make the cost of provision of services by NGOs cheaper.

Though these are some general trends, we may have to see potential pitfalls in this regard. All employees need not internalize the organizational goals or see their work as altruistic. Thus, when NGOs do not or cannot give a salary equivalent to market rates, they may be getting people who may work at lower rates, but these people may be commanding only those wages in the market (implying that their quality is also lower). This may affect the quality of service. The fact that some people are working at below market wages may prevent a realistic evaluation of their services, and what they deliver may be either not of the desired quality or may be influenced by their pet ideas, and need not be one desired by the society. This does not create much problem if their service is in a competitive context—wherein there are others (government and/or private firms) also providing the same service. This is true to some extent in the case of health care (even though there are some geographical areas where one health care provider may enjoy some limited monopoly power).

Charity and Altruism

Charity or altruism was partly behind the actions of NGOs, but these were driven primarily by the goals or ideals of the organizations. On the other hand, altruism can be much more specific: one person's gain (or satisfaction) depends not only on one's own consumption but also on somebody's consumption (or on welfare). In fact the primary space for such altruism is the family. Here one may see some biological or other reasons which encourage people to be concerned about the welfare of others—spouse and children. One can define self-interest in such a way to include the interests of one's own future generations too, and in that sense, what is transferred within the family is driven by self-interest. But family is a terrain within which resources are transferred from one to another without the mediation of a narrowly defined self-interest.

There can also be charitable or altruistic transfer of resources by a person to a community or a wider section of society, within or beyond one's own country. For conceptual reasons, these transfers may be seen differently from what rulers and kings had done in the past. The latter too had supported many social initiatives despite not having any obligation as in the case of a democratic government. However, they were using these means to legitimize their power—one becomes powerful only when others accept such a position. Coercive ways of asserting one's power need not be the best way in all circumstances (or the most efficient way if we use an economics jargon). Thus there can be transfer of a part of the resources mobilized by the king to a wider section of society. We need not consider this as altruistic transfer as there is some quid pro quo involved in this transfer. We have also analysed the non-governmental actions driven by religious or social ideals, and these can also be seen differently from 'pure' altruistic transfer.

It is not that those who carry out such an altruistic transfer do not expect anything from it. It could be due to a sense of belonging. In certain cases, the sense of belonging may operate in a wider circle like the extended family, one's own community, own region or own country. It could also be for one's own satisfaction in doing the 'right' thing—right being decided by one's own preferences. Protecting the environment and wildlife could be seen as the 'right thing to do', or minimizing the death of children could be another one or alleviating the sufferings of the poor or diseased could be yet another. In doing such 'right things', the person derives utility.

It is not that there is no rationality in spending money in this regard. One can see strategies used by such persons to maximize his/her satisfaction. There can be choices and priorities since the resources are scarce. It may not be difficult to bring in efficiency considerations (using the minimum possible cost for reaching a given objective or having the maximum achievement for a given cost) even when the objective is altruistic. However, the altruistic objective of the person may not be always in tune with (or need not be adequate to meet) the requirement of society even within the limited sphere. Moreover, sometimes the feeling of doing the right thing does not necessarily mean the willingness to tread the full distance to see that the whole effort and spending are leading efficiently and effectively to the targeted goals. Thus altruistic initiatives too need to be seen only as complementary to the government initiatives.

Bibliographical Note: The issues of government failure are discussed in Krueger (1993) and also in Stiglitz (2000). Insights on community action can be gained by reading Ostrom (1990). Tabellini (2008) provides insights on economics of values and internal incentives including altruism.

QUESTIONS/EXERCISES

1. What are the probable reasons that make governmental or public sector organizations less efficient?

2. List down one instance (which is not mentioned in the chapter) where people depend on the private sector or the market for their need for public goods.

3. Give a short summary of a community action which you know or have read about. Do you see any relevance of the discussion in this chapter there?

4. Evaluate the work of an NGO, which you know or have read about, based on what you have read in this chapter.

5. Is there a need for worrying about efficiency in an effort driven by charity or altruism? Discuss.

6. A women's self-help group carries out paddy cultivation on land it has leased in. After the harvest, the women pool the profit and divide it equally. The number of women who work in this enterprise depends on whether the income per person from this paddy cultivation is greater than what each one of them can get from outside work (as agricultural worker on others' fields). Is there an issue of economic efficiency here? What are the mechanisms which could be used to address this issue?

7. NGOs like missionary schools/hospitals could provide service (say education/health care) of a given quality at a lesser cost (compared to government or private schools/hospitals). What could be the reasons for this?

NINETEEN

INSTITUTIONS AND DEVELOPMENT

———————•⊶◆⊷•———————

What is an institution? It can be a rule—formal or informal—or a norm, enforced by the state or other public agencies or communities. It can also include the internalized normative behaviour of an individual—that 'I should not waste food' or 'I should not drink alcohol' and so on. Formal rules like 'land cannot be leased out', 'narcotic drugs cannot be consumed or sold', 'anyone constructing a house in the city needs to get permission from the town planners' and so on are enforced by the state. There can be norms such as 'marrying a person from other caste is unacceptable' enforced by communities. Prohibition or restriction on inter-caste marriage can also be internalized by individuals—they follow it even when there is no explicit enforcement.

In our common usage, we refer to a school, college or a hospital as an institution and this may create some confusion. It is better to address them as organizations. Organizations evolve and function within certain rules or legal (and hence institutional) frameworks. Thus organizations, including firms (which produce/distribute goods and services) and individuals, are actors functioning within institutions. Let us take the example of family and marriage. It is better to call family an organization and marriage an institution.

Why are we concerned about institutions?

There are two situations when people think about them. First is when there is an institution already existing. We may be asking whether this existing institution is 'good' or 'bad'. To call something as good or bad, we need to define 'good' and need a 'criterion' to judge goodness. This implies the possibility that certain institutions can be good. Or more specifically, having such institutions is better for individuals and societies in general, rather than their absence. This leads us to the second situation when we are concerned about institution. These are situations marked by the absence of those 'good' institutions. Or there are some problems or inadequacies that we perceive in a given context (something is not fine), and this can be due to the absence of such 'good' institution. Then the question bothering us would be the following: is it possible to design an appropriate institution in the given context, so that society in general is better off?

There are two aspects to institutions. First is the agency which imposes/ enforces the rule and second is the content of the rule/norm. Formal rules are those which are imposed by the governments using its coercive power and sanctioned by the legal system. Informal rules are made and enforced by communities or groups of people having some common characteristics (those belonging to a village, caste, a residential area, members of an association, those who are part of an occupational group and so on). There can also be norms, which are not enforced by others, but are considered by individuals as something worthwhile to follow. Thus there are three generic categories of agencies: state, community (which include all non-state associations) and the individual himself/ herself.

HOW DO INSTITUTIONS MATTER FOR DEVELOPMENT?

Institutions matter in explaining the different levels of economic development of different countries. More specifically, it shows that the absence of certain institutions (well-defined property rights, speedier mechanisms to adjudicate conflicts, proper enforcement of the rule of law, mechanisms to control the excessive cost imposed by the political decision-making including corruption and so on) causes underdevelopment. Studies comparing the economic growth of different countries have confirmed this relationship between institutions and economic growth. Scholars have also explained analytically how certain institutions can hamper or facilitate economic growth. Nobel laureate Douglas North has used institutional analysis to explain the long-run economic performance of nations.

While the above set of studies have looked at the macro-picture (like the economic growth) of a country and the type of institutions existing there, there are also a number of instances where ill-functioning of a governmental programme or a social security scheme can be attributed to the lack of appropriate institution (rules) and organizations. When planners say that only a small percentage of the funds earmarked for poverty eradication reach the real poor this can be due to inappropriate institution. When schools do not work even when teachers are appointed, or when a significant share of students do not have access to education, these are also due to inappropriate institutions. (These may have significant bearing on the development outcomes of a country or a region.)

Whether it is for explaining the differential performance of different countries in terms of economic growth or the inefficiency of specific governmental programmes, institutional analysis is used extensively these days. Hence, different types of institutions, their efficiency and the reasons for the emergence and persistence of inefficient institutions have to be part of the economics knowledge needed for development practitioners. That is the purpose of this chapter.

Content of a Rule/Institution

We have already defined institutions and their enforcers. However, what does a rule say? It prescribes behaviour and this behaviour is likely to be different from the one people would have chosen anyway based on their self-interest. It may be difficult to have a generic categorization of such prescribed behaviour. However, some broad forms can be identified. First, there can be some 'shall not' prescriptions. These are prohibitions or banning of some behaviour like: there should not be any consumption of narcotic drugs; one should not take law into own hands (implying that law enforcement should be left to the state) and so on. There can be different punishing mechanisms for violations—liability, fines, confinement in jails, social estrangement and so on—depending on the agency enforcing the norm or institution.

The state or community can take over the responsibility of carrying out some actions. A government arranging water supply, a residential association arranging solid waste management and so on are some examples. This direct provision or action by the state or community reduces the efforts to coordinate or regulate the actions of individuals or firms. Another category could be fixing limits. Behaviour of certain kinds is permitted but within certain limits. For example, pollution standards do not ban pollution but say: 'yes you can pollute, but not beyond a particular limit'. Drinking alcohol may be regulated in parties and within circles of friends by putting informal limits on consumption to avoid excessive drinking. Individuals themselves may internalize such a limit, the crossing of which occasionally may prick their conscience.

There can also be more liberal rules, which say that, 'yes you can indulge in that behaviour, but make appropriate payments'. Broadly, taxes on consumption that create some externality come under this category. Cigarette smoking incurs payment of higher taxes in many countries, but banning or limiting of consumption of cigarettes is rarely seen, while such a ban exists in public spaces. Waste disposal is not restricted in many developed societies, but one may have to pay for waste disposed. Making the provision of certain information mandatory is yet another form of institutional intervention. Labelling on products, disclosure of audited accounts of the companies, mandatory advertising of the harmful effects of smoking on cigarette packets and so on are examples. Such information disclosure can also be seen in community/informal exchanges. For example, not revealing certain crucial information about a partner before marriage can be reckoned as cheating by the other partner and community forms of 'punishment' (including divorce) may be sought as resolution. Partners in business are expected to reveal certain crucial information to each other even if such a partnership is not based on a formal (legal) contract.

We expect certain actions as a follow-up of the information disclosure. This may be simply aimed at informed exchange. Calorie content mentioned on a food product helps a consumer to decide whether to use or not to use it. However, information disclosure can also address some other problem, including externality. If a factory is made to reveal the pollution levels to the public, people living nearby can check if the actual pollution is beyond permissible limits, and if so, notify the regulatory agencies to take action. Even if the actual pollution level is lower than the permissible limit, people who do not like or cannot tolerate it (for health reasons) can decide to shift elsewhere.

One advantage with the payments (taxes) or information disclosure is that there is greater freedom for individuals or organizations here compared with the banning or fixation of specific limits. Rather than banning cigarettes, allowing them information that 'cigarette smoking is injurious to health' enables smoking by some individuals who value it much more than a reduction in the probability of getting cancer. Some industries, which use old technology, may find it better to pay taxes rather than to control pollution to the prescribed limit, and they have this freedom under the regime of taxes. Some innovative firms may come out with ways of controlling pollution much beyond prescribed limits, and they have an incentive to reduce pollution further if taxes are in place rather than a specific limit. Thus a worldview, which values individuals' freedom, sees taxes and information disclosure as less restrictive compared with bans and limits.

Different Enforcers of Institutions

There are both merits and demerits in the different agencies who are promoters or enforcers of institutions. The state or the government has coercive power, sanctioned by the political process (which can be democratic or non-democratic) and/ or has police, courts and administrative machinery to make and enforce rules. This may minimize the possibilities of free riding as the state can impose behaviour through its coercive power. There can also be some economy of scale in rule making and administration when these are carried out by the state.

However, the state may have limitations in understanding the needs/demands of each individual (or small groups). The rule made by the state is likely to be inflexible (since it may take a lot of effort to change rules made and are in place). Thus the efficacy of the state may vary from context to context, depending on its inherent merits and disadvantages.

The second agency is the communities. We have already seen the prospects and problems of community enforcing rules. It needs cooperation from its members. Cooperation is likely to sustain less if interaction is between strangers, if repeated interactions are not important, and also if people discount future gains heavily and value highly the immediate or short-term gains. (Remember the discussion of 'folk theorem' in Chapter 6.) The third category of agency for creating/ enforcing behaviour is the individual himself. He/she internalizes (or decides to follow) a particular behaviour in a certain context. There can be the use of norms as a substitute for rational calculations at every moment of decision-making. Then there can be congruence of norm-based decision and those of the rational decision-maker. However, there can be some norms which facilitate coordination to address (partially) problems of market failure. Such normative behaviour has certain advantages. This makes the need (and hence the cost of) for external monitoring and enforcement unnecessary. The information processing costs incurred by the decision-maker may also get reduced since he/she is simply following the norm, without thinking about the need for such norms in each and every context. However, the problem with the norm is that there may be situations when following the norm can be perceived to be very costly and under such situations there can be a tendency to break the norm. Thus there can be some unpredictability regarding the consistency of the normative behaviour. Since the social context of norm-based behaviour is sustained by expectations—'I follow the norm as I believe that others are also following it'—any unpredictability or reduced expectation on the norm-based behaviour on the part of some people may discourage even those who are planning to follow the norm.

INSTITUTIONS VERSUS ORGANIZATIONS

We have briefly mentioned, in the beginning of this chapter, the distinction between institutions and organizations and cited the example of marriage (an institution) and family (an organization). Organization can be viewed as part of a larger institutional framework. For example, consider a small bakery. A person can run a bakery by producing most of the items (like breads and cakes) by herself; or she can outsource the production to another person and merely retail the products. The other option is to employ a person and make bread and sell it. When she opts for the latter an organization (in this case a firm) is evolving and if she chooses this to make her life easier, then the firm is an organizational solution of a problem (that is, without an organization her life will be difficult). There are a number of real-world situations where an organization of this kind is better than having every transaction depend on the market (like bakeries buying bread from another person in the market). Thus, you have large firms making many things from planes to cars and even soaps and breads.

One argument for the existence of an organization is the need for minimizing transaction costs. The bakery that buys bread from another person has to ensure quantity and quality to meet its demand. This may not be possible if it buys bread as and when required; there may be a need for a formal contract. There is a need to identify an appropriate bread maker to suit the quantity and quality needs of the bakery; monitor regularly the supply and if something goes wrong the bakery has to take action. The bread producer may have to make investments to produce bread in adequate quantity and quality; and if the bakery does not lift the stocks she may suffer a loss since there may not be an alternative buyer in the locality. After making such investments for bread making if the bakery wants the price reduced (knowing that the bread maker has fewer options to sell bread to outsiders), this may put the bread maker in trouble. These are called contract contingencies. If she perceives such a possibility she may be overcautious while preparing the contract. Or such a contingency may discourage her from entering into a contract. Thus there is some mutual dependence requiring mutual monitoring of action and there is a cost for carrying out the transactions between the producer and the bakery. This cost can be significant. In some circumstances the bakery employing a person to produce bread may reduce the transaction costs. This is an incentive to create and sustain an organization.

There is another role of organization—to work as part of an institution. If the market failure encourages the government to produce and/or supply a service (for example electricity), the agency carrying out this job is an organization. One can cite electricity boards, water supply corporations, highway departments, air traffic control authorities and so on as examples of such organizations. They come to exist as part of a particular institutional framework.

EFFICIENCY AND COSTS OF INSTITUTIONS

Institutions which correct market failure or serve useful purposes described above are effective ones but all such effective institutions need not be efficient. This is so because for each of the purpose mentioned above, one can think of alternative institutions and one of them may be more efficient (that is, it imposes less cost on society). For example, the state has many alternative ways to ensure that poor children get school education: it can open schools, provide fellowships to students to study in private schools or provide grants to private or charitable agencies to start/operate schools. (Each of these corresponds to a rule/policy of the state.) However, the social cost of each of these may be different and one may be the cheapest in a given context. Taking another example, for a city government desiring to provide a cheap cable TV connection (as it may be cheaper to have one company to provide cable TV service but then there is the problem of natural monopoly and hence the need for social intervention), there are multiple options: the city government can start a cable TV service on its own or allow one company to operate cable TV through competitive licensing. There are merits and demerits for each of these options (see Box 19.1).

Box 19.1: What Are the Alternative Forms of Government Intervention in the Case of Natural Monopoly?

GOVERNMENT OWNERSHIP OF THE FIRM

The advantage is that the government can exercise greater control over the firm. Thus, if the government is capable and is serious about its intention to exercise control for social benefit, this is much more possible under government ownership, compared with alternative mechanisms. However, many governments exercise control over public firms with short-term political interests rather than for overall benefits of society. The disadvantage of state ownership is that public sector organizations may not have the incentives to be efficient and effective. There should be efforts to reorganize public-sector organizations (as corporations) with incentives similar to that of a private organization with only the ownership (shares) resting with the government. This is rarely done. True there are well run state-owned utilities but by and large the government owned utilities are known for their inefficiency and ineffectiveness, driven by political interests and lack of incentives for managers and employees.

REGULATION OF PRIVATE UTILITIES

Instead of the government owning utilities, there could be government regulation of private utilities. For example, generation and distribution of electricity could be carried out by a private monopoly in a region regulated by the (regional) government directly or through an independent regulator. This way the government can bring in the efficiency of private companies and ensure a steady supply of power to the consumers. This way it can also control the prices at which power is supplied at socially desirable rates. However, there are problems with this type of regulation too. Certain forms of regulation, which

(Box 19.1 contd.)

(Box 19.1 contd.)

ensure a specified rate of return for the company, may encourage the firm to use more capital than that is warranted. This is so if the rate of return ensured in the regulated sector is greater than that from other opportunities. There is also the problem of asymmetric information between the regulator and the regulated company. Usually the company has better (private) information on the real cost of supplying the service. This may lead to what is called the regulatory capture by the regulated companies.

REGULATED COMPETITION

Even if there is a natural monopoly and only one firm can function effectively, a competitive bidding to grant the license to operate as monopoly can be used to reduce social losses. The bidding can be based on the price of supplying service. The competition at the time of bidding may encourage firms to seek/search for efficient means of producing the service. The problem with the regulated competition is that it requires contracts. There can be contract contingencies and all contracts may be incomplete. There can be ex-post (after the signing of the contract) pressures to renegotiate the terms of the contract. Such pressures can come from the government or the company. One of the parties may be in a vulnerable position forcing it to accept the demand for renegotiation. Contracting parties envisage such contingencies and may take costly precautions.

Source: Author.

Why do we talk only about the costs and not the benefits? Here our concern is about alternative institutions to address a particular problem (or a form of market failure). As mentioned earlier, there are social benefits in solving this problem (or addressing market failure). By and large, the benefits are the same for all the alternative (but effective) institutions that solve a specific problem and hence we need to be concerned only about costs of different institutions and select the one which incurs the lowest cost.

What do we mean by the cost of an institution (or rule or the norm)? There are two types of costs here. First, there are direct costs, which include those needed to make the rule, administrative costs to make it work and enforcement costs to see that people follow that rule (to look for those who violate it, try them, and finally punish the guilty). Thus, if consumption of alcohol is prohibited, then there are significant direct costs for making the law (for which there should be a majority support within the legislature, which in turn may require advocacy by those who think that such consumption should be restrained). Direct costs also include those for enforcement. This includes inspection of possible locations where alcohol is likely to be (illegally) consumed, booking those who are found violating the rule, then their trial and judgement, appeals if any, and final verdict, and also the facilities for collecting fines from those who are proven guilty and/ or for their confinement in jails. Yes, the direct costs of having an institution/rule are substantial indeed.

There are indirect costs too. Certain levels of human activities or transactions between people will be reduced in the presence of an institution. For example, when a tax is imposed on alcohol, it is likely to lead to a cut in production. This may impose a cost on society even if the reduced supply and consumption is beneficial. Considering this cost is thus necessary to see how much reduction in consumption of alcohol can be allowed. Different institutions may incur different costs here. If the objective is to reduce the consumption of alcohol, then each of the following—prohibition, imposing higher taxes, supply through government outlet—have different losses in terms of the foregone economic activities.

There is also an implication due to the costs. It is very probable that under certain circumstances, the benefits of having an institution may be lesser than the costs. Let us take an example. There is a serious problem if people drive vehicles as they please without bothering about others. It is better to have some (traffic) rules and their enforcement to control this. However, there are limits to the enforcement of such a rule. Since traffic police cannot be posted all along a high-way, especially during nights, the actual enforcement is carried out at certain times and there is no enforcement (or there is an institutional void) at other times. However, the cost of enforcement need not continue to be high forever. The relative cost of enforcement may come down due to changes in technology and economy. For example, if the number of vehicles increases drastically, then the per-vehicle cost of monitoring through installing cameras to record traffic violations may come down. This enables greater enforcement of existing traffic rules. Hence, it is not surprising to see the absence of institution and/or its enforcement and such a situation may indeed be desirable, when the costs outweigh the benefits.

INEFFICIENT INSTITUTIONS—WHY DO THEY EXIST?

So far we have discussed the need for institutions and the features of 'efficient' institutions. But there are also useless or costly institutions. How did they come to exist? Why do they continue to exist? What prevents society from changing such useless or even harmful institutions?

Identifying such institutions is not that difficult given the discussions earlier. Those rules/norms, which do not address any clear problem of market failure or any well-articulated issue of distribution or equity or poverty, can be suspected. A greater part of the rules, which formed part of the 'license raj' in India, did not aim at (or succeed in) solving any problem related to the efficiency or growth of the economy or address any well-articulated distributional concerns. (However, these may have helped to distribute resources among some vested interest groups.) Even when a rule/norm is found to be addressing a real problem, it can be inefficient if it imposes a greater cost on society compared to the potential alternatives that can address the same problem, but impose lesser cost on society/ economy.

How do such useless or inefficient institutions come to exist? One can easily blame people and politicians not knowing institutional economics for creating 'bad' institutions, but it is not a persuasive argument. This is not to discount the role of ignorance, incomplete information, ideological or prejudiced reading of reality in the making of (inefficient) institutions. Ignorance and prejudice can play a role (in creating ineffective or inefficient institutions). Even when information is available, what one learns from depends upon their pre-conceived notions. An open mind towards new information is not a very common trait. However, attributing the existence of all or most inefficient institutions to the ignorance or mistakes in their formation may not be a correct approach. Even without the knowledge of institutional economics, reasonably efficient institutions can come to exist. This is so especially when different interest groups compete and articulate their interests, and when such articulation of self-interest of multiple stakeholders can ensure that the cost imposed by the institution on society is minimal, even when society realizes that an institutional intervention is necessary to solve a perceived social problem (or market failure). Thus there should be other reasons for the existence of bad institutions.

One possibility is that some interest groups in society (especially those who are bearing the costs of institutional intervention) whose participation would have helped in creating efficient institutions could not do so for some reasons. What prevented these groups from participating? We can consider an example. In the case of services like irrigation or drinking water, where some social intervention is needed, the decision-making on how to do the intervention is carried out usually by the public sector technocratic departments. We have seen that there is no market-like mechanism to know the demand for such services, as water for drinking or irrigation is not priced like a commercial commodity in many contexts. Thus the demand for such services is assessed by public sector organizations through political means (people demanding through their elected representatives, who in turn express their demands in legislature, which makes ministries act). It is very difficult for any principal (who uses an agent) to make the agent deliver what the principal wants him/her to do. This is more so in a chain of agency relationship as mentioned above. In effect, what the public sector organization (PSO) does can be very different from what people want it to do. Thus it is very possible that institutional intervention made for irrigation or drinking water or many such services, are the ones considered ideal by the PSO, and hence need not be the ones appropriate for the society.

Or more perversely, such institutional interventions may meet the internal requirements of the PSO more, rather than the identified social problems. This problem arises not only in the case of the provision of public services, but also for redistributive purposes. For example, a typical agricultural office in a village in Kerala, spends most of its time in maintaining records of the subsidy to be transferred to people. The total subsidy transferred in a month is less than the total expenditure for the functioning of the office. It would have been much cheaper for the government to distribute the subsidy through postal money orders rather than through an office for this purpose in each village. Such subsidy distribution programme is used for the expansion/functioning of the PSO, and thereby a lot of public money is wasted. It is also possible that some import control regulations come to exist due to the lobbying of a particular industry, whereas such a regulation may force society at large to consume a product or service at higher cost (due to the reduction of import). The emergence of inefficient institutions can be explained to a great extent by the influence of interest groups.

When an institution came to exist, it could be good and efficient, but it could persist for some reasons even after turning out to be bad (inefficient) due to the changes in technological and economic factors. Under this case, the inquiry should be directed at the factors that led to the persistence of the institution. The most quoted example in this regard is the case of the QWERTY arrangement in the computer keyboard. This order of alphabets was used in the keyboards of mechanical typewriters because it minimized the movement of adjacent metal levers (the metal rod moving and hitting the paper to imprint the alphabet). This would minimize the possibility of lever jamming. Such an arrangement is unnecessary in electronic and digital printers. However, the efforts and costs already made by the society in familiarizing itself with this arrangement make it difficult to replace it with potentially more efficient ones. The firms and organizations that are developed to supply products/services of a particular time may prevent the emergence of alternative better products/production systems. This may be happening in the case of electricity-driven cars or even the use of solar energy. A similar pattern may explain the persistence of inefficient institutions.

POLITICAL ECONOMY AND INSTITUTIONS

The description in this chapter is not to give an impression that it is only institutions that matter or that these can be fixed easily. There is some realization that the development of appropriate institutions takes place organically as part of the overall social and economic change of a country, and these cannot be implanted from elsewhere. These changes are also related to the process of political economy—what are the outcomes of bargaining by different interest groups in society through political and other means. Some of these issues are taken up in the next chapter.

Bibliographical note: The key issues discussed in this chapter are based on Santhakumar (2011). A classic work on institutions is North (1990).

QUESTIONS/EXERCISES

1. Why do we need institutions?
2. What are the costs of institutions?
3. Though institutions are desirable, there may be some (rare) situations where the presence of an institution could be costlier than its absence. Discuss.

4. How are norms enforced?
5. What makes an institution inefficient?
6. What factors may cause the persistent of inefficient institutions?
7. Why do we create elaborate rules for the functioning of public organizations (for hiring and procurement)? How do these rules affect their efficiency?

TWENTY

POLITICAL ECONOMY AND DEVELOPMENT

————————◂•◈•▸————————

WHAT IS POLITICAL ECONOMY AND WHY IS IT IMPORTANT?

Politics is the process by which different groups or individuals bargain (or sometimes fight) for a share of public authority and resources. Political economy is about the relationship between political and economic interest. This is a two-way relationship. Political power facilitates influence over the sharing of public resources (or government money) and also on public policies that may have a bearing on private wealth. Economic status of individuals may determine their specific positions in politics.

Political economy influences development in different ways. First of all, it creates the environment within which economic activities take place. Structures of governance and economic environment impact the prospects for economic growth, and this can affect development. Beyond economic growth, development also depends on how resources (especially public resources) are allocated within a society. Are there enough schools and health-care centres provided by the government? Is there an adequate social security for those people who are unable to gain an income from the labour market? The answers to such questions would determine the nature of social and human development in a society. Political economy plays an important role in taking decisions on these matters.

Different Ways of Analysing Political Economy

There are different ways of analysing political economy. An important stream well known during the twentieth century was that influenced by Marxism. In this view, the society is broadly divided into different classes mainly as workers or working class and capitalists. Working class owns only their labour and it is the capitalist class which owns the other factors of production. Thus the struggle in the political economy is driven by the conflict between these two classes. (There is also some consideration of a section of the middle class which may take up a leadership role in mobilizing the working class.) Thus social and political change under this framework is driven by the class conflict of workers and capitalists, and Marxist political economy predicted a move towards socialism through this process.

However, we will not be touching Marxist political economy and the discussion here would be based on what is called the 'new political economy' which is based on mainstream economics (or what is called neoclassical economics). Here, the framework of analysis is individuals or groups of individuals (with similar income, occupation and social position). Their economic interest which encourages them to take specific political positions is considered here. In such an analysis, though the interests of the working class and capitalists are reckoned, society is not considered to be neatly divided into these two categories. More disaggregated grouping of the society based on income or other specific interests (like those holding a particular job, or living in a region) is attempted, and how do their varied interests lead to specific political outcomes is the focus in this political economy. Moreover, it is recognized that individuals may have an interest which may sometimes encourage them to work against the interest of their own group.

Political economy is analysed here with two specific objectives: first, how does it enable/disable allocation of resources to sections of people whose deprivation may have a negative impact on development? Second, how do political–economic factors influence the shaping of rules and institutions in a country and its governance structure? This is particularly relevant in the context of developing countries where governance or institutional reforms are being attempted and the success of such reforms depends on political economy.

ALLOCATION OF RESOURCES TO THE POOR AND UNDERPRIVILEGED UNDER DIFFERENT TYPES OF POLITICAL ECONOMY

Here we consider different types or stages in the political process and how do these affect the allocation of public resources and development in general.

Elite Capture

We discussed elite capture in the section on local governments. In almost all societies some sections of the elite dominate political economy in the early stages of social change. They could be the elite in the economic sense (with ownership of assets) and/or social sense (belong to specific caste/groups which have certain social supremacy). These contexts may be non-democratic but an elite capture can be sustained even under some phases of democracy. In such a situation, a greater part of the resources (including public resources like minerals) would be under the custody of these elites. They create public goods for themselves, collect rent from public resources (like land or other natural resources), use public resources for their own consumption and provide some private goods to the ruled. If their survival does not depend on support from below, a greater part of public resources can be used for the consumption of the elite or for providing public goods for themselves. Major sections of society may support (or may not oppose) the elite since the former has to depend on the patronage of the latter for social/economic reasons. They may serve as 'vote banks', if the context is a democratic one.

There will be resources flowing to the poor and vulnerable (or the ruled in general) to the extent that such resource allocation is needed for the legitimization of the elites. (There could be some rulers from the elite who are benevolent and such benevolence can also influence resource allocation.) However, it is easy to think that sections which are not important for the elites may not get adequate public resources, and their economic position could also remain inferior under such a situation. They may get limited access to public goods but their demand for public goods would be lower since their consumption of private goods is also at a lower level. (The assumption here is of a positive relationship between the demand for public goods and private consumption.) In terms of the economy, this elite capture can manifest in collaboration between the few capitalists and the ruling elite (and this can be called crony capitalism). Capitalists can be from within or outside the country (in the latter case, the domestic rulers share resources with foreign capitalists). Even the rulers and the limited domestic capitalist class can be one and the same.

Counter-Elite Capture

The elites who have captured the state may be overthrown violently or peacefully (through democratic or non-democratic means) by different forms of what can be called counter-elites. For example, such a counter-elite assertion has occurred in Indian states in two ways. First, the caste groups which were in the middle or at the lower levels in the traditional social hierarchy had their rights asserted through political movements (mainly focusing on such groups). For example in Uttar Pradesh, it started with middle-caste groups (say under Mulayam Singh) asserting their power but later Dalits were able to assert their political power. This was to undermine the upper-caste domination. Such a caste-based assertion (or that against a caste) had occurred in Tamil Nadu, Uttar Pradesh, Bihar and so on. On the other hand, a class-based counter-elite assertion had taken place in Kerala and West Bengal under the leadership of the left parties. Such parties mobilized small peasants or tenants (who were not having land titles) or agricultural and industrial workers (under a middle-class leadership).

What are the implications of this counter-elite capture for development? Such a transition leads to the de facto ownership of public resources by the 'counter-elites'. This may change the allocation of private-goods in society based on public resources, which may end up giving more to all or some groups which were not getting much previously. The majority of the ruled may get a greater share of the rent from public resources and they may also consequently demand a greater amount of public goods. Such sharing of private and public goods was part of fulfilling the aspirations of the sections that may have supported the capture of the state from the elites. Hence, counter-elite capture itself can widen the coverage of resource transfer from the state to society. Thus it has to be seen as part of a useful democratization at an early stage of social and economic change. There may not be an improvement in governance from the point of view of liberal democracy. There could be a continuation of corruption and vested interests influencing governance. This may encourage some people to look at the assertion of counter-elites negatively. However, they neglect the inevitable need for such democratization. Such democratization has some implications for the economy. Since a very limited consumption of private goods (including education) of some major sections of society could have a dampening effect on economic development in general, the expansion of private goods facilitated through counter-elite capture may have a favourable impact on economy and development.

Gradually a section of the counter-elites may become elite economically (due to the rent from public resources) and may even become social elite. What could be the relationship between the counter-elites and capitalist class? Though the counter-elite may take an adversarial position against those capitalists who were very close to (or part of) the previously ruling elite, they too need capitalist enterprises to generate wealth (unless they go for a full-fledged state-mediated production enterprises as in the socialist countries). Counter-elites would build up a base for production through state-mediated enterprises or through encouraging another capitalist class or by building new relationship with the prevailing domestic or foreign capitalists.

Moving towards Competitive Democracy

When the previous elites are not eradicated completely and the counter-elites have become new elites, there can be a competition between these sections. If the previous elites have been eradicated, the counter-elite capture may turn out to an 'elite capture' and it may encounter another counter-elite in due course. A competition between in-elites and counter-elite requires widening of support bases. Even if this competition is not manifested through democracy, but through periodical 'regime-changing' (violent or non-violent) revolutions, there is a need for widening the support base.

Where does this competition to enhance the support base lead to? Each group is likely to amass resources from society for distribution among its actual and potential support base. Since the direct tax system is likely to be less developed in such contexts, there will be a greater dependence on indirect taxes but most part of the resources may come from publicly owned assets. The major expenditure with public resources is for the distribution of (or transfer for) private goods. The competition between the elite and counter-elite would mean that the quantum and coverage of such distribution could go up. The competitive populism is a manifestation of this situation.

What is the impact of competition between the elite and counter-elite on the economy? It enhances the consumption of the ruled majority and this can be beneficial for the economy as long as their private consumption is a constraint on economic development. Thus the constraints imposed on economic growth due to undernourishment, illiteracy and ill health of a large section of the society may become less formidable at this stage. Second, competition between the elite and counter-elite may result in some competition among the capitalists. Thus, the social loss associated with crony or monopoly capitalism is also likely to decline albeit marginally in such politically competitive societies.

A special case in this regard is where the 'counter-elites' are a class-based formation like a communist party. Their ascendance to power may lead to much more widespread reallocation of assets and resources to the working class and the poor. However, historically we have seen that such working class parties have tried to monopolize power and have been successful in this regard in certain contexts. This can have a two-fold impact. They may create a governance/economic structure which may not facilitate wealth creation. (It may be noted that it is only during the last two to three decades that China and Vietnam have moved towards a market economy with a political framework dominated by single party.) Such a monopoly power of one party can be harmful. Even for resource allocation to the poor, a monopoly party may allocate resources to only those sections which are visibly aligned with them. Such a situation was noticed in West Bengal under the left front government. On the other hand, where political competition comes to exist between elites and counter-elites and where the latter is led by a class-based party, it may lead to a much more vibrant democracy, and sustainable allocation of resources to the poor as has occurred in Kerala.

POLITICAL REGIMES AND PROSPECTS FOR ECONOMIC GROWTH

The impact of the political regime on economic growth per se could be somewhat different. Whether a country is under democracy or dictatorship or whether it is under elite-capture or counter-elite-capture (or under the control of the working class parties), it need not affect the prospects of economic growth per se. Under any of these regimes, policies that facilitate economic growth can be pursued (or there may be cases where such policies may not be pursed). Economic growth depends on whether the system allows wealth creation and mutually beneficial exchanges. Even if there is one dictator who suppresses all political and human rights (and takes a 10 per cent cut on all deals as bribe), there could be economic growth in that country. There were cases where growth-friendly policies were pursued under dictatorship (Chile was one example from the past and China is a contemporary one). South East Asian countries like Singapore, Malaysia, Indonesia, South Korea and so on, have achieved rapid economic growth under a 'limited' democracy curtailing political and human rights. The growth seen in the Central Asian Republics using oil wealth under not-so-democratic regimes is another example. On the other hand, there are a number of cases where countries have followed policies that drive away investors and undermine economic growth. These can take place under elite-capture, counter-elite capture, competitive democracy and dictatorship. Zimbabwe and North Korea are some of the current examples in this regard.

Even though the relationship between economic growth and the nature of the regime is not so clear, development (in the broadest sense) may face challenges under elite capture. For achieving distribution of resources and providing welfare to the people at large, those at the helm of affairs should be either benevolent or should be driven by an underclass party. The cases of South East Asian countries (formally democratic but there are restrictions on political and human rights) or communist countries are examples in this regard. When such non-democratic countries achieve higher levels of wealth (say through the exploitation of natural resources) a certain level of affluence would trickle down to the larger population. There is also a hypothesis that those countries which depend heavily on natural resources for their income do not have adequate incentives to develop democratic institutions. This is because such incentives develop when people depend on domestic value-addition (production which gives profits to the capital and wages to workers). It is when such value addition takes place within the country that economic actors have an incentive to improve institutions that reduce transaction costs and enhance efficiency. Such incentives may not come about when income comes in through the export of natural resources without much value addition. For example, an oil-producing country exporting most of it as crude petroleum does limited value addition within itself and this can be a disincentive for developing efficient institutions.

WHICH SECTIONS OF SOCIETY DRIVE COMPETITIVE DEMOCRACY?

We have argued that the competition between the elites and counter-elites would lead to competitive democracy. Such a demand for competitive democracy may happen even if elite capture (or counter-elite capture) could achieve higher levels of economic growth and also the distribution of resources enhancing development opportunities for the poor. When people have incomes there would be a growing demand for greater political and human rights (and the success of such demand may depend on how these aspirations can be articulated under the prevailing political system of the country).

Competitive democracy can also mean dominance of some section of voters. One hypothesis in this regard is the influence of the median-voter.

Median-Voter Influence

Think about a context where there are 11 voters (and this example is just to highlight a point and hence this small number is only for demonstration. A similar problem may arise for any large number). Assume that there are two parties in this context: one is a Party for the Poor (PP) and another is a Party for the Rich (PR). Among the 11 voters, some are rich and some are poor and the rest are in between. One can list these voters in a descending order—with the richest at the top and the poorest at the bottom—and then the upper half are relatively richer and the lower half relatively poorer. Thus it is likely that the voters numbering 1, 2, 3, 4 may prefer voting for PR, and voters 11, 10, 9, 8 may prefer voting for PP. However, for either PP or PR to win elections, they need to get more votes. This would depend on the votes of numbers 5, 6 or 7. If No. 7 is with PP and 5 is with PR already, the additional vote determining the win would be 6. In fact, both PR and PP would try to attract the vote of 6, and shape their agendas to suit this voter's interest. The interesting implication is that whether the party is ideologically for the poor or for the rich, it may shape its agenda to suit the same voter. Thus the interest of this 'median-voter' may reflect in the aggregate electoral choice. Moreover, the difference between two parties (one which professes to stand for the poor and the other for the rich) may actually narrow down through political competition.

It is possible that the private goods demands of the median-voter can be given undue attention by the competing parties in a developing economy. (Such an influence can be there in the case of the developed economy too, but here the public goods and tax preferences of the median-voter may be attracting the attention.) However, political economy even in a competitive democracy can create barriers against reforming the economy and governance, especially in a developing economy. It can take place even in developed world. Let us consider some of these barriers in the following section.

POLITICAL ECONOMY AND EFFICIENCY-ENHANCING REFORMS

There can be several instances where a change in public-resource allocation or a change in a specific public policy would enhance the efficiency of an economy (or an increase in social welfare). For example, if a greater part of the money spent on poverty eradication programmes does not reach the poor, a change in the status quo would be better. In a context where poor people do not have access to good quality schools and health-care facilities, but the middle class gets subsidy for consuming electricity or LPG, a change in policy could enhance social welfare. When some goods are not imported to a country (probably due to the influence of a section of domestic producers) and because of that its consumers have to pay a higher price, the removal of import barriers could enhance the welfare for the majority of society. When the government spends substantial sums on government machinery, but if people are not getting good quality public services, a change in the system is desirable. When very high levels of fiscal deficit create inflation and debt-burden for the society (and also causes the increase in interest rates, as noted in Chapter 7), steps to reduce such deficit are desirable for the society.

It may be noted that in all these cases there may be some small section benefitting from the status quo. These may include the intermediaries or the non-poor, who siphon off the support aimed at the poor or specific industrialists who benefit from import barriers or governmental employees who do not have the pressure to perform and so on. Hence any 'reform' could harm some beneficiaries of the status quo (and hence such reforms cannot be called efficient under one notion of pareto-efficient, which would mean improving the welfare of some without harming the other). However, the lack of such a reform may cause aggregate social losses greater than the gains made by these specific sections (and hence reform is efficient under 'pareto-efficiency with compensation criteria'). Hence the reform is desired from the point of view of the society as a whole and probably in the long run.

There are several political economy factors that may prevent or delay such reforms. Obviously there are potential costs or losses to some sections due to such reforms. Hence, these can be delayed if these sections have some way to influence political decisions. Such influence can be through effective lobbying. Some political parties may be depending on specific interest groups for their re-election and survival, and hence may be vulnerable to influence by such groups. For example, teachers unions (even in the developed world) were found to be an important group opposing efficiency-oriented reforms in education. An important issue here is that usually those groups who are likely to suffer from a reform (like a trade union, or a set of industrialists who may suffer due to the removal of import barriers) are likely to be a homogenous and/or organized group, whereas the beneficiary of such reform could be society as a whole. The latter is neither well-organized nor homogenous, and hence they may not be able to exert collective pressure on the political decision-makers. Hence even a small section of the organized group can prevent reforms that may benefit a wider set of population in a country.

There are different types of costs when a policy is in a place that gives benefit to a small group but which is costly to the society as a whole. There were several such policies of this kind during the license raj in India. Limiting imports of a specific commodity to India could be one. This would mean that the domestic firms producing such commodity would gain by the lack of international competition in India. Their gains can be called rent. The major cost is that adequate amount of production will not take place in India, and the price that the domestic consumers would have to pay would be higher. There is consumer surplus forgone here. However, there is another cost due to such policies. Many firms may try to be part of these 'privileged' firms getting a part of this rent. There may be officials and politicians who get a part of this rent as commission/bribe from the protected firms. Thus the reward for such an official or politician could be higher than other people of comparable abilities/positions. Hence many people would try to be such rent-getting officials and politicians. Many people would divert their effort (from socially useful and productive activities) to be in positions where they can get rent. This rent-seeking behaviour is socially unproductive.

We have seen the median-voter hypothesis. It shows that even in a competitive democracy, it is possible that a small section of voters who occupy the median-voter position may be in a position to exert excessive influence in political decision. (One need not be part of a majority to influence decisions in a competitive democracy.) For example, if the middle-class section currently gets some subsidy which should have been ideally used for the welfare of the poor, a targeting of subsidy (for the poor) need not get electoral support if this middle class occupies the median voter position. It may be noted that such targeting need not be opposed by the upper middle class and rich who do not get the subsidy (or for them this subsidy may not be that crucial) and also the poor who may get more subsidy if it is targeted. Thus the possible support (or non-opposition) from the majority may not be adequate to overcome the opposition of the median voter in certain democratic contexts, especially if the two parties competing have their support bases fragmented along income/class basis. (For example, the competition of two coalitions in Kerala follows this pattern, whereas the competing parties in Tamil Nadu do not seem to reflect such a division of voters. The bi-party competition in the US and the UK has fault lines on the basis of income.)

Most of the contesting issues over which reforms are needed pertain to the use of public resources. The pool of public money can be viewed as a common pool resource (like the example of the fishing pond given in Chapter 18). If the common resource is not owned by anybody, we have seen that there would be a tendency to overuse it, even though such overuse harms everybody. However, no one individual (or group) has the incentive to control or avoid the overuse. Public money can also be viewed as a common resource and the tendency is for everybody to demand a greater part of it, without being concerned about the overall amount or the impact of such demand on others. By doing so everybody ends up in a worse off situation in the form of an increase in the fiscal deficit or interest rate or even total debt burden. Avoiding this may require coordination or sustenance of cooperation as in the case of the fishing pond example. Politics is expected to do such coordination but it can fail in many circumstances.

The expectations on the benefits and costs of reforms of some sections of society or the majority too can be a barrier against the reform. There are two types of problems related to these expectations. First could be that people are unsure of the benefits of reforms. When a government says that interest rates would come down if the fiscal deficit is controlled or that it will spend more money on poverty eradication by cutting down spending on other activities, many people need not be certain whether such positive changes would really happen (if they accept the suggested remedies). Hence there could be only lukewarm support to such reforms in society. There is another issue related to expectation. People know that there will be some losers due to certain reforms even if they are sure of the over-all benefits. However, some individuals are not sure whether they would be part of the losers or winners. For example, the proposal to increase the fees charged by institutes of higher education to create a greater number of seats or institutes may be considered beneficial by all. But they may be undecided on supporting it due to the uncertainty involved in the way this change in policy would affect each one of them.

Even when many people perceive that it is desirable to have reforms in the long-run, the fact that it may cause costs of adjustment immediately or in the short-run (whereas the benefits accrue in the long run) may encourage people to delay the reforms. This is like the situation where people may postpone a sur-gery (due to the fear of pain) even though such a delay could be harmful. In such a situation, a crisis could trigger reforms. For example, economic reforms in India were driven by the balance of payment crisis. (When Rajiv Gandhi came to power in the mid-eighties, the government allowed liberal imports and borrowing money from abroad to finance such imports. However, India's reserve of foreign exchange could not go up due to the then prevailing controls over exports. This created a balance of payment crisis in 1990–1991 when India could not meet the demand for US dollars to pay back the loans. This encour-aged the then Finance Minister Manmohan Singh to initiate certain reforms, especially the removal of barriers against exports from India.) Similarly, the changes in the former socialist economies were also driven by crises.

In the absence of crises, how do reforms of government policies or govern-ance take place? Whatever we have discussed here as factors restraining reforms also give us some clues on what may enable reforms. If there are some major stakeholders—who can influence political decision-making either through public discourses or due to their position in the electoral spectrum (say as the median voter)—who want efficient economic policies and better governance, there may be greater political willingness to take those steps. It is generally considered that the growth of the middle class which benefit from economic growth and competition as consumers, professionals, investors and as citizens may facilitate such reforms.

One can see the influence of such middle classes in India too. In the early years of Indian independence, the articulate sections were domestic industrialists, farmers with large farm-sizes or rural landlords, government officials and politicians. The size of the middle class as a whole was limited then. Moreover, most of them were depending on the government. Even industrialists were depending on the state for protection from foreign competition. The licensing policy gave some protection from competition and even from domestic companies too. Thus a major section of the middle class then was benefitting from the state which provided jobs or created policies which provided opportunities for rent-seeking. There was a nexus between politicians, officials and industrialists to sustain such a status quo. On the other hand, the economic growth of the last two to three decades has turned nearly 20 per cent of Indians into a class which is the equivalent of a global middle class. This class does not depend too much on the government for jobs or privileges. They depend on the market for consumption, on the private sector for jobs, and also participate in the capital market as investors. They want better public services in terms of roads, electricity, water supply and so on. They see the monopoly power of some companies (possibly sustained through corruption) in the product or service market as harmful to themselves. They see scams in stock market eroding their gains as investors. They see wastage or siphoning of the public money reducing the availability of resources for public goods and infrastructure needed for them. Hence even if this middle class does not constitute a majority, its visibility in public discourses (especially in English media) enables them to influence debates and governmental and judicial actions. Thus there is much more public posture against corruption and malpractices these days. This is evident from the recent discussions on the Lokpal Bill and also the support base of civil society leaders like Anna Hazare. However, the fact that this class does not constitute the majority in most states would mean that the corrupt politicians can win elections, especially from rural constituencies. Thus, the growing middle class has been making some positive influences on the shaping of government policies and governance per se in India.

Such a middle class has played an important role in the transformation of developed economies in Europe, America and Japan. Karl Marx had predicted that the conflict between the capitalists and working class would sharpen in the future. However, economic growth during the last 100 years depended not only on capital and (unskilled) labour but more importantly on knowledge, technology and human capital. (We have discussed this in Chapter 9.) The people who brought in technology, knowledge and human capital to the production process received a reward much higher than the subsistence wages received by the working class (specified by Marx). The people with human capital could create some limited surplus from their returns. They were visible in public discussions and in certain cases they had electoral clout and hence they could assert themselves in the political sphere too. This has influenced discussions on growth and redistribution.

Regarding growth, such a transition has led to capital market developments which facilitated the provision of capital to new-generation entrepreneurs. Development of merchant banking, stock markets (and markets for firms which enable the owner of a start-up company to sell his company and make gains) and early forms of venture capital and so on have helped even those entrepreneurs who were not born in rich families. People from middle-class families could become successful entrepreneurs (and rich later on). This process of economic mobility was much more evident in the US where the fact that everybody who migrated to that land were trying to build a new life there, and most people who went there initially were not from the privileged sections of Europe. (It is their independence and not the affinity with the royal powers back home in Europe that motivated them to found democratic political institutions in the US.) This new set of entrepreneurs had created social and economic institutions which are more appropriate to them. Bankruptcy laws which enable those who lose everything from their failed enterprises to keep what is needed for their basic sustenance are one such example. Thus the entrepreneurial middle class (or for example, the large number of owners of small size firms) has played an important role in the shaping of the economy of the US.

The emergence of the middle class has also led to social negotiations on what is to be redistributed. This is about how much of the private income has to be collected through taxes by the government to spend for purposes such as social security, education, health care and so on (in addition to public goods).

This negotiation and the social acceptance of taxing a larger part of the income of individuals became much more evident in the European (especially West-European) countries. The countries of North-West Europe (or Scandinavia) which include Norway, Sweden, Denmark and Finland became 'models' in this regard. They tax nearly 60 per cent of the private income and most of the educational (including higher education) and health-care needs of the population are met from the public exchequer. Some of these countries have income from oil production, control over large territories in the North Sea, and their population sizes are small—all these have contributed to ensuring a high quality of life for their citizens.

It is not that these developed economies are not facing any challenges. Globalization poses a serious threat to these countries. There are spheres of protection within these developed economies, and these may not be sustainable in the long run. The fact that these countries have already undergone an advanced stage of demographic transition by which more number of aged depend on the work of a lesser number of adults too causes problems. There may be pressure to rethink or roll back some of their major social security schemes, as evident from the debates in the USA (on Medicare) and in France and other parts of Europe (regarding generous pension schemes and early retirements). The growth of countries like China and India in global economic and political scene may reduce the bargaining strength of the developed world on the terms at which globalization can be charted. These tensions are somewhat reflecting in the attitude towards migrants to these countries. Thus the social and economic transformation currently happening all over the world may pose newer challenges to these countries, and their future may depend on the way these challenges are addressed.

Bibliographical Note: Some issues of elite capture are discussed in Bardhan and Mookherjee (2000, 2006). The political economy factors that may work against institutional reforms are reviewed in Santhakumar (2008).

QUESTIONS

1. How do you analyse the political change and status quo in your own state based on the discussions here?
2. How do you analyse the emergence of caste-based political parties and their ascendance to power and their impact on development outcomes?

3. How do you see competitive democracy playing out in resource transfer to different sections of society? Give concrete examples.

4. How can we develop sustainable strategies to counter corruption in India? Do you see a change in your thinking after learning economics and political economy?

5. Think about any step proposed as part of economic reforms in India. Who opposes it? Who is supporting it? Do you see any scope for a rational analysis here?

6. The Government of India may pass a Lokpal Bill very soon. What could be the effectiveness of such a bill in controlling corruption in India? Explain based on the discussion on political economy as part of this text.

PART VI

ENABLING DEVELOPMENT PRACTICE

◄ TWENTY-ONE ►

USING ECONOMICS FOR DEVELOPMENT INTERVENTIONS

———————

Economics may help us become more effective development practitioners—whether as a government official, politician, NGO volunteer, civil society activist or a social-entrepreneur. This and the following chapter list some 'easy to use' tips for such development actors.

Starting a school in a village (when the existing one is difficult to access), starting a fellowship programme for school students, constructing a toilet in the school, starting a drinking water project in a place where people currently use some unsafe source of water, improving the road to a village, training midwives, a scheme to provide additional food in *anganwadi*s and similar 'small-scale' actions can also be taken as development interventions. These may have a significant impact on reducing infant mortality and enhancing literacy and school retention rates leading to improved indices of human development.

Before starting a development intervention, we need to ask a number of questions:

1. What is the real problem that we are trying to solve or the real need that we are trying to meet?
2. How did we assess the problem or the need? Is the assessment reliable?
3. Why should we intervene here? Isn't this something that the potential beneficiaries of the intervention can solve/manage themselves?

297

4. How can we be sure that the 'solution' in our mind is the one that is really needed? Is the absence of the proposed solution the real cause of the problem?

5. Have we considered alternative ways of meeting the need/solving the problem?

6. Which alternative is the best considering the costs and benefits?

7. If the benefit of an intervention cannot be measured easily (for example, like the one which aims at reducing infant mortality rate), does the alternative selected incur the minimum cost to achieve a given objective?

8. Have we put in place mechanisms to see that the development intervention can continue to perform its expected role during the projected life? What is the source of funding for its operation and maintenance?

The same set of questions can also be used to analyse a development intervention already made by others. The success or failure or efficiency of development interventions depend to a great extent on how these questions are addressed at the stages of planning and implementation.

DEFINING THE PROBLEM CLEARLY AND HONESTLY

Before designing a development intervention, it is important to define very clearly (and honestly) the problem that you want to address. (At this stage you are not considering the causes of the problem or the solutions.) I have seen cases where development interventions are designed to suit the requirements of the funding agencies. Such a practice is not so uncommon in many government or NGO actions, especially those funded by international or foreign aid. Then it is better to say that we design such an intervention since we need money/jobs and these are provided by the funding agency.

Defining the problem at an appropriate level of generalization is useful. For example, many girls in a village do not go to secondary school. For an outsider this could be due to the absence of a secondary school. The lack of school there is a reality. However, there could be other factors that may be discouraging parents from sending their girls to the high school. We will not look for such factors if we frame the problem as the lack of school. On the other hand, if we expand the scope too much, there would be many factors that may come in our way. Hence, a particular development actor may not be able to address them and this may breed cynicism. Thus, framing the problem in such a way that some practical steps can be taken is also important. There should not be any urge to intervene just for the sake of intervention. A reflective practice would mean a proper balance between acting where it is possible and appropriate and 'leaving it to the larger socio-political forces' to sort out the issue when that is the best course of action.

An understanding of whether the problem is one for us or it is for those, whom we want to help, would be useful. For example, beggars may be a problem for us but they may not view it in the same manner. To a great extent, such a dilemma exists in the case of programmes aimed at rehabilitating sex workers. It is not that we should give up even if those who 'suffer' do not perceive it as a problem. There can be two ways of identifying a need for intervention—the first is based on what is 'demanded' by people; the second is when the 'interventionist' feels that there could be a scope for intervention even if people are not demanding. Whatever be the case, a clear and honest articulation of the problem to be addressed is absolutely important.

ASSESSING THE DEMAND: NEED TO BE CAREFUL

There are different ways of knowing about social needs. The first is through a political process, whereby people express their needs through political representatives and they in turn communicate it to the development machinery. Where such political process is ill-developed or inadequate, participatory processes are also suggested in literature to avoid a merely top down approach (by government officials) in delivering development services. (You may get exposure to such participatory appraisal techniques elsewhere.) What is written here is to make you cautious in interpreting what people want as expressed through political or other participatory processes.

There are two ways of assessing what people want: the first is to look at their current behaviour. If they are currently using a source of water, and it is clearly unhygienic (and it gives them health problems), there is clear information that a source of safe drinking water is useful to them. If people use traditional midwives during child delivery, and that leads to infection, there is a clear case of a need for intervention here. In these cases, what we do is to learn from their revealed behaviour. In general economists would give greater weight to the information gathered from such revealed behaviour. There can also be another route to understand what they want. This is based on what they tell us as part of surveys or to politicians or even during participatory appraisal sections. Assume that they expressed the wish to have a small irrigation project; there is some problem in taking this 'wish' at its face value. This is especially so when they know (it is expected in the case of such public services in a country like India) that they are not going to bear the full or major part of the cost of such an intervention, and it would be borne by an external agency—like the government, NGO, charity organization and so on. When they know that they do not have to bear the cost, there may be a tendency to demand something that is not most wanted. What is the problem in providing such a service, even if it is not demanded?

Let us take a very simple example. There are programmes to deliver saplings in schools. If you ask a student whether he needs one, he/she may say yes, and take one or more plants. However, this may not be a very important priority for him or her. For the plant to grow (in his/her backyard) additional care is needed (for watering and protecting it from animals). If this plant is not important for her/him, it is neglected to die. This means that the money spent is wasted. This is a social waste. Coming back to the example of the irrigation scheme, people may have to use complementary inputs like seeds, fertilizer and so on and see to it that watering is done at the appropriate time to reap the benefits of an irrigation scheme. This will happen only when the irrigation scheme is a felt need. What they demand, when they know that they do not have to spend money, need not be a felt need. Thus, a better strategy is to study their cultivation behaviour. If they are getting water from a deep or a distant source, it may be a clear indication that they will use the proposed irrigation scheme effectively. The other strategy used in economics (but not of much use in many contexts) is to ask them, through a properly designed and administered survey, how much they would be willing to pay for having such an irrigation system. Even if they do not have to pay, such a concern about their willingness to pay is needed to instil a cost consciousness on them. This is so because there is an opportunity cost for providing such a public service. Thus, we may get a clearer picture of the felt demand of the people, when they demand something with the knowledge that by doing so, they are losing something else.

WHEN AN OUTSIDER SUPPLIES A SERVICE NOT DEMANDED

Sometimes an external agency or a person from within can provide a social good or service even when people have not sought it. When a product or service or its benefit is unknown, it is likely that people do not express the need. If the people in a village are not sending their girls to high schools and prefer to marry them off, it is possible to have an intervention here. I have mentioned the efforts of rehabilitating sex workers. Such efforts can be made even when the potential beneficiaries do not show an urge to accept these changes.

The rationale is that the efforts made by the interventionist may demonstrate to them that something 'better' is indeed possible. Many poor people who were not really keen on using safe drinking water, hygienic toilet, electricity, vaccination, contraception measures and many such goods/services, turn around after such a demonstration effect. However, their sustained use depends on the willingness on the part of the potential beneficiaries. Otherwise, the intervention is to be carried out by the government, which has some coercive power to make people consume (or not consume) certain services. There are limits even for this coercive power.

If such an intervention is made by a social entrepreneur or by an altruist, then he/she may have an incentive to stop the effort while getting the signal that the beneficiaries are unlikely to accept such a service. However, because of the fact that many such efforts are funded or carried out by the government or NGOs (including international funding organizations), the people who make such efforts do not have the incentive to stop these interventions even when there are adequate signals that these are not going to work. This can lead to the wastage of resources.

WHAT CAUSES THE 'PROBLEM'?

In many cases, the apparent causes of the problem that we see need not be the real ones. There could be a problem even when people 'demand' some public intervention, and also when some socially concerned citizen tries to solve a problem. Identifying the causes of certain problems may require technical or scientific knowledge and here development practitioners may need to take the help of such experts. For example, when a village reports a number of infant deaths, and midwives there are not trained, a non-medical development practitioner should not summarily attribute the deaths to lack of trained midwives. Expert knowledge is to be sought wherever needed. There are many instances where development practitioners, including government officials or generalists, have gone ahead with their pet ideas without consulting experts. There are cases where sericulture was promoted in areas where its productivity was low, tube wells dug without checking the status of ground water table, biogas plants set up without checking whether enough waste was available in the locality and so on. Effective use of technical/scientific knowledge is needed and cross checking of an expert opinion with another expert is also desirable.

There is a tendency among those who work in the government/NGO to consider themselves as experts on every social issue and they find no need to consult an expert. Thus, they identify wrong causes and waste efforts in that regard. There may be a set of economic and social (including cultural) factors that may cause a particular outcome (which we see as a problem), and the non-consideration of all the relevant factors may lead to a wrong diagnosis. A classic example in this case is the practice of dowry which prevails despite its prohibition (which we have mentioned in Chapter 21). The case of not sending girls to secondary school (and that it may not be due to the lack of a school) is another example. In such a case opening of a school may not be adequate to solve the problem.

WHY SHOULD WE INTERVENE AND WHY CAN'T THEY SOLVE THE PROBLEM ON THEIR OWN?

There could be interventions when a social entrepreneur sees an opportunity and then he/she will be like any other entrepreneur. He/she may see a market untapped or not adequately tapped. Or he/she may have a technology which can help to supply a particular service at a cheaper rate or a better quality product at the current rates. All the precautions to be taken by a normal entrepreneur should be taken by a social entrepreneur too. (He/she may not have the incentives to be cautious adequately if there is some funding agency underwriting his/her losses.) It is not that the profit should be the prime concern of social entrepreneurs. However, reflecting on the trade-offs involved (including what they are willing to sacrifice personally to achieve a social goal) and a clarity in this regard is desirable. There are many successful social entrepreneurs in India, who include founders of

NGOs or Ashrams (or neo-religious establishments), and some of them may have had very humble beginnings.

There are cases where an external agency may have to intervene (not as an entrepreneur but more in a paternalistic role) when there is a problem which cannot be solved by those who are affected by it. The lessons from Chapter 5 (where markets or voluntary exchange do not work) are important here. In general, such intervention is for providing public goods or merit goods and addressing externality or of asymmetric information issues. There are cases where external help is needed to improve access to education (including higher education) due to the positive externality. There is some rationale for external intervention in the case of certain private goods since these are merit goods. Helping to produce something on a large scale (by tapping the benefits of economy of scale) without causing social loss of monopoly is also desirable. Simply helping those who cannot help themselves may also be needed. When such help is extended, it is desirable to help them in such a way that they help themselves in the long run. Whatever be the reason, a clear articulation of the reason for intervention (along with a clear articulation of the problem) is desirable.

NEED TO CONSIDER ALTERNATIVES

This is an area where many development interventions carried out by the government and NGOs fails. Many people go with pre-conditioned ideas of solving problems. This reduces the efficiency and effectiveness of interventions. Effectiveness and efficiency should be an important concern in all development interventions. By effectiveness, we mean whether we could meet a particular objective. If the objective is not realized, then the action is useless and ineffective. For example, if money is spent on a project to solve drinking water problem, and the problem remains unsolved even after implementation, it will be the worst outcome possible (since this is equivalent to zero benefit). Efficiency, as mentioned in earlier chapters, is related to the question of whether we get maximum benefits for a given amount of resources spent (or whether we spent the minimum amount of resources for a given level of benefits). In order to be effective and efficient, consideration of alternatives are important. There are many ways of improving the health of pregnant women (so as to reduce maternal and/or infant mortality)—giving cash to such people, supplying more food items at reduced prices, supplying cooked food in *anganwadi*s and so on. All of them may not be effective and efficient in the given context. By going ahead with a pre-conceived idea, we may be neglecting more effective and efficient means. This may lead to a wastage of social energy and resources, which could have been used elsewhere.

BENEFITS AND COSTS OF DEVELOPMENT INTERVENTIONS AND EFFICIENCY

Every private company owner will do an analysis before deciding on new investments. Will the total benefit (discounted sum of benefits received in different years) being greater than the total cost (discounted sum of costs incurred in different years) be a consideration here? Or there can be a calculation of Internal Rate of Return (IRR) to see whether it is greater than the interest rates or the normal returns from other capital investments. This is called a financial analysis. However, this is different from an economic analysis and what a government or an NGO should do in the case of public investments or social intervention. In financial analysis, the private entrepreneur will take into account all paid-out costs and all the revenues accruing to the firm. Thus, if the electricity tariff is ₹1 per unit and he has to pay ₹300 per month, that may be considered as the cost. But an economic analysis is carried out by taking society as a whole. Even though electricity is supplied at a subsidized rate of ₹1 per unit to the entrepreneur, society may spend more to produce and distribute each unit. Thus, the actual cost of electricity and all such inputs used in the production process needs to be taken into account in the economic analysis.

Let us consider another input. For a particular project, the wages of unskilled workers may be fixed by the government at ₹300 per person per day. The financial analysis will take this as a paid-out cost. However, if the region has higher unemployment and if people do not get this much wage rate normally, economic analysis need not consider ₹300 as the paid-out cost. If the prevailing market wage in the region is ₹200, only that needs to be accounted for in the economic analysis. In the absence of the project, local people would have got only ₹200 as wages and it goes up to ₹300 with the project. Thus, the additional wage that local people get becomes a part of the benefit of the project.

Think about a public road where no toll collection is envisaged. In that sense, there is no revenue after constructing the road (and there are only costs for construction and maintenance). Thus a financial analysis which takes into account the paid-out costs and revenue would project it as making negative income. However, here the benefits are for society. Having a new road may reduce the distance or time of travel. It may enable commodities to reach the market, and thus they could fetch a higher price. All these benefits have to be taken into account. Thus, economic valuation of benefits is needed.

There are inputs and outputs for a project or intervention. Whether each of these inputs and outputs are exchanged in a market has some importance for their valuation. For example, the output of a water supply project is drinking water delivered at home or to a community location. Drinking water is not normally traded in markets. (Of course mineral or bottled water is traded, but that is a product with a different quality.) Similarly, a particular intervention may require electricity or kerosene as an input which are not traded in the market. Instead, their prices are decided by the government, which also gives subsidy. In the case of commodities, for which there is a market (like cement which may be used as an input) its market price can be used to calculate the cost of the input. However, in the case of those commodities for which there is no well-developed market, their cost is to be estimated on the basis of an elaborate procedure. This is needed to identify their opportunity cost. One strategy is to see its real cost of production. Otherwise, we may have to see the foregone benefit in using a particular item for this development intervention.

This book does not cover the method of cost–benefit analysis. Doing such an analysis would require specialized knowledge. Even when we are not doing a cost–benefit analysis, we should be concerned about the basic principles. Where the cost is substantial, it is important to take the help of an economist to carry out such an analysis. Based on the cost–benefit analysis, the project which has the highest benefit for a given cost (which has the highest ratio between benefit and cost) needs to be selected.

SELECTING THE BEST OPTION WHEN THE BENEFITS CANNOT BE ASSESSED

However, for a number of development interventions, it may not be possible to assess the benefits in money terms. For example, if a project could reduce infant mortality rates, or another one could improve the nutritional status of children

going to *anganwadi*s, their benefits cannot be measured easily. There are economic insights for doing such measurements, but these are difficult to apply for a
normal development practitioner. However, this does not mean that we need not
be conscious of the cost of such projects. In such cases where benefits cannot be
measured, a strategy would be to use the cost-effectiveness approach. Here, we
are asking whether we use the measure which minimizes cost to reach a particular
objective. For example, there can be several ways to improve the nutritional status
of the children attending *anganwadi*s. A cost-effectiveness approach should
enable us to select the cheapest possible means to enhance nutritional status. (By
using minimum cost here, it is expected that the resources saved can be used for
other equally important social needs.) The measurement of a clearly specified
objective is very important here. The costs of two projects which aim at different objectives cannot be compared. Consider the following three projects: (*a*) that
improves the vitamin A deficiency of 50 children; (*b*) that improves the vitamin A
deficiency of 70 children and (*c*) that improves the vitamin A and protein deficiency of 50 children. One cannot choose the minimum cost project among
these three because these are different projects with different objectives.

ENSURING THE SUSTENANCE OF DEVELOPMENT INTERVENTIONS DURING THE EXPECTED LIFE

In general, it is relatively easy to create or implement a new project—like building a library or a recreation centre, or a school, or even a toilet for the school. It
may be easy to hire a contractor for its implementation but continued operation
and maintenance is very important. If a toilet is built, and if it becomes unusable
within a few months, there are no benefits from this intervention. A simple example of a school toilet is cited here to highlight the fact that maintenance is not a
simple job. A lot of planning is needed. For example, it should have regular water
supply. For pumping water, it may require power (even if the toilet is not used
during nights). A servant is needed to clean the toilets and it should be ensured
that he does his job well. All these cost money and so there should be a regular
stream of revenue.

How do we ensure that this money reaches the person who has to spend it in
time? Can there be a charge for those who use toilets in a rural school? If not, the
school should have enough additional income for maintaining a toilet. If the toilet

is built under a government programme or with the help of a charitable organization, there should be some planning on how to mobilize money for maintenance. Can there be a budget allocation for the school to maintain the toilet? Can the local government meet the cost of maintaining it? Even if there is some understanding on this, how does one ensure that it allocates money regularly and that the money reaches the person (probably the head master) in time? If wages are not paid in time, the servant may stop coming and soon the toilet becomes unusable. Ensuring all these is not that simple.

There are two dimensions to this problem. First, the financial sustainability. This is ensuring that an intervention or project has a revenue stream to meet its operating expenditure until the expected end of its life. Second, there has to be an institutional system for maintenance. Taking the toilet example, there should be some way to ensure that the person cleans the toilet in time. Who will ensure this? Will the teachers or headmaster have an interest in seeing that the children's toilet is clean, if they have a different toilet for themselves? If the headmaster is not doing this job, is there a way by which somebody else (government/parents) can pressurize him to act? These issues are related to institutional or organizational matters and will be discussed in the next chapter. Let us consider financial sustainability here. While designing development intervention, financial sustainability should be an important concern. This is especially so if the intervention is not a one-time activity, like a training session for school teachers. When there is a continuation of the programme or a continued operation of the asset created as part of the development intervention, financial sustainability is to be an important concern.

It may be possible to have a user charge to meet the operating costs and there is a merit in doing so wherever possible. But in some cases user charges are neither feasible nor desirable. The toilet of a rural school is a typical example. We may not like children to pay for using the toilet or even their parents may not afford it. There is an opinion that it should be provided free of cost. This is one reason for not charging user fees. The other reason is that it is difficult to charge a fee for what is called public goods without reducing social welfare. Once it is provided, one person's consumption does not affect others' consumption (for example, street lights). Thus, when it is not costly for one more person to enjoy the service, and if we do not allow him/her to enjoy the service due to the non-payment of a fee, it is not socially efficient. Moreover it is costly to exclude some people. For example, if we do not want a public park to be enjoyed by persons who have not paid a user fee, there should be compound wall, a security guard and a toll gate. In certain cases, the revenue may not even be sufficient to meet such expenditures (like compound wall, security guard and toll gate in the case of a public park).

Places Where User Charge Is Desirable

In the provision of private goods where one person's consumption reduces the availability of the goods for others, and where excluding the non-payer is not costly, charging a user fee is not that difficult. This is desirable, if the people who get such a service are not those whom society at large considers eligible to get the service free of cost. A typical example is piped water supply. This is usually provided by the government or non-private organizations (or through collective effort) since there is some economy of scale. It may be better to develop one major source and one pipe network to provide water to a number of households. In order to avoid the transition of this system into a harmful monopoly, some social control is good. Even if such water supply system is implemented with government money or through a non-governmental initiative, there may be a need for other sources of income for the recurring cost for its maintenance. It is not easy to get grants for such recurring costs, and even if some (like local or district governments) assure such grants, there are many difficulties in India to see that these are disbursed in time. Thus, the maintenance of the water supply system could be very difficult without adequate money available in time. Thus, there is some merit in mobilizing at least part of the money from the users. Moreover, if people do not have to spend any money, they need not be very careful with the system or even with the use of water. They may not close taps after the use or may take excessive water for gardening and so on.

If user charges are neither desirable nor feasible in certain contexts, the proponents of a project or intervention (whether it is government, NGO, collective groups or a charity organization) should ensure that there is adequate money for operation and maintenance. In governmental contexts, there may be an implied understanding that the government would finance such costs. But there can be inordinate delay in the disbursements of such payments, and this may affect maintenance. This would lead to the non-availability of services intended and also the degeneration of the assets created. This would affect the effectiveness of such development interventions. A large number of development assets created do not lead to benefits for the intended population during the expected period because of this problem.

There can be a problem related to political economy here. People who make such development interventions are often interested in creating assets and want to show off that they have done something but are not keen on its maintenance and operation. Creation of an asset is a visible intervention but maintenance is not. Asset creation is often done through contractors who only have an incentive to see its completion but not its maintenance. There is also a tendency to use whatever money that is available for fixed costs (to create maximum visible asset) leaving little for maintenance. Thus to make development interventions effective this issue is to be addressed squarely.

POSSIBLE TRAPS IN ASSESSING THE IMPACT OF AN INTERVENTION

Farmers in a locality were getting very low incomes. An NGO thought that the lack of a tube well was the main problem and got one such well for the farmers. After a couple of years, an outside agency came in and saw that farmers' income had increased and concluded that the tube well project was successful. This is a general problem called attribution error. Here we may be wrongly attributing the increased income to the implementation of the tube well project. There may be several other factors that might have contributed to the increase in the income of farmers. The prices of the commodities that they produced may have gone up (compared with the situation before the implementation of the project). They may be using more fertilizer lately or a different variety of seeds and these could have increased the productivity. Or it is that the crops that they cultivate now are of a different kind (more of commercial crops) than what they were planting earlier. Or the younger generation of these farmers is working elsewhere and sending back money and this too may have increased their incomes. Thus there is a need to separate out the effect of the tube well project. This is not a simple exercise. Thus the first lesson for development practitioners is that they should not easily fall into this attribution error. How to avoid it?

We need to know what we are actually comparing. Let us consider this village of farmers. When we want to know the impact of the intervention/project, we are comparing the situation of the village 'today' with what would have been the situation in the village 'today if there was no project'. How do we get information on what would have been the situation in the village had there been no project? This is a very difficult task. If there was a similar village nearby where such a project had not been implemented, then its current situation could have been compared with the situation of the village where the project had been implemented. It may not be easy to locate a village which has relevant features (type of farmers, their cultivation pattern, and their socio-economic features) similar to those of the project village.

The other possibility is to collect data on all the relevant factors that might have contributed in boosting the income of the farmers. This should be done before the implementation of the project and also at the time of evaluation (after the implementation). (This is possible only if the idea of evaluation was there before the implementation of project and if the required baseline data were collected then.) Then we have the information on the change in all factors (like the prices, cropping pattern, fertilizer use, income sources of the family members and so on) that may have an influence on the income of farmers. By analysing these data with a statistical method called econometrics, one may be able to isolate the impact of the well project. This method is not covered in this textbook. This requires specialized knowledge. The help of a trained econometrician to do the actual data collection/analysis may be taken.

QUESTIONS/EXERCISES

1. If farmers are committing suicide in a village that you work for, how do you plan an intervention?
2. Think about a strategy to intervene, if there is a significant dropout rate among the boys after eighth standard in an area.
3. What are the alternative ways that you would consider, if somebody finds that the non-use of hygienic sanitary napkins is a constraint against the improvement of health and work participation rate among rural women?
4. How do you evaluate a programme that funds rural government schools to have annual excursions?
5. What would be a strategy to operate public libraries in rural areas on a sustainable basis?

⊰ TWENTY-TWO ⊱

USING ECONOMICS FOR ANALYSING AND DESIGNING ORGANIZATIONS AND RULES

———————◦•◦•◦———————

One reason why development interventions fail is that there is no provision for the maintenance and operation. Another important reason is that the organizations responsible for implementing and managing such interventions fail to function in the expected manner. Even when money is allotted, interventions need not be successful. For example, if many schools do not work well, the blame is with the way their affairs are managed. Only a small portion of every ₹100 spent on helping the poor reaches the beneficiaries and this may have something do with the organizations managing such programmes. We presume that organizations or mechanisms that we design will deliver the goods. When they fail we generally infer that 'people are bad' or 'they are morally corrupt' and so on. Even if these inferences are correct, we cannot set right all people to ensure the success of development interventions. So we may have to 'design' organizations and rules, which may encourage or force people to work in the way they are expected to do.

Organizations are part of a larger structure—a framework of 'rules'. As discussed in the chapter on institutions, these rules of the game are called institutions in economics. Some organizations do not succeed because the institutional framework (within which these organizations are created) has some built in problems.

311

Or, organizations do not work because of the failure of institutions. The main focus of this chapter is how to design institutions and organizations that work for development interventions. The same insights can be used for analysing existing institutions (and organizations) which are either successful or a failure.

ARTICULATING THE SPECIFIC OBJECTIVE OF THE INSTITUTION/ORGANIZATION

We should be first clear as to why we need an institution/rule or even an organization. Is there a market failure (as discussed in other chapters, especially Chapters 5, 17, 18 and 19 of this book)? If the context has some features of natural monopoly, public goods, externality, merit good or asymmetric information, then voluntary action or exchange by individuals alone may not be adequate. Then there may be a need for an intervention by society or government (of local or higher levels). The following question needs to be asked: why should there be a social or governmental intervention (or that by an external agency like a charitable organization or NGO) in the given context? This question should be asked even about lack of adequate schooling or non-availability of safe drinking water or the lack of cleanliness in public spaces and so on.

As noted earlier, there can be governmental or societal interventions even when there is no explicit form of market failure. This may be for a distributional reason, that is, to help or transfer some resources to some specific groups for social, political or other reasons. Even when an institution is built for this purpose, a clear articulation of goals is desirable. This is so since many 'distribution-oriented' institutions may neglect their foundational objectives in the long run and survive just to meet the needs of some intermediaries. Some organizations may survive even when its foundational objective can be met by other more efficient means.

There could also be a lack of clarity of objective in certain contexts in the design of organization. Enabling all children in a village to get school education could be an appropriate objective. Establishing a school in the village is not an objective by itself, but is only a means to achieve an objective. A logical framework, as suggested in the previous chapter for establishing the need for a development intervention, is required even for designing a rule or an organization. Is the lack of a rule or organization the reason for the prevalence of the problem that has been identified? Is it enough to close the liquor shop in a village that has many alcoholics? We may not be always sure of such cause–effect relationships but a reasonable effort to establish the relationship is needed. It is not that we should not intervene by creating a rule/organization on an experimental basis to address a problem, even when we are uncertain of this cause–effect relationship. This is similar to a risky investment made by an entrepreneur. (Or an entrepreneur may start producing/selling a product/service to test the market.) However, an entrepreneur making a risky investment (or testing the market) has the appropriate incentive to learn from the signals coming out of the situation (whether it will work or not). On the other hand, such incentives need not exist for a public manager or a politician (or other development practitioners) who may be depending on others' money to make such investments. This may lead to the wastage of social resources.

Ability to Achieve or Meet the Objectives

Another characteristic of an institution/rule is its effectiveness or the ability to meet the objective. (Here too, there can be some reasonable levels of risks and uncertainty.) Once we have clearly articulated the social objective, the next step is to come out with a set of alternative ways of addressing the identified problem. For example, if many children in a village do not attend a secondary school, there can be multiple interventions, such as the following: (*a*) start a school in the village; (*b*) help a private organization to start a school there and (*c*) give financial support to parents to send the children to a nearby school and so on. All these should be evaluated for their effectiveness—whether each one of them is adequate to meet the objective (and here we need not be concerned about the cost of intervention in listing out such alternatives). For example, if there are no schools within a reasonable distance, then option (*c*) cannot be effective. Similarly, if no private practitioner or NGO is willing to work there, even option (*b*) need not be effective. If fathers use the money given for this purpose to meet their private needs (say for alcohol), that would become another reason why option (*c*) cannot be effective. This may encourage us to think about giving the money to the mothers instead.

There is a possibility that there will be excessive focus on certain alternatives and (a neglect of other viable options). There can be several reasons: ignorance, pre-conceived notions, ideology and so on can play a role here. Even when information is available on the possibility of a new option, we may filter information, which conforms to our pre-conceived ideas. Thus, measures to minimize the impact of ignorance and to collect more information, and finally a willingness to be open to assimilate new information (contrary to our beliefs and pre-conceived ideas) are important. However, economics may guide us to take an 'optimal' position in terms of gathering new information. We need to be concerned about the additional costs and benefits of acquiring more information. If greater expertise is available at ₹5 lakh to think about a problem, which creates a social cost of ₹3 lakh, then seeking such expertise may not be efficient.

An important reason behind the non-consideration of some viable alternatives is the influence of some narrow interest groups. For example, when a social problem is identified, the tendency of the public bureaucracy is to propose a solution that would enhance its size. When agricultural productivity was not increasing in Kerala in the seventies and eighties, the agriculture ministry suggested opening of their offices in all the villages without checking whether the lack of such offices was the reason for low productivity. Similarly, research scientists may have an interest in giving an exaggerated picture of the potential benefits of a research investment as a solution to a social problem. Here the institutional arrangement should have provisions for evaluation of such proposals by outside experts who do not have a direct interest in the outcome of the evaluation. Hence there have to be checks and balances considering the likelihood of the influence of narrow interest groups. This is part of the issue of 'conflict of interest' in decision-making and we will discuss it in a later section of this chapter.

ABILITY TO CARRY OUT THE ASSIGNED TASKS EFFICIENTLY OR IN THE MOST ECONOMIC MANNER

Efficiency would imply that the cheapest way of solving the identified problem should be selected for the purpose. This would mean producing a given output through minimum possible cost (effort) or achieving maximum output for a given cost (effort). If all the alternative institutions considered are just adequate to address the given problem, then it is sufficient to pick up the one that costs the least (and one need not be concerned about the benefits here). There are direct and indirect costs in the functioning of an institution (as we have mentioned in

Chapter 19). Direct costs, as noted earlier, include those needed for the functioning of the institution (and the organizations shaped within that). The cost of starting and maintaining a school, financial support to the private organization to run the school or financial support to parents to send their kids to school and so on are part of the direct costs for the example given in the previous paragraph. There are also costs of enforcements: to see that school functions as envisaged (in option [*a*]) or the private school which get financial support provides education to all the eligible students and of the expected quality (in option [*b*]); or to see that the parents who get money send their kids to school (in option [*c*]). Ensuring these may require monitoring and supervision. The difficulties (or the cost or effort required) for monitoring could be very different for these three options. For each of these options, there can be many subalternatives which may incur different efforts to monitor and oversight.

An efficient institution would enable/encourage organizations and individuals to carry out the assigned tasks efficiently. Efficiency can be achieved only through aligning the incentives of actors (organizations and individuals) with the objectives of the institution. You may remember the principal–agent relationship and example of the photocopying operator mentioned in the chapter on strategic relationships. For example, the government which finances a private school (under option [*b*] mentioned above) should see whether it has the incentive to take in all the eligible children in the locality. There can also be incentive systems which are 'self-enforcing'. For example, if the money given to the parents (under option [*c*]) is based on the attendance of their wards in school, it has an inbuilt incentive for the parents to send the children to school regularly. (Of course there may be a certain need for supervision here to see that there is no manipulation of attendance records at schools.) When the grant to the private school is based on the number of students to which it caters, it has an incentive to admit all the eligible students (and hence a monitoring of whether they admit all students may not be needed). Similarly if the funding is based on the number of staff positions depending on the number of students, then the school or the teachers may have an incentive to admit all the children. On the other hand, if there is a lump-sum grant (an amount of money irrespective of the number of students or staff positions), such an incentive may not exist. If the funding is based on the performance of students, the school may have an incentive to deny admission to those students who may not do well in the examinations. Thus self-enforcing or 'incentive compatible' alternatives may reduce the cost of enforcement (and consequently the cost of institution/rule). That is why economists prescribe such mechanisms.

When the school is run by the public agency, there should be a special concern about the efficiency of the working of the organization itself. This concern for organizational efficiency is important for public provision, since public organizations do not have the 'obvious incentives/disincentives' of the for-profit firms to minimize costs and be efficient. However, such concern is not needed when a private organization is supported to provide education. This is so since the private organization has the incentive to be efficient in terms of cost minimization. Here the concern has to be whether it provides the services expected from it. It may try to save costs by diluting the quality. For example, it may try to employ inexperienced teachers by paying low salaries. (If financial support is given on the basis of the number of students it admits, there may not be a need for monitoring the attendance in private schools, but monitoring may be needed to see whether expected quality education is provided.) It may be noted that if there is only one private organization, it does not have the incentive to provide adequate service required by the consumers, and it is unlikely to behave in a customer friendly manner.

The government school may require multiple layers of supervisors to see that it performs its role adequately. None of the actors lose directly by not performing his/her role. Hence, there should be penalties to those who do not do their job well. Teachers who do not come to school, do not take their classes properly and do not complete their expected tasks may have to be penalized. Teachers who do their job exceedingly well may have to be rewarded with positive incentives. In order to do so, higher authorities may have to monitor the teachers. These authorities should have the incentive to do their jobs well. The effort required to see that this multilayer hierarchical system works may be substantial.

If the institutional alternative is a mere rule (for example, the one which says that parents who do not send their kid to school will be penalized or punished), direct costs may include that which is needed for its enforcement. Indirect costs are those which are foregone due to the presence of a rule. For example, if there are some economic activities currently taking place with the help of child labour, these may become expensive by employing adult workers when mandatory schooling is imposed. The costs (direct and indirect) should be an important concern in designing institutions.

In certain cases, the strength of the market (and its freedom of choice) is combined with the 'compulsions' of the regulation. If a government decides that the total pollution of a particular chemical (say carbon dioxide) should not be more than 100 units in a city, it may allocate this as quota to the existing polluters (factories). For example, if there are 10 factories, each may be given a quota of 10 each. Then they can be allowed to 'trade' their quota. If one firm which uses the latest technology of production generates only eight units of carbon dioxide, it has two unused units, which it may sell to others. There may be another firm which uses an old technology, and it may be emitting 12 units of carbon dioxide. It has two options then. Either it can buy two units from the quota of the first firm, and emit 12 units (legally), or it can change its technology of production to reduce its emission from 12 to 10. In certain instances, the former option may be cheaper. Thus the trading of quotas gives an incentive for the first firm to use better technology and emit lesser than it can do legally. It also gives the freedom of choice to the second firm, whether to change technology or to buy unused quota of units from other firms. This is a market-based instrument for solving a market failure. Hence even when regulation is needed, innovative solutions to bring in choice may enhance efficiency.

ABILITY TO BE EFFICIENT UNDER CHANGING ECONOMIC CONDITIONS

A particular institution might have been socially efficient at a point of time but it need not continue to be so under changing socio-economic conditions. There can be several reasons where 'path dependence' or a lock-in occurs by which past institutions continue to persist despite becoming inefficient. The self-perpetuating or self-preserving feedback provided by the organizations developed within that institution could be one reason. Sunk costs, the spreading of incorrect models of reality and so on have also been cited as reasons. Thus, one characteristic required for institutions to be efficient and effective is the ability to change itself in tune with changing realities. This can also be related to the flexibility that the institution sustains in its operations. This too requires design of incentives of actors (organizations and individuals) that encourage them to be in tune with changing economic variables.

We can understand this issue by using the example of schooling discussed here. Let us consider the three ways of funding the private school (under option

[b]): (i) sponsoring a fixed number of staff positions; (ii) giving money depending on the number of students and (iii) providing a fixed grant to the school. It is easy to see that the first two ways help us to change the funding if there is a decline in the number of students going to that school for some reasons. (These may include the fall in the number of children in the locality, students/parents not liking the school for some reason, competitive schools coming up in the locality and so on.) On the other hand, there may be difficulties in reducing the lump-sum grant even if there is a reduction in the number of students. (They may have already employed a fixed number of teachers based on the grant and reducing this number could be difficult.) Whether the rule or organizational structure allows it to evolve according to the changing reality is to be an important concern in the design.

One reason for this concern about dynamic efficiency is the following: sometimes interventions are designed in a specific context due to the absence of a market. For example, there may be a need for social intervention if some people in a village have acute dental problems, but there is no proper supply of dental care services in the villages. The care available in the village could be of spurious nature. However, this situation may change over a period of time. Once such market provision of service is available, how people respond to (use) the socially provided service is something that is to be evaluated. The social provision should be able to internalize the changes in this regard without causing wastage of resources.

CONTRACTING OUT OR EXPANDING THE ORGANIZATION?

It is well known that private firms may decide to outsource certain activities rather than recruiting employees to do the same tasks. In general, private firms are expected to have the incentives to take appropriate decisions in this regard, and these decisions may be driven by their interest in maximizing the profit. However, public or non-profit organizations need not have such an incentive. Thus some rationality-based decision-making may be needed to see whether to outsource an activity or not.

In many small towns in the US, the local administration does not contract out some activities even though they are permitted to do so. Clearing of trees (and removal of snow) falling on the roads during winter/storms is one such activity. Why do they prefer to have their own employees carry out this task was a subject of analysis. Contracting has some inbuilt problems. First, it is relatively difficult to specify the conditions of contract regarding the quantum of activities to be carried out as part of an uncertain natural event or calamity (tree falling during winter). Even if an authorized agency is asked to do this additional task, it may ask for an additional contract clause for this purpose. If the agency is called upon to do the task after the event, there may not be enough time to prepare the contract. Since the county faces a contingent situation (arising out of the urgency to remove the materials so as to open the roads for traffic), the agency may try to extract an unfair deal in this regard. Hence they may wish to do it themselves as it is relatively easy to exercise greater control over one's own employees in such emergency situations. Having one's own employees may be costlier (compared with the contracting out) option, since supervision may be needed to get the expected work from them. However, such an additional cost may be justified in certain cases due to the difficulties in contracting out such services.

In general, it may be difficult to use private companies for emergency purposes. That may be one reason why a fire control service is provided by the state. (But preventing fire has positive externality too since it may reduce the possibility of spreading fire. It has some economy of scale in the sense that it is costly to have a fire extinguisher service in each and every building.) Likewise emergency ambulance services are provided by the state or non-profit agencies in many countries. What if the ambulance company tries to extract an unfair deal exploiting the contingent situation? (It may not be costly for the society to have private [for-profit] firms providing ambulances to transport dead bodies. Why?)

A number of factors may have to be considered while taking a decision on whether to contract out a service or to have own employees. How difficult it is to judge the quality of the work, how important it is to control the transactions/processes of work, the possibility of contract contingencies and so on are some of them.

CENTRALIZATION VERSUS DECENTRALIZATION

Should decision-making in an organization be decentralized or centralized? A certain degree of decentralization in decision-making may be good in itself (which is not related to the efficiency or effectiveness of the organization). This gives a sense of ownership or power to all the participants in the process (participation may be necessary as part of empowerment). There is also a moral position taken by many who view decentralization as good in all contexts. However, such decentralization is usually evaluated in economics in terms of efficiency and effectiveness of an organization. As noted in Chapter 17 on governance, the guiding principle in economics is that if something can be done efficiently at the lowest level (the most decentralized level), it should be carried out there. The decisions and actions should be taken at the higher levels (or more centralized levels) only if it enhances efficiency.

One reason for such centralization is the scale economy. If an action taken for a wider set of stakeholders turns out to be cheaper, then such centralization is desirable. For example, the management of waste disposal systems or drinking water systems in certain contexts may require a centralized organization to ensure efficiency. This may be due to the nature of technology. The use of certain technology may bring down the per-unit cost, but its use may need large-scale systems. It may be cheaper to have a reservoir and water distribution system for a larger area rather than many small systems catering to each settlement. This may require a larger organization too.

Another important (but related) reason for having a larger organization is the need for expert knowledge. If the running of a system requires specialized knowledge, it may not be efficient if each small organization tries to acquire such expertise. This may require a network or a federation of such organizations (or a bigger organization serving a wider constituency) procuring such expertise. It is easy to understand that a clinic serving one or two villages may not be able to procure all medical specialists such as cardiologists, neurosurgeons and so on. However, their expertise may be needed for some patients. One strategy as practised in the government is to have such specialists in a district hospital, to which patients from primary health-care centres may go. But there could be other ways of sharing the times of these specialists so that their services become available to the people in different villages. The use of information technology can play an important role here.

Another conventional system in the government is to have specialists at state-level organizations, and thus create a state-level department to provide public services. Though local governments cannot procure such expertise efficiently, this by itself need not necessitate the state-level organization. For example, different local governments can design/implement their water supply systems, or electricity distribution systems or waste processing units by tapping the experts available at the state or national level on a consultant basis. There are challenges in this regard. You may read one such case (city governments and water supply) in Santhakumar (2011).

CONFLICT OF INTEREST

This is a crucial issue in the functioning of any organization. Are the people taking decisions at any level likely to be driven by their (own) interests that may work against the stated purpose of the organization? It is important for private organizations too at some level. For example, when the ownership of companies is spread out to a large number of share holders, and when private firms depend on markets for capital, providing correct information about the functioning of the firm to the public is essential. That is why independent auditing and accounting reports are needed for corporate governance. What if the auditing firm hired by the private company prepares an incorrect report to suit the interests of the major shareholders of the company? The minor shareholders, lenders and public may be misled about the real financial health of the company. Some of the recent corporate frauds/scams are indications of this problem. Thus, the conflict of interest issues are important even in the case of private companies.

Conflict of interest issues may arise more frequently in non-private organizations. For example, assume that the owner of a private company appoints his son as the senior manager. This should not be a major concern for the public (if they are not the shareholders of the company) since the cost of this decision—an inefficient/ineffective person is appointed as the manager just because he is the son of the owner—is borne by the owner himself. (This may reflect in the profit of the company.) In fact, in such cases, the owner may have an incentive to appoint efficient managers if he cares for the profit. Think about the president of a non-private (public or non-governmental) organization. He is not that much affected by the inefficiency of the organization (unlike the owner of a private company) and hence he may have greater incentive to hire his friends and relatives. This is not a hypothetical situation. If we analyse public sector organizations in India where appointments are not made through the Public Service Commission, one can see political and personal relationships influencing the appointments without much consideration of the merit or the real qualification of the person.

To minimize the conflict of interest, organizational mechanisms are needed to avoid situations where the decision-maker is likely to be influenced by personal interests that are against the interest of the firm. (On the other hand, personal interests which go along with the interest of the organization have to be encouraged.) People with known conflict of interest have to be kept out of specific decision-making process, even if they, by virtue of their position within the organization, are expected to participate in the process. Transparency plays an important role here. By making the decision process transparent, others can see whether any decision was taken with a conflict of interest. Then the remedial measures can be sought for their correction.

SOME ISSUES RELATED TO CORRUPTION

One major source of corruption is when some people are granted monopoly power to provide a license or service. Let us consider the regulation of motor vehicles in India. We need to take pollution control certification and there are many licensed firms providing such a certificate. We do not see much corruption here as there are many firms competing and the charge is also reasonable. The veracity of the certification can also be checked with the help of technology (image of the emissions). But there is rampant corruption in the issue of driving license. Here there is a monopoly department issuing license; there is no competition in the provision of this public service and hence the service provider need not be concerned about the conveniences or requirements of the clients. People do not have any option other than depending on the motor vehicles department. Hence many people (who are qualified or eligible to get the service) pay a bribe directly to the vehicle/driving inspectors (or through the driving school) to get a quicker service. This by itself is not a problem (and this can be like paying an agent to buy something from the market, since the customer does not want to spend the time). However, it is costly on two counts. Given the fact that the motor vehicles department is known for corruption and providing delayed or rude service, everybody is forced to go through the route of corruption. In addition people who do not qualify a driving test are also likely to get licenses using the route of corruption. This can be costly for society due to the potential increase in the accidents created by such unqualified people. Since officers get substantial bribes, there can be a rent-seeking effort to be part of that corruption racket.

One possible solution in such cases is to minimize the need for monopoly (and to bring in some competition). This may encourage service providers to be customer friendly and avoid a delay in service provision. However, it may not be easy to bring in competition in the case of all such (especially public) services. If the issue of driving license is privatized, how can we ensure that licensees do not issue such certificates without proper testing? This may require supervision and oversight by a set of regulators, but what if these regulators are also corrupt.

Punishing a private franchisee for issuing a driving license to an unqualified person may not be that effective in certain situations, where as punishing a government officer for this mistake may be relatively easier (since government has greater control over his work). Hence there are costs and benefits in alternative actions to control corruption, and the decision to use one alternative may depend on the context. This trade-off need not remain static, but the availability of technologies may enable controlling corruption relatively easily. Biometric cards are being used these days to avoid fraudulent practices, which involve misrepresentation of the identities of the people.

What about 'big ticket' corruption like that of ministers and top officials in collusion with capitalists? In general, if there is a discretionary role for the government to select one private firm over the other, there is a greater likelihood of corruption. Hence it is important to reduce such a discretionary role. In those cases where government selection cannot be avoided, it is better to assign that role to independent regulators whose function should be made transparent and accountable. Politicians need to limit their functions to policy choices and the overall oversight of the functioning of the executive. The level of corruption is likely to increase, if they perform micromanagement of implementing agencies. Electoral reforms that reduce the need for political parties to depend on funding from capitalists and also to prevent people with a track record of crime and illegal activities from contesting elections are also important. Greater transparency in decision-making as attempted through the Right to Information Act is also paramount. However, the social pressure or demand to control corruption is also important, and here one has to consider the political economy transformation and the level of economic development of the society. (You may note the discussion in Chapter 20.)

INTERNAL INCENTIVES

We have talked about incentives throughout this book. We have also talked about altruism and other not-so-self-oriented actions in Chapter 18. It is possible that many people are driven (to some extent) by non-material incentives in their work and daily interactions. The joy of doing the right thing or something meaningful can be a driving force. People may not like to work in a context where the superior does not trust him/her (even though people may continue to work there for want of other comparable opportunities). We have also seen the efficiency wage hypothesis—the tendency of employers to give a wage rate higher than what is prevalent in the market to create employees' loyalty to the organization. There are many NGOs (including religious or spiritual or ideological organizations) where people work by getting a material compensation much lesser than what they can get in their respective labour markets.

It is possible to design organizations where the non-material motivations of people can be tapped or used effectively. We have seen several NGOs working (and sometimes degenerating later) on the basis of these 'internal incentives'. However, some periodical reflection of why some people work here with a different set of motivations would be useful. There can be a trade-off between material and non-material incentives and this can be different for different people depending on their preferences and endowments. Even this trade-off can change for the same people over a period of time. Some organizations start with certain ideological/altruistic features which may disappear over a period of time. For example, an organization started with a non-hierarchical structure may motivate some youngsters to join the organization, but they may get demotivated when they realize that such hierarchies are not completely absent. The commitment to an idea or a belief may enable people to sacrifice certain material incentives, but the strength of this commitment itself may change for individual reasons. All these may have a bearing on the quality or the effectiveness of these organizations. Economics may inform that even though such organizations working on the basis of non-material incentives are possible, a rational analysis of the working of the organization as part of a reflective practice is useful to avoid unexpected outcomes.

INTERNAL VERSUS EXTERNAL MECHANISMS OF CORRECTION

In making an organization continue to be effective and efficient, there are two types of strategies used. First is to see whether all its members (employees and managers) have the incentive to be effective and efficient, and if not so, to have penalizing/punishing clauses. This is what we have discussed so far. However, the other strategy used in the case of public organizations is to create mechanisms that will put external pressure on them to be efficient (mainly by its users). Having a well-functioning parents–teachers association in the case of a school is part of this strategy. Here we are expecting the 'voice' of the disgruntled parents to work as a pressure mechanism to make the school deliver (what the parents want).

There are many such mechanisms widely being used these days as part of the rural development initiatives in India. Grama Sabha or the assembly of all villagers is expected to plan and evaluate the activities of the local governments. Social auditing is expected to carry out the monitoring of the creation of assets and generation of work days as part of the Mahatma Gandhi National Rural Employment Guarantee Act (MGNREGA). Some states have also instituted citizens' charters. These charters prescribe a specific time for the delivery of a public service (like the issue of a birth certificate or the issue of building permit by the local government to those who are eligible and have completed all the required formalities). If a particular citizen encounters a delay (of more than what is prescribed in the charter), he/she can complain to the higher authorities. The Right to Information Act is also one such mechanism which can be used to unearth information on the inaction, if any, on the part of public organizations.

These mechanisms which enable citizens to exert pressure on public organizations are important. These give them legitimate rights to express their discomfort with the system. Even if only a few people use such rights, it may put a certain pressure on the employees of public organizations. However, we should not overestimate their potential in our context. We have seen cases where people have not bothered to use these mechanisms even when they encounter poor service from public organizations. Gram Sabhas have not been effective even in states which have a tradition of grassroots democracy. Even when such mechanisms exist, people may use bribes or political influence to get the public service on time. There can be several reasons for this state of affairs. People have to encounter certain costs in using these mechanisms (especially since there are institutional deficiencies in getting redress from higher authorities). These costs need not be trivial. It was shown that the need to forgo the wage of even a single day may discourage working people from attending grama sabhas. There is also uncertainty regarding how effective these mechanisms are. Even if citizens' charters exist, public service need not be delivered at that time, and there can be delaying tactics, even if a complaint is filed before higher level authorities. Thus people may use other means like bribing the official or using the influence of politicians to get the service. When corruption is prevalent, even citizens may use them strategically. They may try to get public service—like the permit to construct a building or a license to drive—even without completing the formalities through corruption. Even those who can complete the requirements easily may follow the route of corruption rather than going through the formal route.

There can be a relationship between the internal versus external mechanisms to make organizations efficient and effective. External mechanisms need not work well if internal mechanisms are defunct. Thus, people may take the informal or illegal route to get what they want from public organizations. On the other hand, if internal mechanisms are reasonably good, people need not use external voice mechanisms very often. They would consider such mechanisms (as RTE, right to attend Gram Sabha and the citizens' charter) as part of citizens' rights, and these would be used only in the case of circumstances where they feel that very unfair treatment is meted out to them.

RULES/ORGANIZATIONS AND POLITICAL ECONOMY

However, it would be a mistake if we neglect the relationship between the performance of organizations and rules (in terms of efficiency, effectiveness and lack of corruption) and the larger social, cultural and political economy of the country, including its state of development. It may be difficult or costly to control the ill functioning of organizations through oversight or rules. On the other hand, it is evident from the international studies on Scandinavian countries or Japan that some cultural factors may be playing an important role in making some of these countries different (for example, in terms of corruption or social cohesion). These cultural factors need not be attributed to the different features of the people living there, but they may have acquired certain habits or traits during a long period of time. There is one argument that the conditions of life (for example, the need for water control in the Netherlands or the coordination in small-scale irrigation in Japan) had forced people to develop certain habits of cooperation (which discourages them from free riding, even when there are opportunities for them to do so) and these might have shaped the social milieu of these countries. Countries like India, which had sustained a higher level of inequalities in the past between those having material assets and social privileges and those who do not have them, may witness a struggle by those deprived sections to acquire similar privileges (including the license to use public resources for one's own benefit) as part of the process of democratization.

Many people do not see corruption as a harmful trait in countries like India. We have already discussed the role of the middle class in taking some social positions against corruption. The evolution of this middle class is part of the development process of a country.

QUESTIONS/EXERCISES

1. What is dynamic efficiency? Why is it important?
2. What are the external mechanisms to control organizations? Describe why these may not work well in our contexts.
3. Think about an organization which is known for corruption. What would be your proposal to reduce corruption there?
4. What is an incentive-compatible mechanism? Describe one such case where such a mechanism can make an organization relatively more efficient.
5. What are the considerations before outsourcing some of the activities of an organization? Think about an organization where these insights may be applied.

APPENDIX

———◆◆◆———

RESPONDING TO CRITIQUES OF ECONOMICS AND DEVELOPMENT

Anyone reading popular writings on economy or on development may have come across numerous criticisms of economics or the economists' ideas of development. Even extreme views like 'economics is the root cause of all social and environmental problems we are witnessing' are not unheard of. People criticize economics from different points of view. Some of these are based on an incorrect understanding of economics but many well-known economists too are among the critics of the discipline. Criticism is important for any growing discipline since these would highlight certain issues of concern which are yet to be understood or addressed. These may encourage researchers to focus on new issues and problems.

Given that critics of economics share many viewpoints, we may not be able to consider all such views in this short essay. However, we take up some well-known critical views on economics and mention how each one of them is taken into account within the discipline. Before getting into some of the more serious criticisms, let us consider some not-so-serious ones first.

NEGLECTING THAT ECONOMY AND ECONOMICS ARE DIFFERENT!

The distinction between economics and economy should be obvious to readers of even this introductory book. However, there are some who consider problems of economies (inequality in consumption, environmental problems, price rice, monopoly and so on) as the 'problems' or 'limitations' of economics. Some may even consider 'profit-motivation' or 'self-interest' as a product of economics. Economics is a science or a set of tools used to analyse the economy. The economy has existed and grown even before the growth of economics. Problems, related to economies like inequality or monopoly, have prevailed even before the birth and growth of the discipline called economics. 'Profit-motivation' and 'self-interest' are attributes of (some, if not all) people in our society noted or studied by economists. These are not traits inculcated by economics.

Critics who attribute all the undesirable problems of economy to economics are actually exaggerating the role of economics. Even if economics had not evolved as a discipline, economy would have evolved by and large along the same lines that we witness today. The contribution of economics to the way economy evolves is rather modest. Economics remains by and large as a way of understanding economy, rather than a tool of designing economic behaviour or channelizing the movement of the economy.

DEVELOPMENT IS A WESTERN IDEA!

To be fair to the critics who hold this view a few features of what is considered 'modern economy' are visible predominantly in Western developed economies. The level of material consumption (or the objective of enhancing material consumption) of these countries cannot be compared to that of the developing economies. There is a perceptible individualization that has occurred in most of these countries. To that extent, community and kinship linkages that existed in these societies have become weaker. Liberal democracy is the overall framework of institutions and a substantial part of the social interactions are based on formal rules and institutions. They sustain a capitalist or market-oriented system of economy.

Mostly, the developed economies (in a relative sense) until the middle of the last century were from the Western world (comprising mainly North-Western Europe and North America). They had the features described in the previous paragraph. However, the last 50–60 years have seen the emergence of developed economies in many other parts of the World.

Though countries from Southern Europe, like Spain and Portugal, could amass wealth during the colonial period and established colonies mainly in Latin America, they did not do well as North-West European countries. Catholicism

(of Southern Europe) was not viewed as enabling as protestant ethics for industrialization (of North-Western Europe). The church played an important role in
political life of the Catholic countries where democracy was not deep rooted.
However, one could not see much difference in terms of material consumption
especially among those with means in these two sets of countries.

A few countries from East Europe emerged powerful under the socialist model.
However, they could not sustain their economic and political models and they have
started following the capitalist (and democratic, even though these countries struggle hard to be as democratic as North-Western Europe or the US) during the last
two decades. Japan was the first developed economy in Asia. There is not much
difference in the material consumption between Japan and the North-Western
Europe (or the US). However, there is an argument that the 'culture of household
savings' in Japan is still prevalent strongly and this influences its economic growth
trajectories. It is not that the households in Western Europe were not saving. In fact,
it is argued that the habit of saving and re-investing was part of Protestant ethics
which put Western Europe economically ahead of other countries. However, household saving has declined in these countries and this may be at least partly due to the
social security schemes implemented by the governments.

Though Japan is capitalist and democratic, some of the long-standing cultural features of the country continue to influence the social, economic and
political life of the people. Community linkages seem to be strong even today.
Patriarchy is much stronger in Japan compared with Western Europe.
Management observers note that acceptance of hierarchy and preference for life
time jobs continue in Japan. Some of these may be changing, albeit slowly.
South East Asian Countries (Taiwan, South Korea, Singapore and Malaysia)
have caught up with Japan during the second-half of the twentieth century. One
cannot see much discernible trends in these countries in terms of material consumption. However, there is something 'Asian' in their political and social life.
Democracy is not as free as in the Western world. Until recently, the government and the capitalists enjoyed a close relationship in the management of
economic affairs and such a close relationship was facilitating economic growth
for some time. Social life in these countries may be closer to that of Japan
rather than that of Western Europe and America. However, there are demands
to expand the scope of political and human rights in these countries.

The evolution of Latin American countries by and large followed the route of
their south European colonialists. The dominant role played by the church, unstable

democracies, periods of turmoil and (sometimes brutal) dictatorships are notable. Higher levels of inequality and tension between indigenous populations and the younger generations of colonialists were also visible. Though there were periods of affluence (mostly financed by the extraction of natural resources), they did not lead to a sustained improvement in the life of the whole population or the development of democratic institutions.

The need to enhance material consumption is there in almost all societies. This is evident from the recently growing countries or from the consumption pattern of the affluent in the developing world. This need not be due to the spread of the 'idea' that material consumption is a good thing. This could be driven by internal incentives. The rich and the powerful had a higher level of material consumption even in traditional societies. If they could not use their own jet planes and Cadillac cars, then they could construct massive tombs to commemorate their loved ones. The spread of this consumption pattern from the royal and feudal ones to the people at large might have been part of the democratic aspirations of the people. Even when consumption is minimal, the few may get 'satisfaction' from the concentration of power. Hence, the emergence of material consumption could be part of the spread of affluence to the wider society. Similarly, if some developed countries are not truly democratic, it may not be the intentional choice of most people living there. Some sections of society may be bearing the costs of these non-democratic systems and there may be pressures to change.

All societies need not have to emulate the consumption pattern and also the social and political models of the Western world to ensure development. If every individual in the world consumes as much as an average US citizen does, the burden on resources would be unbearable. However, we may not reach that situation because prices would go up and hence people may be forced to find alternatives to specific items of consumption and also alternative ways of seeking satisfaction. It is not that the cultural and social traits of all societies have to be like those of the US or Western Europe as part of development. The history of development shows that economic development may go hand in hand with multiple social and cultural traits (and some of these change even in Western Europe/ US based on the internal requirements of societies and the changing aspirations of individuals). What is important for economics is that it can explain diverse ways of economic development. However, rubbishing development as a Western conspiracy is far from the truth.

ECONOMICS BREEDS INEQUALITY!

Economics is concerned about efficiency (and the first fundamental theorem talks about competitive economy leading to efficiency under certain conditions). However, if we do not like the distributional outcome of competitive economy (since it is highly unequal), the second fundamental theorem of economics would argue that there should be redistribution of initial endowments. It is social and political forces that facilitate or thwart such redistribution. We have also seen the situations under which inequality changes.

However, of late, an attempt is being made to address some issues related to inequality. We have mentioned the details in the chapter on inequality. Further research is needed to address the growing inequalities in developed and developing worlds, especially those related to the differential access to education.

ECONOMISTS NEGLECT ENVIRONMENTAL HAZARDS!

This was a genuine criticism in the seventies. Economists did not think seriously about the potential impact of economic activities on nature and environment. This situation has improved drastically during the last three to four decades. Efforts are on to fully understand the complex relationship between ecology and economy and thanks to the development of environmental economics, a number of insights on the economic or institutional causes of environmental impact have been highlighted. There is also a growing understanding on which policy instruments may work (which may not work) in containing the negative environmental impacts or the unsustainable use of natural resources. We have already discussed a number of these insights in Chapter 16.

ECONOMISTS SUPPORT EVER-INCREASING CONSUMPTION AND USE OF NATURAL RESOURCES!

Increase in consumption (and consequent production) helps boost economic growth but there are many reasons why such a growth need not be undesirable. A substantial section of world population does not have even the basic minimum consumption. Thus, an increase in the consumption levels of even these people (and not merely the increase in the consumption levels of those who already consume very high) can also result in economic growth (especially in the developing world). If consumption/production uses a resource which becomes increasingly scarcer, its price would go up (if it is not artificially kept low). This may provide incentives to use substitutes or develop technologies to reduce the use of the scarce input. In fact, one can see a trend where the material input of certain consumption items coming down over a period of time, and compensating with the technology/knowledge input. The size of some electronic devices (including computers) have become smaller and smaller but their processing capacity has increased dramatically. Thus the natural resources used for making such items have not increased, if not declined.

Increase in consumption does not have to reflect in 'material consumption'. It can be in services. For example, consider the aged people. Their number is going to increase all over the world due to the increase in life expectancy in most societies. Caring of the aged was previously considered a household task, but that is changing rapidly. On the other hand, adequate institutional (including private) facilities for caring for the aged are yet to develop in many parts of the world. Services of this kind may emerge in the future and these may absorb significant sections of people as employees. Such service sector growth need not be natural resource intensive, but at the same time can enhance the welfare of consumers. Hence economic growth need not always lead to the depletion of natural resources.

MAINSTREAM ECONOMICS IS BAD, AND WE NEED ALTERNATIVES!

In any developing discipline, there will always be certain strands of enquiry which are much more meaningful for certain issues and times than others. These may change over time too. Thus it is not at all surprising if we see some people not excited about certain streams of (ways of acquiring) knowledge within a discipline. This is much more possible in the case of social sciences where the outcomes cannot be predicted precisely as in the case of natural sciences or technology. We have seen that human behaviour is influenced by a wide set of tangible and intangible factors, and the challenges in predicting them correctly.

However, certain broad lessons can be learnt. There was a conflict in economics between socialist strategies (or those who focused on central planning) and market-based strategies. However, this is not a serious conflict these days for a number of reasons. First of all countries which have focussed heavily on socialist strategies have themselves moved out of that framework. Even communist countries like China and Vietnam depend more on markets for organizing economic activities these days. Hence the conventional claims of the socialist economic planning are no longer relevant. On the other hand, no serious economist would say that markets alone can solve all economic problems. The need for an effective and efficient state (government) is well recognized by those who study economics seriously.

However, there are some contemporary debates on the methods of economics. Recent recession has brought back attention to the role of Keynesian strategies of increasing government expenditure (even by creating fiscal deficits) to enhance employment and consumption of people. (See the discussion in Chapter 7 in this book.) There are some who argue vehemently for enhancing government spending, whereas there are others who are concerned more about the consequences of fiscal deficits created through such enhanced government expenditure. There is some political debate too in the US. The Republicans oppose such an increase in fiscal deficits, whereas the Democrats want such an increase, at least for a short term. It is very clear that the expected benefits of increased government expenditure in the economy of a country need not be derived in a globalized context since a substantial part of this spending may be used to buy goods and services from elsewhere. Thus, the boost in spending by the US government may benefit companies of China and India, and gains in employment within the US may be modest. However, when many people in society are unemployed or homeless at a time, increasing government expenditure is unavoidable to some extent. Anyhow, this debate is something that needs to be watched.

There are also contesting points on how to regulate the financial sector and also on using other strategies (like the historical evidence) in economics research. There is an initiative called Institute of New Economic Thinking (INET) which supports research using unconventional methods. The results of these experiments have to be keenly watched. Experimental economics (rather than predicting human behaviour on the basis of a theoretically constructed rationality) has become an important part of the discipline. Controlled experiments are being used these days to decide the efficacy of development interventions (Banerjee and Duflo, 2011).

ECONOMICS FAILS TO ANALYSE SOME REAL-WORLD PROBLEMS!

This is a genuine criticism, but this is not at all unusual for a growing discipline. After all, the systematic development of economics as a professional discipline is not even 100 years old. Considering the importance of economy in the life of people today (and this importance goes up exponentially as more and more people participate in market-based production/exchange system), when people see problems in the functioning of this system called 'economy', they have heightened expectation from the discipline of economics. They become frustrated when economics does not come out with answers to every issue that may affect the functioning of the economy.

There is nothing wrong in a growing discipline to have a set of less understood domains. Once everything related to the economy is well understood, probably economics may become a dead discipline, and it may be like the Bible—a set of answers given from above. Moreover, economics, for genuine reasons, wishes to focus on a rigorous methodology to analyse the world. Even this methodology may evolve or change to address future challenges. When such a rigorous method has to be used to evaluate an issue, many issues may remain unexplained for several reasons: some issues are not amenable to that method; enough data or information is not available on certain issues and so on. These may become amenable to economic analysis as more information is available. Thus, it is not at all surprising that economics does not have answers currently to a number of real-world problems.

PEOPLE ARE NOT RATIONAL, PEOPLE SHOULD NOT BE RATIONAL

Some may argue that people are really not rational, and hence economics is not right. Some may even say that people should not be rational but trustworthy, altruistic and caring of others and hence economics which 'glorifies' the rational behaviour is problematic. Does economics glorify 'self-interest' and 'profit-motivation' as desirable traits, especially when economists say that these may lead to efficiency under certain circumstances? There can be two responses to such an 'allegation'—(a) Economics valorizes certain rational behaviour (which we have already discussed in the previous chapters) but the requirements of this rational behaviour are very limited (and for which people do not have to be narrowly or selfishly self-oriented). The ability to arrange options and a purposive behaviour in selecting the best-possible option depending on the endowments and constraints are the basic features of such a rational behaviour. Such behaviour is not that rare among human beings. (b) Assume that only a small section of people is 'rational' in the way economists think and others are not rational and are altruistic, caring and not at all interested in the self. (It may be noted that even if people are not rational, this does not make them all trustworthy, altruistic or caring of others.) However, a design of a development intervention or organization on the basis of the assumption that people are 'self-interested' may have some virtue, even when only a few are of such type. When we assume that some people are self-interested we may take adequate precautions in the design of the interventions and organizations. This may ensure that these would work normally. On the other hand, if we design interventions/organizations with an assumption that all people are concerned only about others, then it may make these dysfunctional when a few behave selfishly.

ECONOMICS WORK AGAINST COOPERATION, ALTRUISM, TRUST AND OTHER NICE BEHAVIOUR AMONG PEOPLE

We have seen that the rational behaviour highlighted in economics need not be in conflict with cooperation, altruism, trust or other 'nice' behaviour. In fact, trust is very much valued in an economic exchange. Imagine two potential partners in an exchange process. If one thinks that the other is not trustworthy, the former has to take extra-precautions before and after entering into an economic relationship with the latter. This would increase the transaction costs. This may discourage certain transactions. Thus, people want to participate in exchange with people known for their trustworthiness. Even in a modern globalized economy, many transactions take place between people known to each other directly or indirectly, and here trust plays an important role.

We have already seen that people cooperate in certain situations, and this need not be against rationality. On the other hand, if some people blindly cooperate without thinking about others' incentives (to cheat), it may lead to losses. Moreover, we need public or social mechanisms to deal with cases of market failure, wherein people cooperate voluntarily or due to the coercion (by the state) or the persuasion by others. It will be very useful if people cooperate voluntarily and this reduces the costs of the provision of such services in the context of market failure. The habit of frequent free-riding is not desirable, even though economic analysis would search always whether the context permits such free-riding. The fact that economists analyse free-riding does not mean that they 'encourage' free-riding.

We have also seen that one can be rational even when the objective of the individual action is altruistic or not to meet self-interest. Altruism can also be for self-gratification—for the feeling of doing the right thing. Given the scarcity of resources, there may be multiple ways of reaching an altruistic objective. Thus selecting the best possible option which maximizes the benefits for a given cost (or that minimizes the cost for a given level of benefits) is important even here. Hence economists' concern about efficiency cannot be brushed aside, even if the objective is to help others.

WE SHOULD GO BACK TO NATURE

This is yet another strand of thinking which poses itself as a counter view to the process of economic development that takes place in the world. We have seen that economic development has put pressure on natural resources and environment. However, economists would argue that we continue to depend heavily on some natural resources and pollute the environment since we do not pay the 'real price' of these amenities. Thus, we need to put in place institutions and policies that encourage us to bear the real cost of using natural resources and the environment. Moreover, economists would see some positive signals in the world regarding the need for protecting nature, and also may not agree that all people who consume less (for example, poor) use environment in a benign manner. Poverty and damage to nature can also go hand in hand. Economists would argue for a certain level of material consumption for all as a basic necessity for achieving social and human development. Thus, they may not see a reduction in material consumption below this basic level (if it is needed as part of 'going back to nature') as desirable.

Economics as an analytical tool has no issue if people are willing to protect nature or environment in its pristine forms. They may insist that such willingness should be backed by the readiness to bear the cost of such action—forgoing the benefits of consumption. Economic value of a piece of natural resource can increase even if it is not used in a consumptive manner (like cutting down a tree). The value of a natural asset would increase even if it is kept as such, but if people are willing to pay more and more for its preservation. It is a wrong idea that economic value can go up only when resources are 'used'.

Thus, people who advocate 'going back to nature' should encourage people to forgo the benefits of consumption. Once people accept such a prescription, it need not create much conflict with the analytical prescriptions of economists.

WE SHOULD GO BACK TO 'INDIAN' VALUES

We have seen that economic development that takes place in a country may incorporate certain elements of the cultural and social ethos of that country (as evident from Japan or other Asian countries). Some of these 'local' values may change over a period of time due to internal reasons. For example, there may be pressure within Japan to change its patriarchal attitudes. It may be noted that nearly 50 per cent of women do not marry in Japan, since they do not want to enter into such patriarchal relationships. Though people remain unmarried in the West, there one can see a greater willingness to be part of other relationships like living together. Thus, it is not at all inconceivable to think about a process of economic development in India which reflects certain 'Indian' values.

However, what some of us may consider as 'Indian' values may not be good for (or liked by) all Indians, and hence their persistence may have serious implications for the country's social and human development. A major part of the so-called Indian values are coded in the form of social norms (what are socially or morally desirable and what are not). These norms are nurtured through community linkages. But these communities are, to a great extent, divided according to caste lines in the country. There is strong persistence of the caste system in India, despite the efforts of social reformers and also through law. Inter-caste marriages are yet to take place to any significant extent in the country, even among modern, well-educated and urban population. Though the continuation of the caste system may be beneficial to the upper castes, it could be harmful for the so-called lower castes and Dalits. The continuation of caste divisions may lead to a systematic deprivation of assets for a substantial section of the population in India, and this could be a major reason for the high level of poverty and underdevelopment that we witness in the country today, despite having impressive rates of economic growth.

A related issue is the status of women. One of the celebrated 'Indian values' (based on a common sense understanding especially among the NRIs living in the Western developed world) is the focus on families. This may be encouraging the NRIs settled in the US to take trips to India to get brides for their sons and also to take their daughters 'forcefully' to marry them off to Indian bridegrooms. However, high level of gender discrimination could go along with these 'nice family values'. As noted earlier, gender discrimination manifests in terms of access to assets, wealth and education, and also with regard to social/family preferences on work participation and occupational choice. There would be pressure to change these values as more and more women attain a certain level of empowerment.

Thus, the demand for changing certain Indian values and for adopting a pattern of development that respects individual freedom and rights can be driven by the internal needs of our society. This need not be due to the imposition of a 'Western path of development' from elsewhere.

BIBLIOGRAPHY

Agarwal, B. (1994). *A Field of One's Own: Gender and Land Rights in South Asia*. Cambridge: Cambridge University Press.

Akerlof, G. (1976). The economics of caste and of the rat race and other woeful tales. *Quarterly Journal of Economics*, *90*(4), 599–617.

Balakrishnan, P. (2010). *Economic Growth in India: History and Prospects*. New Delhi: Oxford University Press.

Banerjee, A. and Duflo, E. (2011). *Poor Economics: A Radical Rethinking of the Way to Fight Global Poverty*. New York: Public Affairs Books.

Bardhan, P. and Mookherjee, D. (2000). Capture and governance at local and national levels. *American Economic Review*, *90*(2), 135–139.

———. (Eds). (2006). *Decentralization and Local Governance: A Comparative Performance*. Cambridge: MIT Press.

Basu, K. (1997). *Analytical Development Economics*. Cambridge: MIT Press.

Bowles, S., Gintis, H., and Osborne, M. (Eds). (2005). *Unequal Chances: Family Background and Economic Success*. Princeton, NJ: Princeton University Press.

Chenery, Hollis and Srinivasan, T.N. (Eds). (1988). *Handbook on Development Economics*. New York: Elsevier.

Deolalikar, A.B. (1981). *The Inverse Relationship between Productivity and Farm Size: A Test Using Regional Data from India*. New Haven: Economic Growth Center, Yale University.

Dreze, J. and Sen, A. (1998). *India: Economic Development and Social Opportunity*. Oxford: Clarendon Press.

Frank, R.H. (2005). *Microeconomics and Behavior*, 6th ed. New York: McGraw-Hill.

Frey, B.S. and Alois, S. (2002). *Happiness, Economy and Institutions, Institute for Empirical Research in Economics*. University of Zurich, Switzerland.

Gangopadhyay, S. and Santhakumar, V. (2013). *Law and Economics: Theory and Practice*. New Delhi: SAGE Publications.

Hayami, Y. and Godo, Y. (1997) (republished in 2010). *Development Economics*. New Delhi: Oxford University Press.

Krueger, A.O. (1993). *Political Economy of Policy Reform in Developing Countries*. Cambridge, MA: MIT Press.

Meier, G.M. and Stiglitz, J.E. (Eds). (2001). *Frontiers of Development Economics: The Future in Perspective*. Washington D.C.: The World Bank.

Mookherjee, D. (2006). *Market Institutions, Governance and Development: Collected Essays*. New Delhi: Oxford University Press.

North, D. (1990). *Institutions, Institutional Change and Economic Performance*. Cambridge: Cambridge University Press.

Ostrom, E. (1990). *Governing the Commons*. Cambridge: Cambridge University Press.

Ray, D. (1998). *Development Economics*. New York: Princeton University Press.

Russell, C.S. (2001). *Applying Economics to the Environment*. New York: Oxford University Press.

Samuelson, P. and Nordhaus, W. (2004). *Economics*. New York: McGraw-Hill.

Santhakumar, V. (2003). Citizens-action for protecting the environment in developing countries: An economic analysis of the outcome with empirical cases from India. *Environment and Development Economics*, *8*, 505–528.

———. (2008). *Analysing Social Opposition to Reforms*. New Delhi: SAGE Publications.

———. (2011). *Economic Analysis of Institutions: A Practical Guide*. New Delhi: SAGE Publications.

Santhakumar, V. and Chakraborty, A. (2003). Environmental costs and their impact on the net present value of a hydroelectric project in Kerala, India. *Environment and Development Economics*, *8*, 311–330.

Sen, Amartya. (1962). An Aspect of Indian Agriculture. *Economic Weekly*, Annual No. February.

———. (1999). *Development as Freedom*. New York: Knopf.

Silberberg, E. (1990). *The Structure of Economics: A Mathematical Analysis*. New York: McGraw-Hill.

Stiglitz, J.E. (2000). *Economics of Public Sector*, 3rd ed. New York: W.W. Norton.

Tabellini, G. (2008). The Scope of Cooperation: Values and Incentives. *Quarterly Journal of Economics*, *123*(3), 905–950.

INDEX

acid rain, 231
Adhaar, 189. *See also* Universal Identity
  Number
agent, relationship between principal,
  84–85
agricultural GDP, 90
agriculture, Indian, 121–22
  economy development impact on, 164
  EGS impact on supply of labour, 183
  government efforts to increase
    production, 161–63
  outcome of infusion of technology, 7
  public investments in, 163
  subsistence, 121, 123, 146, 156
  tenant, 153
  villagers involvement in traditional,
    147
altruism, 261–62
*anganwadi*s, 297, 304, 306
arithmetic average, 108
Arthasastra (Kautilya), 14
assessment of people demand, 299–300
automatic delivery machines, in developed
  countries, 38

backward bending supply curve, 53. *See
  also* labour markets
bad institutions, 265
bankruptcy, 94, 252, 291
banks
  annual interest on saving deposits, 82

current interest rates, in Indian banks,
  50
  mobilization of deposits by, 54
  need to regularization of, 55–56
  recovery of loans from defaulters, 94
benchmark effect, 202
Bihar, MP, Rajasthan, UP and Jharkhand
  and Chhattisgarh (BIMARU) states,
  116, 208
BIS certification, 258
borrow of money, by government, 99, 101
Brundtland, Gro Harlem, 228
budget constraint, 252
Buffet, Warren, 203

capital-intensive technology, 38
capital investment, 7–8, 91, 97
  in developed world, 96
  for economic growth, 121
  production of commodity, 40
capitalist mobilized savings, 123
capital market(s), 54–57, 70, 150–51, 167,
  169–70, 197, 290–91
cash reserve, 56, 97
cash-support schemes, 166–67
cash transfer, 187. *See also* Public
  Distribution System (PDS)
caste-based assertion, 281
Central Finance Commission, 247
centralization of decision-making, in
  organization, 319–20

342

ABOUT THE AUTHOR

V. Santhakumar is currently teaching Economics for Development Practitioners at Azim Premji University, Bangalore. He had been on the faculty of the Centre for Development Studies, Trivandrum for 15 years from 1996 and he is a Visiting Professor there currently. He has received the research medal and the outstanding research award of the Global Development Network during its initial years. In addition to publication in international journals, he has authored books titled *Analysing Social Opposition to Reforms* and *Economic Analysis of Institutions: A Practical Guide* (both published by SAGE). He is co-author and has co-edited the two-volume series on *Law and Economics*, brought out by SAGE in 2013.